THE LONG PARTY

SAXON HOUSE

THE LONG PARTY

High Society in the Twenties & Thirties

Stella Margetson

By the Same Author:

JOURNEY BY STAGES

LEISURE AND PLEASURE IN THE NINETEENTH CENTURY

LEISURE AND PLEASURE IN THE EIGHTEENTH CENTURY

FIFTY YEARS OF VICTORIAN LONDON

REGENCY LONDON

With love to darling Eileen and Bill

Saxon House, D. C. Heath Limited, Westmead, Farnborough, Hants, England.
© Stella Margetson, 1974

ISBN 0 347 0002 9

Library of Congress Catalog Card Number 74–21198

Printed in Great Britain by W & J Mackay Limited Chatham

Designed by Peggy and Drummond Chapman

Filmset in Imprint by Servis Filmsetting Limited, Manchester

The illustrations used on the endpapers, title spread and contents spread were
supplied by Illustrated Newspapers Group.

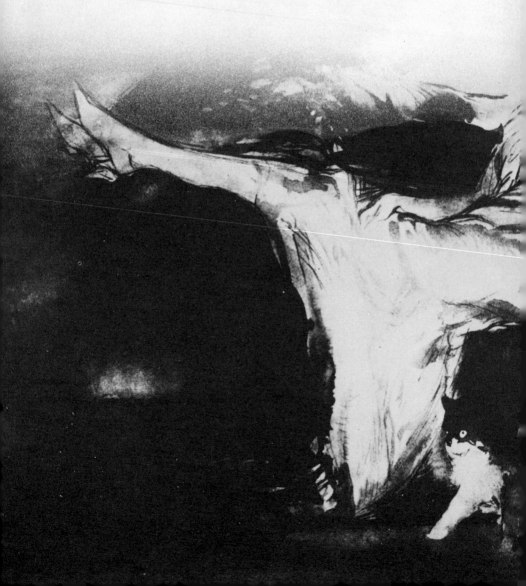

CONTENTS

1 KING GEORGE V. AND THE COURT 1
2 THE PRINCE OF *WALES* AND THE SMART SET 27
3 THE *ARISTOCRACY AT* HOME 53
4 HIGH SOCIETY *AND* CAFE SOCIETY 79
5 STAGE AND SCREEN 105
6 LITERATURE AND ART 133
7 THE *AWAKENING* CONSCIENCE 163
8 THE ENGLISH *ABROAD* 193
9 A CRISIS FOR THE NOBILITY 215
10 THE LAST YEARS OF PEACE 239
BIBLIOGRAPHY 259

1 KING GEORGE V AND THE COURT

The maroons sounded and the pigeons in Trafalgar Square—prosaic doves of peace—rose on clumsy wings into the November sky. With no radio and no television, only the paper-boys shouting and running through the streets, news of the Armistice spread from mouth to mouth. Office workers dropped what they were doing and rushed out of doors, stunned and excited. A crowd gathered in Whitehall. Union Jacks appeared from nowhere, and a man in uniform was hoisted off his feet. Someone started to sing . . . The War to end war was over. More than one million British dead lay in the earth or at the bottom of the sea.

The survivors danced and sang in the streets with a hectic, wild sense of relief, a clownish gaiety very close to the deliberate suppression of pain. All business ceased as the day went on. The crowds thickened like flies round a jam pot. Omnibuses and taxi-cabs were embedded in a mob of seething, shouting, gesticulating humanity; and at night when the lights went up after four years of darkness, the jubilation increased. The sober, reserved English were letting themselves go. Soldiers, sailors and airmen linked arms with the civilians and careered up and down, singing and laughing at anything and everything in the biggest bank holiday bonanza they had ever known. Women danced with their skirts thrown over their heads and according to one very young Guardsman, Sacheverell Sitwell, were rolled along the platform at Waterloo Station like so many barrels of beer.

Class distinction for once was forgotten. The news belonged to everyone, to high society and the *hoi polloi*, to the rich celebrating in champagne and the poor downing their pints of beer. And the news spelt out the prospect of Life with a capital letter, an

1 *The Royal Family. Seated are the Princess Royal and Queen Mary. Standing, from left to right, are the Prince of Wales, Prince Henry, King George V, the Duke of York and Prince George. (Syndication International)*

end to the appalling harvest of death, to the mud and the filth of the trenches and the dreary war-time restrictions of the civilian population. It meant—or so it seemed in the euphoria of the moment—back to 'the good old days' and forward into the future, into a better world, 'a land fit for heroes'—for very few of the revellers that night paused to wonder whether the world they had known was not already dead and the promised land of the future a treacherous question-mark. They were suspended out of time as they cavorted in the streets and rushed in a horde across St James's Park to swarm up the Queen Victoria Memorial and hug the gates of Buckingham Palace. King George V and Queen Mary did not disappoint them. In the light shining from the room behind, they came out on the red and gold velvet-draped balcony and with a wave acknowledged the cheering multitude.

The King was fifty-three, dapper, bearded, no longer young; the Queen gracious and handsome, her hair piled up in stately curls, her figure superbly erect. While most of the crowned heads of Europe were in distress, hurrying into exile with the bedraggled remnant of their dismembered courts, King George and Queen Mary stood proudly together at the head of the British Empire, buoyed up by the loyalty and patriotism of their people, whose victory now seemed to herald a return to the pre-war days of power enjoyed by the nation since the time of Queen Victoria. Revolution in Russia, defeat in Austria and Germany, disruption in Greece and the Balkans had left the British monarchy by contrast more stable than ever; and the King himself, by his rectitude, his simplicity and his devotion to duty, had done more than any other sovereign to identify the Crown as much with the interests of his ordinary subjects as with the traditional privileges of the exclusive aristocracy, thus broadening the basis of esteem and ensuring its continuance into the unforeseeable future.

His Court was a model of decency and sobriety—rather dull in the eyes of the late King Edward VII's entourage. For even before the War had curtailed the social activities of the upper classes, the extravagance, the luxury and the sometimes vulgar display of the previous reign had diminished as a result of King George V's more simple tastes, formed in his boyhood and constant throughout his life. He did not care very much for the high ritual attached to his exalted position, though he believed in its necessity as part of the mystique of the monarchy and always carried out his ceremonial duties with impeccable dignity and a sharp eye for any deviation in the behaviour of his attendants. He did not care, either, for what his grandmother, Queen Victoria, disapprovingly called 'the society of fashionable and fast people', so notoriously popular with his father as Prince of Wales and King, for he had none of Edward VII's zest for wining and dining among the rich or playing for high stakes at the baccarat table, none of his overwhelming delight in the company of elegant and alluring women, whose veiled sexuality was so stimulating. He preferred instead a domestic life of ordered routine with his beloved wife at home—and home meant York Cottage on the Sandringham estate, to everyone else by far the least attractive of all the royal residences.

It was small and cramped and rather ugly, built originally to house the overflow of his parents' guests when as Prince and Princess of Wales they entertained large parties in the big house for the shooting season. The gabled, Victorian Gothic exterior, tricked up with pseudo-Jacobean chimneys and mock Tudor beams, was surrounded by a garden heavily planted with laurels, rhododendrons and thick, dark fir trees, which overshadowed a pond where a few dejected water lilies strove to bloom. The interior was equally dark and cluttered with Victorian and Edwardian knick-knacks: lampshades with bows on them, carved mantelpieces with intricate little balconies supporting countless ornaments and souvenirs, sofas and chairs with excruciatingly uncomfortable upright backs, and small tables with tortured legs, each bearing its weight of family photographs in silver frames and all reflecting the taste of Queen Alexandra in her heyday as the mistress of Sandringham. Nothing, indeed, could be changed without her supervision, and nothing much was changed, because to King George his 'darling motherdear', until her death in 1926, was still the adored and sacred symbol of his boyhood.

How hard this must have been for Queen Mary with her superior intellectual and aesthetic taste, when, as Duke of York he first took her to Sandringham as his Duchess and his bride in 1893, no one was ever to know. She never complained of her mother-in-law's interference and strove patiently to endure the unkind and critical jibes of her sisters-in-law when her natural shyness made her the butt of their family jokes. Reticence, however, was only one among the many great qualities she possessed as the wife of the heir to the throne and then his Queen. Her own sense of duty combined with her intuitive understanding of her husband's dependence on the strength of her devoted companionship in the lonely eminence of his office, made her vigilant in protecting him from any untoward disturbance in his private life. If his aversion to change sometimes irked her and the discipline he had learnt in the Royal Navy made him something of a martinet to his family, she was far too diplomatic to let him observe her distress. She sought rather to suppress her own feelings and to maintain the outward calm he expected of her.

At Sandringham the King had learnt to ride his first pony and at a very early age had been taught to shoot. Every corner of the estate was filled with sentimental memories of his elder brother, Prince Eddy, heir to the throne until his death in 1892, of his own gaiety and fun before that event put an end to his naval career and changed his whole future, of his father and his mother and his sisters and dear Canon Dalton, his tutor. At Sandringham as Duke of York, he had lived the life of a country squire. He knew every inch of the ground, all his neighbours, all his tenants and all his gamekeepers. He loved the bracing Norfolk air and the Norfolk countryside, and some of his happiest days were spent out shooting with the local sporting gentry and half a dozen or so of his most intimate friends among the aristocracy. This was the society he liked best and where he felt most at his ease.

In London, at Buckingham Palace, his function in society was rather different and not always so pleasurable. The demands made on his time and energy by the official and unofficial engagements traditionally associated with the monarchy often weighed heavily upon him, though he never hesitated to accept them as part of his responsibility. After the Armistice there was a Service of Thanksgiving at St Paul's Cathedral. He then went north to Edinburgh to review the Fleet assembled in the Firth of Forth and over to France to visit the troops, and instead of spending Christmas as usual at his beloved Sandringham, was forced to remain in London to receive President Woodrow Wilson and his lady on their state visit to Britain.

They arrived on Boxing Day and were met by King George and Queen Mary at Victoria Station, from whence they drove

2   *King George V in relaxed mood. His preference was for quiet, unpretentious pleasures, rather than the world of glamour. (Keystone)*

through the beflagged streets crowded with cheering spectators in a procession of open carriages to Buckingham Palace. Both ladies were enveloped in ankle-length fur coats: Queen Mary wore a velvet toque; Mrs Wilson carried a sable muff and sported the wing of an aigrette in her pork-pie hat. The President, smiling benignly, repeatedly raised his shining silk topper in response to the welcoming crowds, who saw in him a prophet from the New World about to deliver the utopian dream they all hoped to enjoy; and if, with his strict Presbyterian upbringing and his belief that he was the Servant of God and the People, he felt slightly out of place being entertained in a royal palace by a British monarch descended from King George III, his wife had no such qualms and undoubtedly enjoyed every minute of their royal progress.

As at this time there was no hint of Woodrow Wilson's tragic failure to get the support of the American people for his Fourteen Points in the Versailles Treaty or for the League of Nations he had conceived with such idealistic fervour as the perpetual guardian of peace in the world, he was at the height of his eminence and the state visit was a success. King George found him 'quite easy to get on with' and thought he made 'a nice speech' at the banquet given in his honour.

Much of the pre-war ritual of the Court was revived for the occasion. Buckingham Palace, after being neglected during the War, was spruced up, and even the most die-hard Democrats in the President's suite who viewed the ceremonial splendour of the monarchy with disapproval, could not fail to be impressed by the sight of the white and gold ballroom where the banquet was held. With its pendant chandeliers, its neo-Classical mouldings and door frames and the gold-embroidered canopy of crimson velvet lined with rich Indian silk draped above the throne, it was a magnificent setting. The handsome gold candelabra and gold plate designed for the Prince Regent one hundred years earlier for the Peace Celebrations after the Napoleonic Wars, glittered on the spotless white napery, though fortunately the behaviour of King George V to his guests did not in any way resemble that of his self-indulgent and extravagant predecessor. Then, the venality of the Court, the intrigue and above all the vain and easily ruffled temper of the Prince had almost wrecked the purpose of the banquet; now, dignity, calm and good-will prevailed, at least on the surface of things.

The Gentlemen-at-Arms in full court dress, carrying their wands of office, and the King's bodyguard of the Yeomen of the Guard in their Tudor uniforms were in attendance. The Lord Steward, Lord Farquhar, was a neighbour of the King's at Sandringham and a very good shot; Lord Sandhurst, the Lord Chamberlain, a gentleman of the utmost discretion. Both belonged to the upper-class English gentry and were typical of the unspectacular but dependable members of the Royal Household who surrounded the King and gave him confidence. Their duties were simplified by his faith in them, for no sovereign was ever more loyal to his friends or more steadfast in his appreciation of their services. His Private Secretary and most intimate counsellor, Lord Stamfordham, served him for thirty years; Sir Charles Cust, his friend since 1877 when they were naval cadets together in the *Britannia*, was his Chief Equerry until 1931; Sir Frederick Ponsonby, Treasurer to the Household, was the son of Queen Victoria's Private Secretary—and all these trusted servants of the Crown upheld the traditions of the past which the

3 *President Wilson driving with King George V during his state visit to London, December 1918. (Central Press Photos Ltd.)*

4   *The ballroom at Buckingham Palace during a state dinner, such as that given for President Wilson. Even the most Democratic among his train were impressed by such splendour. (Illustrated London News)*

King respected and believed should be continued. As courtiers they were never obsequious, never ambitious for themselves or in any way connected with the more raffish or dubious members of high society. They kept their own counsel and the Court eminently respectable.

The banquet was attended by the Archbishops of Canterbury and York, both of whom sincerely believed that God was on the side of the victorious Allies; by members of the War Cabinet and the *Corps Diplomatique*, the Dominion statesmen, the Viceroy of India, the chiefs of the armed forces and a number of hereditary peers of the realm who filled the high offices of state. Mr Lloyd George, the Prime Minister, flushed with the victory of his Coalition Government in the recent

General Election, was there, so was Mr Asquith, who had lost his seat at East Fife after years of devotion to the Liberal Party. Lord Northcliffe sat rather far down the long table, looking furious with everyone. Winston Churchill and his charming wife were present, and according to one observer 'the brilliance of the assembled company brought back glorious memories of pre-war days'. No one noticed that the younger generation for whose benefit President Woodrow Wilson, Mr Lloyd George and that angry old tiger M. Clemenceau were shortly to rearrange the frontiers of the world, was scarcely represented at all. The Prince of Wales and his brother Prince Albert (later Duke of York and then King George VI) were abroad with the armed forces; only the King's younger sons, Prince Henry (later Duke of Gloucester) and Prince George (later Duke of Kent), and their sister, Princess Mary, were present among the middle-aged and elderly peacemakers—and this omission, though no one realized it at the time, prefigured the immediate post-war conflict between the generations as the young became increasingly resentful of the 'nanny knows best' attitude of their elders.

The King's relations with his grown-up sons were already none too happy. Perhaps in his preoccupation with the cares of state, he was not even aware that they were no longer children to be teased in the gruff and boisterous manner of the quarter-deck, which he seemed to think was an appropriate way of controlling their high spirits, when, in fact, it absolutely terrified them. Perhaps, though a sensitive man himself, he was unable to realise that the Prince of Wales, now twenty-four years old, was equally sensitive and rather more imaginative, and that, being young and of a restless kind of temperament, he was eager to explore the world of the future instead of being content with the autocratic and stultifying ways of the past. Undoubtedly the King was very fond of 'dear David', and in a letter to Lord Stamfordham he wrote: 'I believe he will be a great help to me.' But like so many middle-aged parents of his time he felt that the new generation growing up had a distinct inclination towards frivolity and that the young needed more of the discipline he had been subjected to in his own youth. Otherwise he feared for the ideals of duty and obedience which he had always believed to be right and was determined to instil into his son's character.

His anxiety was not unwarranted. Times were changing, he could see that for himself from his inner knowledge of the up-heavals caused by the War in Europe and everywhere else. Yet he could see nothing out of date in the pre-war conventions and standards of behaviour he was accustomed to, and as he grew older his adherence to them in his family circle became more rigid, though strangely enough, this inflexibility towards those nearest to him did not show itself in his exhausting and arduous work for the state. Here his judgement remained impartial, unclouded by prejudice or intolerance, and with his vast experience of political matters, he was able to adapt himself to changing circumstances without any loss of his high principles. He received Mr Ramsay MacDonald and his colleagues of the first Labour Government in 1924 with equanimity and took immense trouble through Lord

Stamfordham to see that those who could not afford £70 for the full court dress uniform to be worn at their first levee, were enabled to hire the whole outfit of trousers, coat, cocked hat and sword for half the sum from the obliging Messrs Moss Bros. Thus arrayed and somewhat overawed by the crimson and gold magnificence of his surroundings, Mr J. H. Clynes, the ex-millhand turned Lord Privy Seal, had expected to find His Majesty stiff and unbending, but instead reported that he was 'kindness and sympathy itself'.

With his only daughter, if not with his sons, this kindness and sympathy of the King's predominated. Princess Mary was gentle and undemanding and like her father had little inclination for the gaiety and liveliness of metropolitan high society. She dressed quietly in a style of her own which could not be called rich or fashionable and she was rather shy in public. During the War and immediately after it, however, she accompanied her father and mother on every suitable occasion and was their constant companion at home. Then in 1921, at the age of twenty-four, she became engaged to Viscount Lascelles, eldest son of the Earl of Harewood, a wealthy Yorkshire landowner with a

5 *King George V at the Conference on Ireland, with Lloyd George, head of the Coalition Government. (Press Association Ltd.)*

vast mansion near Leeds, designed by Robert Adam and filled with innumerable treasures. 'They are both very happy and Mary is beaming,' the Queen wrote to her brother, the Marquess of Cambridge, adding: 'We like him very much and it is such a blessing to feel she will not go abroad.'

The wedding took place in Westminster Abbey on February 28, 1922 and as the first big royal pageant since the War, aroused immense popular excitement and enthusiasm. It was headlined in the daily newspapers as the 'Nation's Wedding' and the 'People's Wedding of our beloved Princess', and as there were no news films, television pictures or radio commentators, ordinary people could only participate in the event by going out into the street to watch it. This they did, in large numbers, determined to enjoy themselves and to get their fill of gaping at the highest in the land as if they were Derby winners or a different species of mankind from a more exalted planet. With the class distinctions of the old world still accepted as the fundamental basis of society, class hatred and envy were less widespread than they were later to become, so it was fun for the lucky ones in the assembled crowds to watch the aristocratic guests arriving at the Abbey: Lord Lonsdale conspicuous in his spanking primrose yellow and black Daimler with liveried chauffeur and footman in front, Lord Derby familiar from his pictures at all the race meetings in the country, the Duke of Devonshire with his Duchess in a feathered hat, all the nobs and the snobs in high fettle sweeping through the great west door to the faint sound of the organ playing within. Then the delicate and pretty-looking bridesmaids appeared, followed by the Princes and Queen Mary and finally the King with his daughter on his arm, 'a radiant bride', according to the newspapers the next morning, in a silvery gown strewn with seed pearls and a *bouffant* veil.

'Mary was calm, doing her part to perfection—a very great ordeal before so many people,' her mother wrote afterwards. But the King was heart-broken when he said goodbye to his daughter after the wedding festivities were over and wrote in his diary a few days later: 'I miss darling Mary most awfully.' Prince Albert, now Duke of York, was aware of another aspect of the situation. 'Things will be very different here now Mary has left,' he said, writing from Buckingham Palace on the same day to the Prince of Wales, 'and Papa and Mama will miss her too terribly, I fear,

6   *The panoply of royalty; King George V leads his two sons, the Prince of Wales and the Duke of York–later King George VI–on his way to the Horseguards' Parade for the Trooping the Colour. The period is apparent from the fashions of the privileged onlookers in the courtyard of the Palace. (Camera Press)*

but it may have a good effect in bringing them out again into public. I feel that they can't possibly stay in and dine together every night of their lives . . . and I don't see what they are going to do otherwise, except ask people here or go out themselves. But we shall know more about this as the days go on.'

The young Duke's optimism was disappointed. The King did not ask people in, or go out very often. He preferred dining alone with the Queen and if he had no more work to do on his 'boxes' of state papers, poring over his stamp collection until the ornamental clock in their private sitting-room chimed 10.15 and it was time to go up to bed. That this routine was not much fun for the rest of his family never seemed to occur to him. The Queen, though she still enjoyed dancing and going to the theatre, was willing to forego her pleasure in such diversions for the sake of her husband, who was often a very tired man. The younger members of the family, not unnaturally, were less self-sacrificing. For them an evening spent at home was far from gay and the King's unfortunate habit of interrogating his sons about what they were doing and where they had been, did not help matters.

His own duties towards society, he believed, were discharged by his regular appearance at the semi-state and state functions of the year that were gradually revived as the War receded into the past. In February 1920 he opened Parliament, driving in state to Westminster in the glass coach with the postilions and outriders in scarlet and gold lace, white silk stockings and buckled shoes; and he was extremely gratified by the high attendance in the House of Lords of so many peers and peeresses in full regalia, not apparently noticing the strong odour of moth balls which emanated from their crimson and ermine robes. In March of the same year he held his first levee since the War, noting in his diary that 'it was refreshing to see the old full dress uniform again', though perhaps he really meant 'reassuring' since, like Polonius, he thought 'the apparel oft proclaims the man' and had a particular obsession about the correct clothes for the correct occasion with a corresponding horror of some of his eldest son's bizarre sartorial experiments. In April the Court moved to Windsor and on the morning of Easter Monday, as in Queen Victoria's day, the band of the Royal Artillery played a selection of popular music on the terrace. But at night, after the King had gone up to bed, the younger members of the house-party rolled up the carpet in the billiard-room farthest from the royal bedchamber and danced to a portable gramophone though the atmosphere of the ancient Castle was not very conducive to much gaiety in the proceedings.

In June both the King and Queen were present at Epsom for the Derby, and at Ascot, later in the month, the royal carriage drive down the course was resumed to the flower-decked royal pavilion, guarded by the King's Indian orderly officers in their red turbans and green uniforms. The Royal Enclosure was crowded, the birth and breeding and respectability of the ticket-holders having been scrutinized by the Lord Chamberlain's Office weeks before the event and any person divorced or otherwise disgraced excluded. 'Dress,' according to the Ladies Page of the *Illustrated London News*, 'was not extravagant, because that implies bad taste, but it was costly and it was styleful. Lace and embroidered net dresses held complete sway . . . and long circular lace cloaks were worn.' Lady Dorothy Macmillan, the Duke of Devonshire's daughter who had recently married the young Mr Harold Macmillan, wore a cloak of white lace lined with chiffon, 'having a border and an intersecting band of black gauze'; and everybody carried a sunshade, 'albeit there was little occasion to use them until late in the afternoon'. One parasol was 'black with transparent bands of russet embroidery like an Etruscan frieze', another of yellow silk, brocaded in lines of pale bright gold, 'as flat as a plate and not so very much larger'; a third was of black ostrich feathers opening from a stick of carved coral and still others were 'domes of taffeta of one colour with deep flowered borders in different shades'. All of them were pretty, elegant and quite useless where a shower of rain came on, and the men 'on duty with their brollies' quickly had to protect all the lace and the chiffon and the fluffy headgear of their feminine companions from disaster.

But Ascot was Ascot, the high point of the Season, and it was both nostalgic and heartening after the long years of wartime economy to see the Royal Enclosure reanimated by fashionable society, even if taste was sometimes more 'extravagant' than

7   *The formal house party was still a feature of the social round in the early twenties when the Prince of Wales visited Canada. The Prince is pictured at a party given by the Duke of Devonshire in Ottawa in 1922. (Press Association)*

'styleful'. One lady appeared in a very bold dress in blue and yellow silk, the skirt looped up at the sides to expose a great deal more of her beautiful legs than had yet been seen at a public race meeting. Having topped the effect with a large picture hat worn down on her nose, she looked like an exotic tulip bloom with a mysterious lid on it. The Twenties had arrived. New fashions were coming in and before long parasols would be going out as the young no longer wished to hide their blushes or to protect their delicate complexions from the enquiring rays of the sun.

Fashion likewise dominated the first Court for six years, also held in June 1920, though here the rules laid down by the Lord Chamberlain's Office had to be strictly observed. Sketches were on view of what was acceptable to be worn by young girls, young married ladies and ladies presented on titles changed or conferred. Short skirts and scanty bodices were eliminated because it was necessary to adhere to the required measurements; therefore, as the *Illustrated London News* again commented, 'the women to whom these abbreviated frocks are dear must have one specially for the Court', and it was hoped that the restrictions would have 'a beneficial effect on fashion by limiting extremes, which are not either pretty, refined, or, indeed, modest!'.

The Lord Chamberlain decreed that trains and feathers could be dispensed with in the interests of economy, but the court dressmakers were happy enough with the intense activity engendered among them by the renewal of this pre-war function. Madame Lucile, otherwise Lady Duff Gordon, the first society lady ever to open a smart dress shop in London way back in the 1890s and a sister of Elinor Glyn, the passionate red-haired novelist, welcomed prospective debutantes and their mothers to her elegant pink and grey salon in Hanover Square with charm and practical wisdom. The distinguished house of Reville & Rossiter, also in Hanover Square, designed a dazzling gown of net thickly embroidered with irridescent *paillettes* for Queen Mary and another 'in old gold metal cloth embroidered in *diamenté* and coral' for the Marchioness of Headfort, the handsome and delightful ex-Gaiety girl Rosie Boote, who had successfully married into the peerage. Mrs Lloyd George, who presented her young daughter Megan, wore pale grey satin 'in her usual quiet taste', but a lady from Cheltenham allowed her local dressmaker called 'Margot' to override the Lord Chamberlain's

8 *The glories of Ascot were revived in the early Twenties and the royal carriage drive along the course was resumed. Here the Prince of Wales is seen with King George and Queen Mary. (Central Press Photos Ltd.)*

decree, since her elaborate dress of 'silver lace over turquoise georgette with side panels of brocaded georgette caught with jewelled ornaments, was completed with a brocaded train hung from the shoulders of the corsage'.

The King wore the full dress uniform of Colonel-in-Chief of the Coldstream Guards with a row of medals and diamond stars on his chest and the sky-blue sash of the Order of the Garter. The Queen's superb crown and matching collar of diamonds and emeralds worn with a pendant diamond necklace and still more diamonds and emeralds blazing on her corsage, flashed in the light as they walked in procession through the state apartments to the Throne Room, followed by the Mistress of the Robes, the Master of the Horse and other high Court officials and all the gentlemen of the *Corps Diplomatique* in a fantastic array of foreign uniforms. The brilliance of the jewels and the brightness of the colouring vied with Aladdin's cave; yet for the debutantes themselves it was a rather frightening climax to months of preparation, practising the curtsey, wearing a new dress, waiting in the Mall in a long queue of motor-cars and queuing again in the long corridors of the Palace.

Some of the girls were beautiful; daughters of the English aristocracy, with the bloom of youth in their eyes and rose petal cheeks untouched by rouge or face powder. Some were awkward-looking and very angular in their long dresses, happier in the hunting field or playing hockey at Roedean. Most of them wore their long hair in a shapeless kind of bundle, puffed out in the front and looped up behind, with perhaps a small diamond spray nestling somewhere in it. Many of them were shy and very nervous, goose pimples breaking out on the bare patches of their arms above the long white kid gloves they wore, as they shivered with fright in the rooms kept cool by a primitive method of pumping air over a screen of ice blocks. None the less it was an occasion, a glittering and beautiful sight, and when the curtseying was over, supper in the Green Drawing-Room was very enjoyable. And there were advantages from being presented at Court that could not be obtained by any other means. It gave the debutantes the entrée into what was still a very closed circle of upper-class society at home and at the Embassies abroad, while from a snobbish point of view it conferred a certain prestige on them and improved their matrimonial chances—or so their mothers believed.

It was expensive, of course. Renting a house for the Season in Mayfair, Belgravia or Kensington if you did not already own one, was a game those hard-headed men who had made big profits out of the War always won. Property in London in the immediate post-war boom was at a premium and the situation aggravated not only by the numbers of people trying to find new homes, but by the numbers of houses in disrepair. The spacious and lofty Victorian houses of Queen's Gate, Holland Park and Bayswater had been allowed to run down, or were being divided into narrow compartments, all height and no depth, euphemistically called 'bachelor flats'. No self-respecting upper-class family could any longer dwell in them, nor could they be termed 'a good address', which was still essential; for although the wearisome and complicated permutations of leaving visiting-cards had died a natural death during the War, stamped note-paper and handsomely-printed invitation cards still predominated over the telephone as a means of communication.

Some of the great London houses of the nobility with their

9   *Debutantes at Queen Charlotte's Ball at the Dorchester, May 1931. The Season meant a house in town, rounds of garden parties and the thrill of presentation at Court. (Radio Times Hulton Picture Library)*

splendid marble staircases, patrician dining-rooms and ballrooms hung with eighteenth-century family portraits, were reopening their doors: Crewe House behind its delectable garden in Curzon Street, Bridgewater House on the Green Park, Derby House in Stratford Place and Lansdowne House with its own private passage into Berkeley Square. Others like Devonshire House and Grosvenor House were rumoured to be at the end of their days. Staff was a problem. Young men, who had seen death in the trenches, did not settle very easily into a new job and were not interested in serving in the pantry or the dining-room; young women, who had earned high wages making munitions, were even less interested in the kitchen or the housemaid's cupboard. They wanted, or seemed to want, better quarters, better money and more freedom, and they had little or no respect for the old rules of behaviour. Footmen whistled in the corridors and smoked in their bedrooms; maids, dressed to the nines, rushed off in the afternoon to go shopping at Selfridges or Swan & Edgar's. As one aristocratic lady was heard to say: 'The bottom's coming up, my dear, and the top's coming down', and the adjustment was difficult on both sides, though in the end the aristocracy proved to be remarkably flexible in adapting its way of life to the modern world.

For the time being, however, the debutantes' dances, formal dinner parties and fashionable weddings of the Season in 1920 continued to belong more to the old world than to the new, and so did the comments of the press. 'Many a great name in the peerage, many distinguished political men and members of the Diplomatic Corps, in fact, all the men and women of note in the Social World and in the circle of the Controlling Classes,' according to the effusive reporter on the *Illustrated London News*, 'were guests at the wedding of Lord Curzon's daughter, Lady Cynthia, to Mr Oswald Mosley', and those who could not get into the Chapel Royal for the ceremony were entertained afterwards at the splendid reception held in the Curzons' town house in Carlton House Terrace overlooking St James's Park. King George and Queen Mary were there and so were the King and Queen of the Belgians, who had travelled from Brussels by air to Croydon, well wrapped up in flying-helmets, goggles and mufflers against the potential hazards of the journey.

That Lord Curzon should be so honoured was not surprising, since his power and prestige after the War were even greater in Europe than in England, where his high and haughty manner made him enemies as well as friends, but was not inconsistent with his forceful leadership of the Conservative Party in the House of Lords. By a cruel irony of fate it was this very distinction that robbed him of the highest political prize three years after his daughter's wedding, when the King realized that a Prime Minister in the House of Lords would be unacceptable to the new Labour members in the House of Commons and instead of inviting Curzon to fill the office, called instead upon Mr Stanley Baldwin, the comparatively unknown, middle-class Member for Bewdley. Lord Curzon never got over this singular disappointment and his rejection signified the way in which democracy was steadily and greedily eating into the power of the House of Lords in the government of the country whatever the *Illustrated London News* may have thought about 'the circle of the Controlling Classes'.

The King's decision was made after much careful consideration and it showed remarkable foresight in anyone of so conservative a nature. He admired Lord Curzon and knew very little about Stanley Baldwin, yet he saw what was apparently good for the health of the nation in the confused post-war political situation. And to some extent he made a similar attempt to broaden the basis of the next social function at the Palace. Invitations to the Garden Party in July were distributed among a far wider section of the community than for the Court held in June. Many visitors from the Dominions overseas, the Canadians, Australians and New Zealanders, whose loyal support during the War had so heartened the mother country, mingled with the guests on the lawn, hiring top hats and morning coats for the occasion. Very few of them had much chance of talking to Their Majesties unless they were sufficiently eminent to be presented to them individually, but the King and Queen made an extensive tour of the lawns and then stood in front of the Durbar tent so that everyone could get a good view of them, while the brass band of the Coldstream Guards played in the distance. Afterwards there were cucumber sandwiches and strawberries and cream in a large marquee under the trees and friends gravitated together in little clusters to gossip and comment on each other's news. It was all very decorous, very pleasant and very English, and it all belonged to the aristocratic English way of life that, in spite of being interrupted by the War, was again beginning to flourish.

Garden parties at Hurlingham and Ranelagh for the polo, garden parties at Lords for the Eton and Harrow match and garden parties at Henley were all fashionable events of the Season: an instance of the indomitable optimism of the English upper classes towards the vagaries of their climate and of their preference for a way of life which belonged to the country rather than to the town. Indeed, before the War London had emptied out abruptly at the end of July and for anyone belonging to high society to be seen about town in August was quite out of the question. The blinds of the houses in Park Lane were drawn down, dust-covers spread over the handsome furniture within and a skeleton staff, with perhaps the kitchen cat, left as caretakers. Even now when things were changing, everyone who could afford it went on to Goodwood and then to Cowes before travelling north for the grouse shooting in August.

Goodwood was quite different from Ascot. It was a country race meeting, set in the glorious folds of the Sussex Downs and surrounded by groves of beech trees. From the Trundle Hill, where the *hoi polloi* picknicked happily for the races, the spire of Chichester Cathedral, the sea and the cliffs of the Isle of Wight were visible on a clear day and if the weather was fine, the mood of the racegoers always seemed to be gay and relaxed. Ultra-fashionable clothes were not worn and there was nothing formal about the parade in the paddock; some of the women wore sensible shoes and most of the men light grey or brown bowler hats.

The King and Queen stayed with the Duke and Duchess of Richmond in their large eighteenth-century house which was sheltered from the north by a beech wood called the Birdless Grove and surrounded by lawns, dotted here and there with rare cork trees and the umbrageous Cedars of Lebanon planted by a previous Duke. In the walled gardens there were peaches, nectarines and fig trees, and melons ripening in the hot-houses; in the dairy fresh milk drawn from the Duke's herd of black and white cows, and in the stables horses the guests could take out riding before breakfast. But Queen Mary, who always took every opportunity of pursuing her one great hobby of studying the arts when staying in the country houses of the aristocracy, was more interested in the superb Canalettos of the River Thames, painted for the 4th Duke who was the artist's patron when he first came to London in 1746, and she also visited the Folly half way up the Birdless Grove, where a former Duchess had painstakingly arranged the interior entirely of multi-coloured shells. Later she motored over to Arundel Castle, the historic home of the Duke of Norfolk, where there were more treasures to be seen, and one morning very early, she startled an old antique dealer in Chichester by arriving on his doorstep with no one in attendance except a lady-in-waiting to look at some Grinling Gibbons carvings he had salvaged from Halnaker House.

In the Isle of Wight, the Queen was well known for her sudden forays into the antique shops in search of items to add to her growing collection of *objets d'art* and historical mementos of the royal family. She disliked the sea and found Cowes rather boring. But for the King to miss the Regatta week was unthinkable: after Goodwood, he went aboard the Royal yacht *Victoria and Albert* at Portsmouth and sailed across the Solent willy nilly, in good or bad weather. Cowes was never again to be quite what it had been in its pre-war glory when the yachts of the Tsar of Russia and the Kaiser were anchored in the Roads and King Edward VII, as the leader of cosmopolitan high society, held court on the lawns of the Royal Yacht Squadron, the most exclusive club in the world. The balls and receptions, the brass bands and the fireworks, the flowers and the flags and the white sails of the immaculate boats scudding along the Solent all had a glamour that was unparalleled elsewhere; and King George loved the memory of the Regatta as he had known it in the days of his youth as much as he enjoyed its revival in the Twenties. The sea was in his blood. At the helm of his racing yacht, *Britannia*, he was young again, carefree and content, proud of his skill and his training in the Royal Navy, never more genial. All his old friends gathered round him and even the young found his gruff kindness and humour encouraging.

For them Cowes was a romantic and beautiful setting for their experiments in growing up—less bewildering and less overwhelming than the confined atmosphere of London in the Season. Outside the exclusive formal entertainments at the

10   *Queen Mary, stately and self-possessed in her famous toque, with King George V and the Duke of Richmond and Gordon, 1922. (Popperfoto)*

Royal Yacht Squadron, there were impromptu dances and parties aboard the yachts, with forbidden cocktails instead of sherry, portable gramophones playing jazz records, and walks in the moonlight with the beflagged boats lit up and riding at anchor like jewelled moths on the velvet dark sea. What more could the young want? Already artful in dodging the eye of the elderly chaperone, the aunts and the married sisters playing gooseberry, they did—apparently—want more. They were restless and excited. The War was over, the weeds of mourning had been put away and life was just beginning. They wanted more freedom and more fun—a gay time in the uncertain new world waiting to be discovered.

2 THE PRINCE OF WALES AND THE SMART SET

For millions of the young of all classes everywhere the slight figure of the Prince of Wales very soon became a symbol of their longing and their determination to break away from the stuffiness of the old world into the air and the daylight of the new. With his fair hair, bright blue eyes and a winning smile, he was extremely attractive: a boyish figure, full of vitality and charm; a modern young man interested in modern ideas; a royal prince, who was also a good mixer. 'It's the smile of him,' one American newspaper reported after his first overwhelmingly successful visit to the United States in 1919, 'the unaffected modest bearing of him, the natural fun-loving spirit that twinkles in his blue eyes, and that surest of all poses, the recognition of duty to be done triumphing over a youngster's natural unease and embarrassment. That's what does it.'

Wherever he went—and he travelled over 100,000 miles round the world by sea and land between 1919 and 1923—it was the same story. His popularity was sensational. He was mobbed by the Canadians, pinched and buffeted by the enthusiastic Australians, and even in India, where Mahatma Gandhi and his followers attempted to boycott his visit, suffocated by the crowds who turned out to watch him play polo at Allahabad. The official programme of these tours was relentless and the glare of publicity something which few individuals and certainly no other prince of the blood royal had ever been called upon to endure. Day after day, week after week, he was on show—or, as he wrote later in *A King's Story*: 'Whenever I entered a crowd it closed round me like an octopus . . . Midnight often found me with wearied brain and dragging feet and the orchestra blaring out the by-now hackneyed tunes. If, mindful of next morning's programme, I were to suggest leaving a party early in order to make up some sleep, or if in an unguarded moment my expression betrayed the utter fatigue that possessed me, my hosts, who no doubt had spent weeks preparing an elaborate and expensive party in my honour, would disappointedly attribute my attitude to boredom, or, what was worse, bad manners. And so I drove myself many a night to the edge of exhaustion, lest unfounded rumour create the suspicion that I was an *Ungracious Prince*.'

Yet there were compensations as well as difficulties. Popularity had a stimulating effect on the Prince and gave him a new feeling of confidence. The frustrations of the War years, when he had found it galling as an officer of the Grenadier Guards to be kept out of the front line because he was heir to the throne, were largely forgotten in the comparative freedom he now enjoyed as the King's ambassador overseas. He had his own staff of sympathetic and lively bachelor friends and he was out on his own for the first time after a sheltered boyhood, dominated by the conventional Victorian concept of upper-class family life and further restricted by the tight harness of royalty. So it was all the more exhilarating to receive a noisy ticker-tape welcome in the streets of New York, to be entertained by the grand ladies of American high society and quizzed through their lorgnettes at the Metropolitan Opera House, and to end up at the Ziegfeld Follies. That all this did not go to the Prince's head and make him intolerably conceited was much to his credit; through it all, the unaffected modesty, which so endeared him to the public everywhere, remained his most distinctive characteristic.

At home, however, King George followed his eldest son's progress round the world with a somewhat anxious eye. Remembering his own tours as a young man in the Dominions and the never-to-be-forgotten splendours of the Coronation Durbar in Delhi, the unhurried state drives in an open carriage, the staid ceremony of Government House receptions and the comparative privacy of travelling in the royal train, he was alarmed and disconcerted by the press reports of the Prince's informality. Accustomed to a diet of the *Times* and the *Morning Post*, he was startled by the brash comments of the American and Dominion newspapers and it was in vain that his closest friends and advisers begged him not to pay too much attention to them. He was not

11   *Lady Diana Cooper, one of the outstanding beauties of her generation, played the rôle of the Madonna in* The Miracle.

amused by the story of the Prince at a rodeo in Saskatoon jumping on the back of a bronco and riding round the ring to the ecstatic applause of the assembled crowds. He was shocked by the playful suggestion that his son sometimes took evasive action when confronted with the wives of the officials at Government House, preferring to dance with girls of his own age, or to disappear altogether, no one could say where, with his young cousin, 'Dickie' Mountbatten. Even the photograph published in the newspapers of the Prince and Mountbatten enjoying themselves in the swimming-bath on board the *Renown*, though it only showed their heads bobbing above the water, moved the King to write that it was 'not decent—you might as well be naked'.

Queen Mary, also, was anxious about her eldest son. She often protected him from his father's wrath and managed to find excuses for what she called his 'fads', but her innate shyness and reserve made it difficult for her to reach any kind of intimacy with her grown-up children. 'She is really far too reserved, she keeps too much locked up inside herself,' the Duke of York commented at a later date when the King was ill. 'Through all this anxiety she has never once revealed her feelings to any of us'—and this was a fact of which the Queen herself was sometimes aware, admitting that she found it easier to express her feelings in writing to her husband and her sons than face to face with them. 'What a splendid reception David got in New York,' she wrote to her husband on the occasion of the Prince's visit in 1919, 'he really is a marvel in spite of his "fads" and I confess I feel very proud of him, don't you?' But when the Prince dined with her one evening in his father's absence, she wrote: 'David dined with me in the evening, we talked a lot but nothing very intimate.'

Unhappily the barrier of shyness persisted between them. Queen Mary disliked excitable people—they caused so much trouble. She had spent a great deal of her youth attempting to calm her mother, the Duchess of Teck, whose irresponsibility had so often upset the Court and caused a furore among the royal family, and perhaps she saw more of the old Duchess's volatile temperament in her eldest son than she thought was good for him. She worried because he seemed 'quite played out' when he came home from his travels and was apparently living on his nervous energy, rushing about all the time on pleasure as well as in pursuit of his duties. Thanks to her persuasion the King had allowed him

12 *Men's fashions were reflected by the Prince of Wales and his younger brother, Prince George – later Duke of Kent – seen here on their way to Buenos Aires to open the British Empire Exposition in 1931. (Keystone Press Agency)*

to set up his own establishment at York House, a rambling and inconvenient set of rooms in St James's Palace, which had not been properly modernized since the King and Queen themselves had lived there as Duke and Duchess of York in the 1890s; but although this gave the Prince some kind of independence when he was in London, rumours of the way he used his freedom had an unhappy knack of filtering back to Buckingham Palace and raising a storm there. 'I see David continues to dance every night and most of the night,' the King wrote. 'People who don't know will begin to think that either he is mad or the biggest rake in Europe. Such a pity.'

People—the young in particular—did not, of course, think anything of the sort. They loved the informality, the energy and the light-hearted gaiety of the Prince; they loved him above all for being one of themselves, happy to dance every night and all night in the dancing mania that possessed them all. That this might be a natural reaction from the horrors and miseries of the War, or, in fact, a healthy reassertion of life after the long years of wastage and death, would have seemed utter nonsense to the King, who also could find no reason or excuse for the restlessness of the new generation, their 'flying about' in fast motor-cars, their week-ends and their wild parties. It was all so different from his own youth and so disappointing. He had been so proud of his boys when they shot their first rabbits at Sandringham; now the Prince after a day or two out with the guns in the shooting season, 'rushed off to his tiresome golf'. Riding, too, became a bone of contention. The King had been delighted with his son's courageous horsemanship in the hunting field, but when he took to steeple-chasing with every chance of breaking his neck, it was not at all what the heir to the throne should do. 'The time has come when *I must ask you to give up* riding in the future in steeple-chases and point to point races,' he wrote in 1924 after the Prince had suffered quite a serious fall, and none of the arguments the Prince put forward in his own defence had any power against his father's decree.

The other problem, and the worst problem concerning the heir to the throne, could not be so easily solved by the King laying down the law; it was far more difficult. Having been so fortunate in each other, both of his parents were anxious that their eldest son should marry and settle down to enjoy a quiet family life. But in the post-war chaos of Europe, who was there in what the Prince privately called the 'grab bag' of the royal marriage market for him to take as his bride? Obviously no German princess would be acceptable to the nation after four years of hostilities—they were so inclined to be frumpish, anyway; and except for the Scandinavians, all the other royal houses were involved in one way or another in the political struggle for existence in their own countries or in exile. Even Queen Victoria had come to realize that dynastic marriages could be dangerous and lead to awkward confrontations, and it seemed to King George and Queen Mary better for their son to look for a wife among the English nobility. The Prince of Wales, however, like the prince in *Lac des Cygnes*, was not at all interested in any of the debutantes his mother paraded before him; he danced with them once politely and left them wondering, pretty as they were and charming as they might become when they grew older. 'There were,' he wrote later, 'moments of tenderness, even of enchantment' in his life at this time, but he was determined not to be hurried or to be forced into a loveless marriage.

His brother, the Duke of York, more like the King in

temperament and less exposed to the fierce publicity forever pestering the heir to the throne, was fortunate enough to fall in love with Lady Elizabeth Bowes-Lyon, a daughter of the Earl of Strathmore, who was descended from the ancient Kings of Scotland. Lady Elizabeth was so natural and so sweet she completely disarmed her future father-in-law at their first meeting and after the wedding at Westminster Abbey in 1923, the King wrote to the Duke of York: 'You are indeed a lucky man to have such a charming and delightful wife as Elizabeth . . . I trust you both will have many years of happiness before you and that you will be as happy as Mama and I am after you have been married for 30 years. I can't wish you more . . . You have always been so sensible and easy to work with and you have always been ready to listen to any advice and to agree with my opinions about people and things, that I feel we have always got on very well together. Very different from dear David.'

The Duke and Duchess of York were extremely happy and there were great rejoicings in the family when their first child, Princess Elizabeth, was born in 1926. Meanwhile 'dear David' continued to go his own way and to find his father's criticism of his behaviour more than a little irksome. From his travels in the

13 *Here is the epitome of the British Raj: the Prince of Wales on his royal elephant leads the procession of state elephants at Gwalior, India, in 1922. (Press Association Ltd.)*

younger countries overseas he had learnt to enjoy a more spontaneous way of life than was possible in England and his eager curiosity had been stimulated. 'My life had become one of contrast and commotion,' he wrote, 'whereas order and perfection ruled my father's and his seasonal migrations were as regular as the revolving planets.' Sandringham in January, London in February for six months of official and social engagements, with visits to Windsor for Easter and for Ascot; Newmarket for the Jockey Club race meetings, Goodwood, Cowes, then Balmoral for the grouse shooting and the deer-stalking; London again in October, interrupted by journeys to Sandringham for the partridge and pheasant shooting parties and finally the family gathering there at Christmas—this was the King's routine to which the Prince could not readjust himself. He admired 'the well-ordered, unostentatious elegance of the Court' and was bored by its unending formality. 'Nothing ever seemed to be forgotten, nothing ever seemed to go wrong.'

For a young man with a lively interest in the infinite possibilities of the modern world, it was not enough; it was stifling, and not surprising if he sought his amusements elsewhere, in hunting and playing golf or polo with the friends of his own choosing. Invitations poured into York House for week-ends in Melton Mowbray and the great country houses, and for the sumptuous balls of the London Season at Londonderry House, Wimborne House, Derby House and Hampden House: evenings of pre-war splendour and opulence, which seemed to indicate that the English aristocracy was unassailable in spite of the changing mood of the twentieth century and to suggest that nothing could damage the exclusiveness of a society so rich and so highly privileged. Hostesses vied with each other to capture the Prince, the most eligible bachelor in the kingdom, as the star turn of their entertainments. They measured their own success by the length of time he stayed dancing in their ballrooms or sitting with a girl in the supper-room, and very often they quite overpowered him with their effusive attention, so that he became rather good at inventing another engagement which enabled him to continue the evening elsewhere in more intimate surroundings.

Night clubs were the outcome of D.O.R.A., the Defence of the Realm Act passed during the War to regulate the licensing hours for the sale of drinks. There were vicious clubs in damp,

14 *The Prince of Wales at Accra, receiving homage at a palaver of chiefs of the central and eastern provinces during the African tour of 1925. (Conway Picture Library)*

overcrowded cellars round the back streets of Soho and Leicester Square, and fashionable night clubs in Bond Street and Piccadilly which were quite respectable. The police raided them all from time to time without any discrimination, entering through the skylights if the doors were barred against them and arresting everyone on the spot. One night they raided the Kit-Cat and only missed the Prince of Wales by twenty-four hours; more than once they descended on Kate Meyrick at the '43', but this did not deter her customers; it only added to the spice of life and made going to a night club all the more daring and exciting. Even the sleazy clubs attracted smart, rich people in evening dress to mingle with the prostitutes and their clients, the roughs and the toughs and the pedlars of drugs and sex; for it was all experience and frightfully modern, part of the brittle gaiety of the new world that teetered on the brink of hysteria with the jazz bands beating out their syncopated rhythm in the foetid atmosphere until four o'clock in the morning. The young were determined to have their fling. 'Jix', as they irreverently called William Joynson–Hicks, the Home Secretary in Mr Baldwin's second administration in 1924, was their enemy, his non-smoking, non-drinking, self-righteous virtue matched by the Victorian frock-coat he always wore; and they hooted with laughter when he failed to cleanse what he condemned as 'the social sewers' of London. In fact, night clubs were too profitable for their owners to mind if the law caught up with them or not, and their attraction persisted.

Those that were patronized by the Prince of Wales immediately became the focus of the smart young people he numbered among his friends, the most exclusive—and the most expensive— being the Embassy Club in Old Bond Street. It was approached through a long narrow tunnel between two shop-fronts, closely guarded by an impressive looking commissionaire and run by Luigi, an Italian restaurateur, whose discretion was never at fault. He knew the likes and dislikes of his distinguished clientele, to whom he could give credit and to whom he could not, and the exact position *vis-à-vis* a husband and wife sitting at separate tables and ignoring each other's presence. The decor was elegant, the dance floor small enough to be glamorously crowded, while Ambrose and his band played the hot and sentimental music of the hour 'too divinely'.

The Prince usually arrived at midnight in a party that invariably included the Hon. Mrs Dudley Ward, a dark-eyed beauty with sleek short hair, a slim figure and a rather wistful air

15   *Let them eat cake! One of the most prominent charities of the time was the 'Not Forgotten Association'. Here the Prince of Wales hands round the refreshments during the Association's annual party in 1922. (Radio Times Hulton Picture Library)*

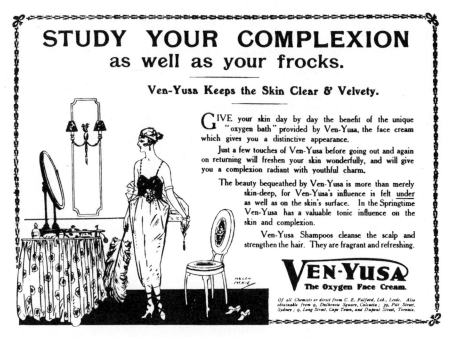

16   *Advertisements such as this reflected the increasing use of cosmetics and creams by the modern woman. (Illustrated London News)*

of melancholy, which besides giving her a most alluring quality, encouraged men to feel protective towards her. She dressed well in the romantic, diaphanous chiffon of the early Twenties, appearing at the Embassy one night in a backless evening-dress worn with a long scarf and a spray of very expensive artificial flowers on the shoulder, with five or six wrist chains and bracelets encircling her bare arms. Soignée and elegant in a new way, her style was imitated and quickly became fashionable, so that before long every young woman contrived to look as slender as an adolescent boy and they all had their hair cut short, deliberately flouting the traditional idea of how a woman should look *en grande tenue.* Gone was the piled-up coiffure, frizzed with curling-tongs, of their Edwardian mamas, the tight-lacing that pushed up the bosom and accentuated the hips, the over-elaborate, bejewelled corsage and the long satin skirts embroidered with beads trailing on the floor. The new silhouette was simple and strangely inno-cent in its daring; and the 'new woman', with the contrast of her soft femininity and her boyish looks, captivated the tired men who had survived the War and were old at the age of twenty-five and the gay young men growing up. Even the old men looked sideways

37

at the pretty arms and long legs revealed by this new phenomenon, while fulminating against her nakedness, her chain-smoking and cocktail drinking, her dancing into the small hours of the morning and the utterly shameless way in which she gloried in her new image.

The more sophisticated appearance of the chic young woman of the Twenties was achieved not only by lighter, more flexible clothing—and a minimum of underclothing in place of the long drawers and petticoats of the past—but also by make-up. Before the War only the *demi-mondaine* ladies of the town and the giddy queens of the music halls had painted their faces. 'Nice' women sometimes used *papier poudré* to enhance their complexions and a white lip-salve as a so-called medicament to prevent chapped or sore lips. Now every girl experimented with mascara, rouge and lipstick of a bright or cherry red, and they all plucked their eyebrows into a thin, provocative line. In America, where it all began, there were only two persons in the beauty culture business paying income tax in 1917 and ten years later there were eighteen hundred, while in Britain a similar escalation occurred after the opening of the first beauty salons in Bond Street. Cosmetic advertisements became bolder. 'Study your complexion as well as your frocks', the makers of VEN-YUSA OXYGEN FACE CREAM suggested. 'Give your skin day by day the benefit of a unique Oxygen Bath. Just a few touches of VEN-YUSA before going out will give you a complexion radiant with youthful charm.' And why not improve on nature? It gave the young confidence and the not so young a new lease of life. Only the old fogies sunk in the leather armchairs of the clubs in St James's Street and the spinsters immured in Kensington disapproved. The boys found the slender young women they hugged on the dance floor enchanting, and once the dancing had begun it looked as though it would never stop.

The friends of the Prince of Wales were the pace-setters, and as regular habitués of the Embassy formed their own élite. They had their own code of behaviour, their private jokes, their nicknames, their upper-class foibles and follies, which all seemed terribly 'amusing' and were food for the gossip writers of the glossy magazines. 'Fruity' Metcalfe, a dashing ex-Indian Cavalry officer, married to a daughter of Lord Curzon, was a voluble talker and a leading figure in the hunting world of Melton

Mowbray, who continually egged the Prince on to enjoy himself in his time off from his official duties. 'Burghie', the Earl of Westmorland, was another racing and hunting man, who combined a devil-may-care attitude with considerable business ability and all the social graces. 'Dickie' Mountbatten, handsome, debonair, highly ambitious to further his career in the Royal Navy, and the gayest of companions on the Prince's tour to Australia in 1920, was now married to Edwina Ashley. As the grand-daughter of King Edward VII's old friend, Sir Ernest Cassel, she had inherited his mansion in Park Lane, filled with eight hundred tons of Italian marble and malachite, together with a major share of his vast fortune. She was vivid and no fool, impatient of the narrow, autocratic conventions of the aristocracy, and quite fearless, with eyes like dark sapphires and an inexhaustible vitality geared to the post-war mood of freedom and independence. Her sister, Mary, married to Captain Cunningham Reid, had a more fragile kind of beauty with Titian-coloured hair and a skin like alabaster, set off by the huge aquamarines she wore in the evening—a mere bauble when set beside her income, which was said to be in the region of £50,000 a year.

Money, however, was not the key to the society that patronized the Embassy. Style was more important: that indefinable quality of upper-class elegance and self-assurance the modern generation had inherited from their forbears and were intent on interpreting in a new way. The dowdier debutantes, if they had the luck to be taken there, suffered an acute sense of inferiority when faced with the immaculate grace of the Hon. Mrs Richard Norton and her sister, Lady Brownlow, or with the exotic élan of the young Vicomtesse de Janzi, a great grand-daughter of King William IV and Mrs Jordan, whose high cheek-bones and huge pale aquamarine eyes rimmed with a sharp line of black gave her a mysterious Slavonic air, like a character from one of the Diaghilev ballets, which continued to excite the *cognoscenti* and to influence their taste.

It was necessary, also, to be a rebel, to defy the old order of high society by doing something outrageous that had not been done before: like Paula Gellibrand, a seductive, golden-haired beauty, who took a job as a mannequin and appeared at the Ritz in a hat covered in wisteria, before she married the Marquis de Casa Mauray, an audacious Cuban of Castilian descent and an ex-pilot of the Royal Flying Corps with a passion for motor-racing. Or like Poppy Baring, who was escorted everywhere by Prince George, the youngest of the royal brothers, and who opened a dress shop brazenly called 'Poppy' to exhibit the latest fashions designed for the new boyish figure. Other society girls opened hat shops in Mayfair, filling their windows with the cloche hats that were indispensable to the modern young woman, or gift shops, where everything was cute and very expensive. And although all these activities when viewed from a distance were really quite ordinary and rather naïve, at the time they were an exciting bid for freedom and a sensational move against the conventional upper-class view of how far a well-bred girl could go without becoming *déclassée*.

But by far the most beautiful and the most glamorous rebel of them all, with nothing ordinary about her, was Lady Diana Cooper, the youngest of the Duke of Rutland's daughters, and still as the years go on, the most beautiful woman of her generation. With fair gold hair like spun sugar on top of a very rich soufflé, an exquisite oval-shaped face, a luminous complexion and magical blue eyes, faintly startled and wholly innocent in their expression of divine inconsequence, this was how Helen could have looked walking the walls of Troy.

Before the War, as Diana Manners, she belonged to the 'Coterie', a set which included all the ardent youth of England, the gay sons and daughters of the Asquiths, Sir Herbert Tree, the Grenfells, Listers, Horners, Tennants, Charterises and Herberts, honourable upper-class families, whose sons all scrambled into the fight in 1914 and all too soon were decimated. Wild parties to keep their spirits up when they came home on leave, nursing at Guy's Hospital and the mounting agony of loss and despair, offset by hysterical orgies 'at the Cavendish Hotel, with Mrs Lewis leading her Comus crew around and around and into a room where a man was dying (not *in extremis*) "to take his mind off", or to fetch from the cellar Lord Somebody's champagne'; dancing all night to the first negro bands; halcyon picnics with Duff Cooper in the Surrey woods eating caviar and strawberries; a broken leg and the terror of who next would be killed and lost for ever—this was Diana's War, from

17 *A photo-portrait of Paula Gellibrand, style-setter and habituée of the Embassy, the*
    most expensive and the most exclusive Night Club in London. (Cecil Beaton)

which she emerged a little older, not much wiser and more ravishingly beautiful than ever.

She married Duff Cooper in 1919, after a sad and bitter feud with her mother, who thought a clerk in the Foreign Office too poor and too uninteresting as a husband for her beloved daughter. Yet the Duchess of Rutland, an artist and a sculptor of great talent, was herself a rebel against the conventional straight-jacket of the aristocracy and was later to be seen on top of a ladder painting a fresco of Chinese birds and butterflies in the bathroom of Diana's new house. It was not in Mayfair, it was in Bloomsbury. '*What* a quarter!' Lady Scarborough was heard to exclaim, and indeed, it was surrounded by rather seedy-looking hotels and boarding-houses. But the Duff Coopers made their home in Gower Street more beautiful and more exciting than any of the mansions in Mayfair. Lady Diana's flair for improvization, her originality and her style gave her parties a singular enchantment. Long before floodlighting became a technical possibility, she illuminated the garden on summer nights by projecting light from the top of the house, while Chaliapin sang with a quartet of Russian musicians, Hilaire Belloc and Maurice Baring sat together under the trees and Viola Tree danced as a naiad on the lawn.

Style was instinctive in Lady Diana—a superb style that made even her most eccentric forays seem perfectly natural. From her seaside home at Aldwick, she could set out to ride down the Bognor High Street on a grey mare, dressed as a cowboy in leather trousers, red scarf and wide-awake hat, her blue eyes scanning the horizon as if she beheld the Rocky Mountains there instead of a row of seaside houses offering bed and breakfast. At Max Reinhardt's Palace of the Prince Archbishop in Salzburg, when he wanted to try her out for the living statue of the Madonna in *The Miracle*, she tied her head up in a pair of chiffon drawers and safety-pinned two skirts together into a draped garment to disguise herself and her nervous apprehension of what he was going to think of her. He was not disappointed; and later he told her that he too, as a young actor, had been unable to play a part until he had disguised himself by wearing a beard, whereupon she commented in *The Rainbow Comes and Goes*: 'My drawers and pins were my beard and no doubt he divined it.'

Lady Diana's success in *The Miracle* in America in 1924,

18   *Lady Diana Cooper selling tickets at a garden party, 1924. As a society figure, she outshone the rest by her natural style and originality. (Press Association Ltd.)*

and later in London at the Lyceum Theatre, caused a sensation. Her beauty was breath-taking. The poise and stillness of her body in its 'cage of stone' and the grace of her movement when the statue of the Madonna came to life, cast a spell over everyone who saw her, though few people in the audience realized the nervous strain and the iron control she needed to carry the performance through. Some—a very small minority—thought it was not quite 'nice' for a duke's daughter to be seen doing it at all. But Lady Diana could violate all the rules without losing her balance, and by appearing on the stage for money, she threw an airy bridge from the old established aristocracy across into the disorientated world of the new society. Her radiance defied criticism—as it still does; and when she floated into the Embassy Club, her rare appearance there transformed the champagne cooling in the ice-buckets on the tables into the nectar of the gods, even if it made the smart young women dancing on the floor look like animated dolls. Or as Mrs Patrick Campbell, then in her own words 'older than God' and perhaps a little envious, once said to Beverley Nichols: 'One should never meet Lady Diana socially; as soon as she comes into a room one should be allowed to retire behind the curtains, and *gloat*.'

But the dancing at the Embassy and elsewhere went on, becoming more hectic to match the still shorter skirts and flesh-coloured stockings that drew attention to the elegant, or not so elegant, legs of the dancing girls. Jazz band leaders became rich and famous. Gramophone records sold like hot toffee and sounded like it, hammering out the sticky negroid jungle of noise with drums and rattles and saxophones. It was old-fashioned not to have a stately and rather expensive cabinet gramophone on legs that could be wound up any hour of the night or day to start the ball rolling. New tunes from America—from Gershwin, Cole Porter, Irving Berlin and Jerome Kern—swept into London like a March gale across the Atlantic, and the hit tunes from *No, No Nanette* and *Stop Flirting*, which brought Fred Astaire and his sister dancing into Shaftesbury Avenue in 1923, were vamped on the piano in the drawing-room at tea-time, supper-time and bed-time.

New dances—the Jog Trot, the Vampire and the Shimmy— were followed by the Blues and then the Charleston, which roused a storm of indignation among the Puritans and the press. 'It is neurotic! It is rotten! It stinks!' shouted the Vicar of St Adrian's at Bristol, while the journalists described 'Nights in the Jazz Jungle' as 'degenerate, negroid and freakish' and probably leading to 'a permanent distortion of the ankles.' There were some red faces in Fleet Street when the Prince of Wales learnt the Charleston and danced it with Mrs Dudley Ward at the Café de Paris. It was noticed that he wore black suede shoes, which served as a useful red herring to divert criticism away from his dancing to his unconventional footwear.

The Café de Paris in Coventry Street off Leicester Square was opened by Poulsen, the Danish head-waiter from the Embassy Club, and quickly became another very fashionable and very expensive rendezvous for the new élite. The underground, oval-shaped room was a somewhat macabre choice in decoration, being a replica of the palm court of the ill-fated *Lusitania*, with a balcony all round it and a double staircase curving down to the dance floor. This, however, formed a stylish background for the cabaret artists Poulsen engaged to entertain his smart clientele. Gwen Farrar, a well-bred young lady with straight black hair and horn-rimmed glasses, who sang in a baritone voice and should not have been singing in public at all according to her family, appeared with her accompanist, Norah Blaney, and was a wild success. Delysia, gorgeous and provocative in a sheath of sequins, descended the stairs, waving her ostrich feather fan like a royal banner. Jack Buchanan, Bea Lillie and the outsize 'red hot momma' from the States, Sophie Tucker, all showed how a single entertainer with talent could excel in the intimate atmosphere of a restaurant. For cabaret was a new feature of West End night life and new high-class restaurants with dance floors and a cabaret show at midnight were opening everywhere—Sovrani's, Quaglino's and the Hungaria, where romantic gipsy music was sometimes a pleasant change from American jazz.

All these kept within the law. Kate Meyrick, the most notorious of the night club owners, did not. She was Irish and the mother of six children when her husband deserted her in 1919. The boys were at Harrow and the girls at Roedean—something had to be done. For a time she went in with a Mr Murray Dalton, who ran a dubious dance club in Leicester Square, then in 1921, she branched out on her own in the basement of No 43 Gerrard Street, a house which had once been inhabited by the poet Dryden. It was damp, ill-lit and dangerous; the police raided it almost at once, and this, perhaps, accounted for much of its attraction, since the threat of interference created a delicious feeling of excitement. Yet there was more to the '43' than that. It had a bedraggled kind of cosiness, which comforted the disillusioned and encouraged the romantic fantasies of the young. Dancing there, cheek to cheek, or sitting hand in hand, with a bottle of champagne and a packet of Abdulla' cigarettes, the realities of the world outside were excluded; and the night, it seemed, might never end, blurring painlessly into eternal night in the haze of tobacco smoke, the half light and the champagne winking at the bottom of the glass.

Kate Meyrick had a remarkable personality. She was completely without glamour and dowdily dressed, with an old velvet cape or a tatty piece of fur draped round her shoulders: a dark, spidery little woman with sharp eyes and a sharp face, belied by the warmth and vitality of her smile when she welcomed her 'boys', as she called all her clients, into her web. The list of her members at the '43' read like the pages of *Debrett*, interspersed with a mixture of Bohemian artists and writers, boxers, jockeys and *nouveaux riches*, like the Lancashire millionaire, Jimmie White, who brought six Daimlers full of show-girls one night to a champagne party costing £400. Prosecutions, fines and imprisonment in Holloway in 1924 failed to suppress Mrs Meyrick's indomitable Irish bravado. When the '43' was closed down, she opened the Manhattan and then her grandest club of all, the Silver Slipper in Regent Street, where the dance floor was made of glass. In 1928, however, she was involved in a more serious criminal charge when a police officer of the C.I.D. vice squad, Sergeant Goddard, was accused and found guilty of accepting bribes from her and another night club owner called Luigi Ribuffi. Kate Meyrick went into Holloway again for a longer stretch and when she came out, was surrounded by a mob of excited Bright Young People singing an absurd little ditty:

> Come all you birds
> And sing a roundelay
> Now Mrs Meyrick's
> Out of Holloway.

Twice more she went to gaol, but in 1932, again in front of the bench, she gave 'an honourable undertaking to have no more to do with night clubs'—and a year later she was dead, though not before she had married three of her daughters into the peerage: one to the racing motorist Lord Kinnoull, one to Lord de Clifford and the third to the Earl of Craven. She left £58 and no successor, for by then bottle parties were more popular than night clubs.

'Bright Young People' was a headline first used by the *Daily Mail* for the gay set in London, whose unusual behaviour had news value, and the label stuck. Like the police, the press did not discriminate between the fun of the original leaders and the more sinister goings-on of the fringe people and social climbers trying to cash in on the Mayfair merry-go-round. Any wild party or Bohemian rag in the West End was attributed to the Bright Young People and was written up for the middle-class readers of the newspapers as an outrage against the common decency of the 'little man'. Yet the leaders of the group were far from stupid and it was because they were bored with the formal functions of the Season that they invented childish and silly amusements to quench their youthful high spirits.

Lady Eleanor Smith, the clever daughter of a very clever father, Lord Birkenhead, and the Jungman sisters devized a

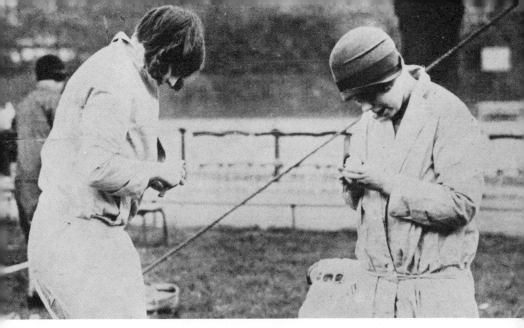

19   *The General Strike: Lady Mary Ashley-Cooper and Lady Carmichael-Anstruther peeling potatoes in Hyde Park to help the food-transport workers. (Illustrated Newspaper Group)*

series of hoaxes, which they found highly diverting. Lady Eleanor had cards printed for 'Miss Babington Gooch, Amalgamated Provincial Press' and went around conducting spoof interviews with the celebrities staying at Claridges and the Savoy. Theresa Jungman, known to everyone as 'Baby', masqueraded as a Russian Princess, arriving at a garden party with two borzois on a leash and a casket of jewels, which she said she had saved from the Bolshevik Revolution and must sell to educate her non-existent 'poor little boy'. It was all great fun and fairly harmless. No one was hurt in the process.

Treasure hunts, too, were a new diversion invented by Lady Eleanor and her friend, Loelia Ponsonby, whose father was Treasurer to the King and lived in St James's Palace. Each hunter contributed to the prize money and they would all meet on Horse Guards Parade or in Piccadilly Circus at 2 a.m. before careering off all over London in fast motor-cars, looking for clues in the most unlikely places, ending up sometimes as far afield as Maidenhead or the Café de Paris at Bray when dawn was breaking. 'Treasure hunts were dangerous and scandalous, but there was no sport to touch them,' Lady Diana wrote in *The Light of Common Day*. 'Quick thought, luck and unscrupulous driving might bring you first to the coveted prize.' And whereas 'Duff disapproved and disbelieved in the wild ecstasy . . . one night when the meet was at Gower Street and the Prince of Wales to be a hunter, having joined in, he caught the fever and shouted: Faster! faster!' as they roared recklessly round the empty streets in their open car.

Such fun and such folly made still bigger headlines in the newspapers and so did the so-called 'bottle parties' of Mayfair. In fact, Loelia Ponsonby gave the first of these quite by chance. Being alone with her brother in St James's Palace and hard up, she invited her friends to drop in one night and to bring their own food and drink. Michael Arlen arrived with a dozen bottles of pink champagne and other friends with bottles of gin and whisky, and the impromptu evening was such a success, the idea caught on. Everyone, also, went mad about dressing up. There were carnival nights and masquerades, circus parties, Russian parties, Greek parties, the notorious Baby party, and parties where everyone dressed as someone else, all on the spur of the moment and for the fun of doing it. Guests were encouraged to improvize their own entertainment by doing a cabaret turn or wicked imitations of their friends, and some of the lively young men just down from Oxford—Evelyn Waugh, Brian Howard and Patrick Balfour—joined in the gaiety. 'They had a splendid zest for life,' Cecil Beaton wrote, 'and an ability for expressing it.' But it was this uninhibited zest pouring out of the young in high-spirited nonsense and wild frolic that the older generation, born to a more stable world, could not understand or forgive; nor could they see that their children might well be the victims as well as the cause of the disequilibrium of society, for the world was shifting under their feet and they could only learn their way about by experiment.

Their morals were fiercely attacked, though it is doubtful whether the Bright Young People were really any more immoral than Edwardian high society in its hey-day. Then it did not matter much what you did so long as you were not found out; now it did not matter what you did so long as you got talked about. A paragraph in the *Sketch* or the *Tatler*, or a comment from the improper pen of Lord Castlerosse, could give you a boost and build you up into a personality; and everyone knew—or thought they knew—about everyone else's love affairs. It was daring to talk about them and more daring still to be honest about sex in a deliberate attempt to flout the most sacred taboo of the older generation, schooled in the days of whalebone to ignore anything so common. Moreover, the young women of the Twenties no longer had the Edwardian sword of Damocles poised above their heads ready to drop on their necks if they were foolish enough to be caught in a compromizing situation. A 'reputation' lost, which had meant ostracism in high society and a quick withdrawal abroad to recover, had ceased to be a cardinal sin and divorce, except in the eyes of the Court, could be gone into without too much fear of the social consequences.

Yet in spite of the freer attitude of the young, sex was still clothed in the glamour of romanticism. Sex appeal, or 'It', the name coined by Elinor Glyn for the erotic allure of her cat-like and mysterious heroines dressed in purple chiffon and writhing on a tiger-skin rug, was seldom so brazenly exhibited as the novelist suggested. In the cloud cuckoo-land of the new society perilously emerging from the old, the bald discussion of sex tended to be more seductive and exciting than the adventure itself. The sex-kitten of the screen, the little girl image and the vamp were all imitated, but with much more smoke than fire. To be in love was the fashion; to consummate a passionate affair quite another thing altogether, for skating on ice was more amusing than falling into the depths.

The young man about town of the Twenties, however, unless he had a craving for his own sex, no longer had to look for his fun in the shadier brothels round Soho, or to practise the subterfuges of his father in keeping a wife and a mistress in separate compartments. The girls and young married women of his own class had suddenly blossomed into gay companions, ready for a lark anywhere at any time; and they were less expensive to take around, for even if they drank a lot and smoked too much through their long cigarette-holders, compared with their guzzling mothers and fathers packed with poached salmon, grouse in aspic and asparagus in season, they only nibbled a mouthful of *pâté de fois gras* when they felt like it, sitting on a divan or a pouffe on the floor. They were teasing and enigmatic, covering their arms with bangles and bracelets, exposing their knees and flicking their sensuous eyelashes with maddening disdain. But they loved fast cars and driving with the wind in their hair, they liked the new and exciting flying-machines, plunging into swimming-pools and whizzing about in motor-

20 *Two volunteer undergraduates take charge of the chief signal box at Bletchley station. All such help was welcome during the General Strike. Note the Fair Isle jerseys and 'plus fours' so fashionable at the time. (Illustrated London News)*

boats. Slim and athletic, the girls were 'good chaps' and girls into the bargain, which was something no one had ever thought of before. If this was shocking, no one cared. It was all part of the fun.

And it never occurred to the Bright Young People of Mayfair that the most shocking thing about them was their completely self-centred view of life. Not since the post-war era of Regency society had the frivolous pursuit of pleasure so blinded those who set the pace to what was going on in the rest of England. Even the opulent Edwardian aristocracy had combined their lavish party-giving with some good works among the working classes. Now, except for some hilarious charity shows which gave everyone a chance to show off in fancy dress, there was never any thought of what was happening in the industrial cities outside London. Poverty and social injustice were ignored. The Webbs and the Fabians and Bernard Shaw were figures of fun. News on the wireless, still in its days of crystal sets and cats' whiskers, was brief and never alarming. And the press was not taken seriously either—or, as Loelia Ponsonby put it: 'From time to time I wrote cheerfully in my diary that we seemed to be on the brink of a bloody revolution, but it was a possibility which had been in the

21 *The General Strike : Ladies more at home in the society pages feed special constables who had come to Scotland Yard to report while on duty. (Illustrated Newspaper Group)*

back of the minds of the upper classes ever since the days of Marie Antoinette and which they had got quite used to, so in the next sentence I went on to describe how I was trimming a hat or arranging a dinner party.'

Then, suddenly, in May 1926, the workers struck. Negotiations between Mr Baldwin's Government and the T.U.C. broke down. The transport workers and the rank and file of all the Unions came out in support of the miners. The General Strike was on.

No one knew quite what it was all about. A single newspaper, the *British Gazette*, appeared, breathing Churchillian fire and brimstone down the neck of the workers. The Bolsheviks were blamed. Mr Baldwin spoke on the wireless and the situation looked grave. Armoured cars escorted convoys of lorries carrying food through the London streets and a battalion of the Grenadier Guards marched into the docks. Young men from Oxford and Cambridge poured into the capital to volunteer as bus drivers, train drivers and special constables, and the Bright Young People rushed in to join them. It was just another lark for most of them and terribly amusing to get filthy driving a train, even if it needed courage to run the gauntlet of bricks and stones thrown by the militants. It meant tearing about on duty, snatching drinks and sandwiches in between, or begging a bed in one of the upper-class houses thrown open to anyone patriotic enough to keep things moving and break the strike. Even the great mass of the working classes seemed to enter into the spirit of the thing, much to the amazement of foreign observers searching for dramatic incidents of the imminent revolution. Bus rides with the windows boarded up and the driver shut in a cage of barbed wire behind a Union Jack waving on the bonnet, became a joke and if passengers bound for Liverpool Street found themselves at Waterloo instead, no one minded very much, least of all the young blood who was driving.

Lady Diana, though she thought she could hear 'the tumbrils rolling and heads sneezing into the baskets', used her car as a taxi. Edwina Mountbatten and the Hon. Mrs Richard Norton manned the switchboard at the *Daily Express*, Winston Churchill chewed on his cigar in the offices of the *British Gazette*. And when it was all over—it ended as suddenly as it had begun—the *Illustrated London News* commented rather smugly: 'We feel that the heart of England must be sound . . . when we read that Mr C. E. Pitman, the Oxford stroke, is driving a train on the G.W.R. from Bristol to Gloucester, the Headmaster of Eton (Dr Allington) and about fifty of his assistant masters have enrolled as special constables . . . Lord Chesham is driving a train and the Hon. Lionel Tennyson is a special.'

The upper classes, with their strange instinct for doing the right thing at the right time and with the middle classes behind them had won. There was no revolution—only a sour taste in the mouth which embittered all future relations between the T.U.C. and the Tory Party. For the time being, the workers went back, looking rather sheepish; all except the miners, who continued their strike for another six months until starvation and despair forced them to accept the Government's terms of lower wages and longer hours. In Mayfair everyone had a story to tell of the Strike and then it became old hat and rather boring, and as Loelia Ponsonby commented: 'We went on precisely as if nothing had happened.' None of the Bright Young People had ever seen a mining village, and few of them wanted to. They were much too busy enjoying themselves.

3 THE ARISTOCRACY AT HOME

It has been suggested that if the French *noblesse* of the eighteenth century had learnt like the English aristocracy to play cricket on the village green, fewer heads would have fallen under the guillotine and rolled into Mme Tussaud's blood-stained basket; and indeed, it was characteristic of the great patrician families in England that, instead of remaining totally aloof from the lower classes, they deliberately chose to share their sporting pleasures with the ordinary people of the countryside. Cricket on the village green, with Lord John Sackville playing for Kent, and Rumney, the head gardener at Knole, as captain of the team, was only one of their pursuits. Hunting and horse-racing drew the cultured aristocracy and the rural population together in a bond of fellowship and good feeling that became a traditional feature of the British way of life; for the wealthy landowners of the eighteenth century with their splendid houses, their glorious gardens and their highly developed taste in the arts, were as easy in the stables with their grooms and huntsmen as in their state apartments when giving a ball or a banquet, and their affection for their horses and their dogs endeared them to the common people.

The dukes and other lords of the nobility were on nodding terms with everyone in the village. They could ride for miles over their own acres without crossing the boundary into anyone else's territory and very often they owned most of the property in the neighbouring towns as well. If a village spoilt the view from their windows, they could—and did—move the entire community to another site, or if a hill stood in the way of some new vista they thought could be improved, they simply flattened it out. Yet, with all this, they seldom abused the immense power and privilege they enjoyed. Their heart was in the land they owned and unlike their continental neighbours, they were never absentees from choice, only from necessity when high office in the affairs of the nation called them away to London or abroad; or as Richard Rush, the American Ambassador to Britain in 1819, observed: 'The permanent interests and affections of the most opulent classes here centre almost universally in the country. They have *houses* in London, in which they stay while Parliament sits and occasionally visit at other seasons, but their *homes* are in the country . . . where they flourish in pomp and joy.'

Their homes were magnificent. The Palladian mansions designed by Lord Burlington and William Kent and the elegant country houses designed or refurbished by Robert Adam were a superb setting for the paintings, the porcelain, the antique marbles and other works of art which the English Milords had collected in their youth on the Grand Tour and never stopped adding to as the years went on. The romantic parks and gardens conceived by 'Capability' Brown and Humphrey Repton in harmony with the contours of the landscape were never to be equalled or surpassed anywhere in the world. Peacocks paced the terraces at Blenheim, deer flicked their tails in the drowsy summer heat under the shade of the trees at Knole, a luminous lake winding through the verdant grass reflected the high white clouds of the English sky at Longleat. Rose gardens, hot-houses with grapes and melons and tropical plants, mellow brick walls with peach trees and pears, orchards of apples and plums, opulent fields of corn, lush meadows and groves of trees dazed the visitor seeing all this affluence displayed with such style and feeling.

Moreover with their mania for improving their estates and their absorbing interest in new agricultural methods, the outlook of the aristocratic landowners was almost always progressive and they left the land richer than they found it—a priceless heritage for their successors. They married their daughters to neighbouring landowners and endowed their sons most often with a sense of duty towards their great possessions in particular and to the service of the nation in general; and when their noble work was done, they were laid to rest in the village church beside their recumbent ancestors clad in crusading armour, to be remembered ever after as the creators of England's golden age of taste.

Even the dynamic changes wrought by the Industrial Revolution in the nineteenth century did little damage to the territorial grandees. Some of them in the North and the Midlands increased their wealth by exploiting the rich deposits of coal and iron lying beneath the surface of their land, or by collecting huge sums in compensation from the new railway companies, whose iron tentacles spread like an octopus through the countryside. The 16th Earl of Derby, a direct descendant of the 1st Earl created after the battle of Bosworth in 1485, besides owning some 70,000 acres of agricultural land in Lancashire and Cheshire, had property in Liverpool, Manchester, Preston, Blackburn, Bolton and many other towns, which under pressure from the rapid expansion of the new age of steam, rocketed in value. The Duke of Devonshire owned 186,000 acres of Derbyshire and Yorkshire, rich in minerals, and the Duke of Rutland had mining interests in Leicestershire. Financially the aristocracy was still in clover and what Richard Rush had observed in 1819 was equally true in 1899—the upper classes still flourished in pomp and joy, in spite of the two Reform Bills extending the franchise, in spite of the upsurge of the Victorian middle classes and the sprawl of the new built-up areas in and around the towns, and in spite of the back-to-back houses and the appalling poverty of the helpless men, women and children slaving in the factories.

Revolution was always somehow averted, partly because even the most Radical leaders of the people were ambitious to be taken for gentlemen, and also because the highest aim of the upstart industrialists and self-made bankers was to buy an estate somewhere in the shires and, by doing so, to become members of the landed gentry. Disraeli, in his fight for power in the Tory Party, bought the manor of Hughenden in Buckinghamshire with money he borrowed from Lord George Bentinck; and several members of the fabulous Rothschild family, grandsons of a Jew Street pedlar in Frankfurt, were his near neighbours. Baron Lionel owned the seventeenth-century manor of Tring and his two brothers, Anthony at Aston Clinton and Meyer at Mentmore Towers, lived *en prince*. 'The Medicis were never lodged so in the height of their glory' was Lady Eastlake's slightly acid comment on Mentmore Towers, Meyer's luxurious Anglo-Norman castellated mansion designed by Paxton and surrounded by groves of trees, rich pastures, racing stables and a stud farm, though she was not averse to enjoying the carriage drives and the Lucullan picnics of lobster mousse, quails, soufflés and champagne, which provided a continuous round of bucolic pleasure in the lush green beauty of the English countryside.

Some of the older country families resented this invasion of the shires by the *nouveaux riches* and the *parvenu* industrialists. But Edward VII as Prince of Wales and King was not so particular and his capacity for bending the rules of society without ever quite overstepping the mark or losing his dignity was remarkable. The charming sons of Baron Lionel Rothschild, Natty, Leo and Alfred, became his closest friends, their names appearing in the Court Circular as frequently as those of the hereditary peers of England. They went racing, hunting, shooting and yachting in the English manner and gave magnificent parties, where it was nothing for the ladies to find some exquisite jewelled ornament wrapped in the lace napkins beside their places at the dinner table. Indeed, the Rothschilds' hospitality was inexhaustible. With more than a touch of oriental extravagance and with a shrewd and calculating brilliance, they bought their way into the highest circles of Edwardian society and were accepted by almost everyone in it. The 5th Earl of Rosebery went so far as to marry one of them—Meyer's eldest daughter Hannah, who inherited Mentmore Towers from her father and thereby enriched her husband's family to such an extent, that her son, the 6th Earl, was able to keep up one of the biggest racing stables in the country all through the Twenties and the Thirties.

Other members of the nobility looked to the New World across the Atlantic when in need of improving their bank balance, in spite of the comments of one autocratic and elderly lady who was heard to say: 'I like the Americans very well, but there are two things I wish they would keep to themselves—their girls and their tinned lobster.' The 8th Duke of Marlborough, whatever his views may have been about tinned lobster, had no inhibitions about girls, American or otherwise. His ardent admiration for his beautiful American sister-in-law, Lady Randolph Churchill, was extremely embarrassing for everyone; and after his first wife had divorced him for Lady Aylesford, whom he promptly abandoned, he married a not so young and very stout American widow, called Lily Hammersley. The New York press unkindly described her as 'a common looking and badly dressed woman

22 *Nannies and nurseries are mostly past history, but in their heyday the park was the gathering place for the dignified custodians of the aristocratic young. (Illustrated London News)*

with a moustache', and noticing the brand new luggage the Duke arrived with, remarked that 'everything his Grace of Marlborough brought with him was clean, except his reputation'. But Lily Hammersley had an annual income of 150,000 dollars, which enabled her to feed her spaniels on fricassé of chicken, cream and macaroons, and the Duke to make some very necessary repairs to the roof of Blenheim Palace, so that even his high born and haughty mother made her welcome.

The 9th Duke also went to America in 1895 in search of an heiress and brought home Consuelo, the daughter of William Kissam Vanderbilt, whose fortune ran into millions of dollars and again served to strengthen the fabric of Blenheim, though this marriage ended in 1920 in another divorce case for the Marlboroughs, which received a great deal of unpleasant publicity. Consuelo then married a handsome French aviator, Colonel Jacques Balsan, who had distinguished himself in the War and moved to Paris, where her elegance and charm brought her many new admirers among the younger generation. The Duke took another American bride from Boston to add to the number of duchesses, whose portraits hung on the walls at Blenheim in line with Sarah Jennings, the first and most termagant Duchess of all.

Consuelo in her youth belonged to the Fifth Avenue set of multi-millionaires with brownstone mansions in New York, summer houses at Newport and palatial yachts on a par with those belonging to King Edward VII and the Kaiser. It was a closed circle, more snobbish and more rigid than anything to be found in England; for American high society owed its existence to the wealth of the original speculators in railroads, banking and commerce and its continuity to keeping everyone else at bay, whereas in England birth and breeding were of more importance than money and the aristocracy took their superiority for granted. There were no battles for precedence among the English families as there had been among the Astors and the Vanderbilts in New York. The order of society this side of the Atlantic, headed by the Royal Family, was fixed by the ancient lineage and titles inherited from one generation to the next, so that even if the individual moved outside the circle of his inheritance, mixing himself up with less exalted company, nothing he did altered the fact of his noble birth.

In New York, things were different. The Fifth Avenue set would not tolerate anyone from the rich Park Avenue set of the next generation and they looked on the new millionaires from Detroit and Chicago as provincial outsiders of the worst and most pretentious vulgarity; or as Cornelius Vanderbilt Jnr., himself a rebel against his parents' narrow circle, commented: 'Both money—barrels of it—and connections—no end of them—were tried on more than one occasion by the people who wished to leave their own and break into the Fifth Avenue set. Tried lavishly and magnificently. Tried unsuccessfully.' Only foreign royalty and certain members of the European nobility were allowed to penetrate into the rich interiors of the brownstone mansions; everyone else was excluded and the door firmly shut. For the Fifth Avenue set had neither the genius for survival of the English upper classes, nor their capacity for adapting themselves to change while appearing to ignore it altogether. Thus, at the end of the nineteenth century, when some of their daughters married titled husbands and settled in England, the association made little difference to the society they had left behind; but when the English went to America to choose their wives, they deliberately set in motion the loosening up process in their own society, which became increasingly noticeable before 1914 and by 1920 had gathered pace like an avalanche sliding down a mountain.

How, in fact, could the English aristocracy adapt itself yet again—and this time to the disorientated post-war world, with democracy on the prowl and the age of the 'little man' just round the corner, to say nothing of the new proletariat nurtured on the doctrine of Marx and Lenin? Never, it seemed, had the traditional English way of life of the upper classes looked so insecure, never had it been so threatened by the forces of change. Yet in the country it still went on. The Duke of Rutland turned pale whenever income tax was mentioned, but at Belvoir Castle the hounds met in the forecourt and the huntsman's horn was heard echoing through the Vale, where the bare winter trees stood in silence and the fox ran for his life. At Chatsworth the roof needed repairing, the corridors were cold, Paxton's great glass conservatory was in ruins and the cascading waters of the fountains fell among weeds. Indoor and outdoor servants were hard to come by; only the very young and the very old were available, the middle rank having been decimated in Flanders as the village memorial testified. Yet here, and at Bolton Abbey in

23　*Wedding presents of Lord Romilly and Diana Sackville-West on display, 1929. Society weddings were an occasion for lavish spending and a rich galaxy of gifts from friends and relations. (Central Press Photo Ltd.)*

Yorkshire, the 8th Duke of Devonshire, on his return from Canada where he had served as Governor General, entertained King George and Queen Mary with all the splendour his ducal authority could command.

The sumptuous state apartments at Chatsworth were hung with priceless tapestries and furnished with works of art that had been in the family since the eighteenth century; a different dinner service appeared for every meal and the sideboards, carved by Grinling Gibbons, were loaded with wonderful dishes of fish and game, vegetables and fruit and bonbons for the ladies. At Bolton Abbey, hampers of food and wine followed the shooting party to a simple cottage on the moors, where the ladies, arriving in a horse-drawn break, joined the gentlemen for a picnic luncheon served by liveried footmen on plates bearing the ducal crest. And when the new levels of taxation pressed heavily on the Duke after the War, it was the historic house in Piccadilly made famous in the Regency by the beautiful and turbulent Duchess Georgiana that he sold for £1,000,000, rather than part with any of his acres in Derbyshire. He needed somewhere to sleep in London, of course, when business in the House of Lords claimed his attention, so he bought a mansion in Carlton Gardens when Devonshire House was demolished, which by comparison served him as a modest *pied à terre*.

The Earl of Derby also kept a large town house in Stratford Place which he used very seldom as he grew older; but when someone asked him if it was worth his while to go on keeping it up, he replied quite naturally that 'Lady Derby must have somewhere to change her dress when she comes up from Cowarth [their home in Sunningdale] to go to the play', and the idea that this might be a rather extravagant way of dressing for the theatre never crossed his mind. Lady Derby served Queen Mary as a woman of the bedchamber and the Earl was one of King George's most intimate friends. He had no intellectual interests and very little aesthetic taste, but he combined a vast knowledge of public affairs and a great deal of common sense with a genial disposition and a progressive outlook.

Knowsley Hall, the Earl's ancestral seat half way between Liverpool and Wigan, had been in the family since the Middle Ages and was one of the largest houses in the kingdom, each generation having added bits and pieces to it, including the

24 *Only on Ladies' Night were wives – and perhaps girlfriends – allowed into the cigar-scented rooms of that male sanctum, the club. (Illustrated London News)*

gigantic dining-room in the Gothic style built by the 12th Earl in 1822, which was so hideously cold it had to be abandoned in the winter. Except for a superb Rembrandt and a series of Dutch sea-scapes, there were no treasures at Knowsley to be compared with the glories of Chatsworth and Woburn, but the upkeep of the house was a formidable item of expenditure even with Lord Derby's very substantial income. A man of the utmost integrity, he never failed to discharge his responsibilities with a princely generosity, the house overflowing with friends and relations and the neighbouring gentry, and on occasions with the more humble members of the Lancashire community whose problems he understood better than anyone else. When he entertained King George and Queen Mary for the Grand National in 1921, forty guests sat down to dinner in the dining-room and with the visitors' servants added to those in residence at Knowsley, sixty took their dinner in the steward's room and another fifty in the servants' hall.

The Earl's enthusiasm for racing made him extremely popular with all classes. He won the Derby in 1924 with Sansovino and again in 1933 with Hyperion, and his stud farm at

Newmarket was as successful as his racing stable. At all the big race meetings he was to be seen in the royal box or in the paddock enjoying himself in close consultation with his trainer and his jockeys, his sportsmanship known to everyone and his judgement highly esteemed. He was a stickler for fair dealing on the Turf and, as a leading member of the Jockey Club, saw to it that the honourable traditions of his ancestor who founded the famous race at Epsom were upheld in the more diffuse and complex commercialism of the post-war world.

After his second term of office as Secretary of State for War in Mr Baldwin's Government from 1922 to 1924, Lord Derby more or less retired from active politics, though he continued to exert enormous influence behind the scenes and to act as a go-between for the people of Lancashire and the central government. He was a Privy Councillor, a Knight of the Garter and Lord Lieutenant of the County, which was no sinecure; for he devoted his time and energy to the promotion of every good cause in his own locality and by doing so, earned the respect and the affection of everyone, while continuing to enjoy his own rich and comfortable way of life. Even through all the industrial strife of the two decades after the War, he emerged as the uncrowned King of Lancashire, his portly figure, his sense of fun and his practical wisdom radiating good will and the very best, benign instincts of the born aristocrat.

The Prince of Wales stayed at Knowsley when he toured Lancashire in 1921 and found the Earl a good deal more sympathetic than his own father. Knowsley was not one of the great houses where, as the Prince wrote later, 'youth walked warily'. Lord Derby was on good terms with his two sons and his daughter, and his grand-children all adored him. But there were some ancestral houses of the nobility where youth never dared to walk at all. At Woburn the Duchess of Bedford, who was deaf, sat at one end of the huge dining-table and the ageing Duke at the other without uttering a word. The Duke's evening trousers were frayed at the bottom and he wore a long black tail coat, a stiff shirt and a black waistcoat, looking not unlike the ancient butler who served him. After dinner he sat for ten minutes with the Duchess and then disappeared into his study; during the day they seldom saw each other while the Duchess was working at the Hospital she had established at Woburn for the wounded and continued to supervize as a special surgical and radiological unit throughout the Twenties. Their only son, Hastings, had become a pacifist conscientious objector, a fact which so enraged the Duke he had not seen him or spoken to him since before the War; and he would have nothing to do with his grandson, either, until one of the Russell relations arranged for that startled and wide-eyed young man to visit Woburn in the early Thirties.

The Duchess, driving a very high and very old green Rolls Royce, met him at Woburn Sands railway station, inspecting him with her keen bird-watching eyes as if he were another specimen to add to her list of rarities, and since she drove very fast and could not hear anything coming along the road behind her, the drive to Woburn Abbey was quite terrifying. In the park, 3000 acres and more in extent with a brick wall eleven and a half miles long running all round it, the young Lord Howland saw for the first time the Duke's rare herds of bison, deer and Highland cattle roaming freely across the meadows and browsing among the trees. And it all seemed 'quite lovely and somehow not part of the world at all'.

25   *The Grafton Hunt at Brackley, 1922. Lack of formality had not extended to the hunting field. The ladies still rode side-saddle, and the breeches cult was to come. (Radio Times Hulton Picture Library)*

His grandmother, meanwhile, had discovered on her first flight in an aeroplane in 1926 that the acute buzzing in her ears was miraculously relieved by the change of atmospheric pressure in the air and this encouraged her, at the age of sixty, to become a pioneer airwoman. At first she hired an aeroplane and a pilot, called Captain Barnard, but she soon learnt to pilot a plane herself and in 1930 the two of them set off to fly to the Cape and back in seventeen days. On the way home flames from the exhaust burnt a hole in the heater pipe and the Duchess became unconscious from the carbon monoxide fumes that filled the cockpit; then, having barely recovered from that disaster, Captain Barnard had to make another forced landing in the Sudan owing to a violent thunderstorm, and to tramp a mile through the lion-infested jungle with the indomitable Duchess before they could find shelter. 'We were immediately surrounded by a weird collection of natives dressed in girdles of beads only, very black, but very cheerful-looking, and apparently quite as much amused by my appearance as I was by theirs,' she noted in her diary, adding later, after the tumultuous reception given to her when they finally landed safely at Croydon: 'I was so little tired on arrival that I could easily have flown back to the Cape the next day.'

The 'Flying' Duchess, as the press called her, disliked the publicity that surrounded her, yet her courageous example did much to promote the science of aviation at a time when the risks were incalculable. Nothing daunted her and her enthusiasm never wavered. By 1937 when she was seventy-one, she had done 199 hours and 5 minutes of solo flying, and one afternoon in March she set off alone in her own De Havilland Gipsy plane from the hangar she had built at Woburn to complete her 200 hours. A heavy snowfall set in and she was never seen again. Duke Herbrand lived on among his servants, with his son's ex-governess, Miss Green, and her pekingese, dry rot creeping through the fabric at Woburn, dust darkening the Canalettos and the vast rooms empty and silent, except for the pattering feet of the mice in the panelling. Death duties hovered over his tired head, and it remained for his grandson as the 12th Duke of Bedford to reverse the process of decay by his dynamic vision of Woburn as a popular tourist attraction for foreign visitors arriving by motor-coach and crowds of midland mums and dads in cardigans and plastic macs, with their kiddies sucking sweets and ice-cream, all gawping happily at the wild animals in the safari park and at the bed the 'Flying' Duchess had not died in.

The public had always been admitted to a limited extent to some of the great English country houses. Belvoir Castle was open three days a week and Bank Holidays in the time of Lady Diana's grandfather, the 7th Duke of Rutland. 'He loved his tourists,' she wrote, 'they represented to him England and liberty and the feudal system and were a link between the nobility and the people . . . He would uncover his head and bow very slightly with a look of pleasure and welcome on his face . . . and Mrs Smith, the housekeeper, in black, would show them round the house.' Anything, however, on the scale of what has been done since had not been thought of. It needed a second World War

26   *The photographer Cecil Beaton at his home at Ashcombe. His unusual bed was created from fairground objects. (Radio Times Hulton Picture Library)*

and its aftermath to forge a new kind of relationship, which brought the people streaming into the palaces and parks of the nobility to picnic and to stare and to buy souvenirs and stickers for their cars. In the Twenties and the Thirties, though more people than ever before were moving around, the holiday explosion had scarcely begun and the tourist trade was confined largely to the well-to-do Americans 'doing' Europe. None of the great houses had become a commercial proposition and, except for those that were administered by the National Trust, no payment from the public was expected or received.

It was Noel Coward with his marvellous capacity for mocking the thing he loved, who first called the great country houses 'the Stately Homes of England' in the witty number he wrote for *Operette* in 1938, pin-pointing the predicament of the eldest sons, born to inherit what had become for some of them a burden and a nightmare. There was nothing then to show how these apparently irresponsible and wild young men were later to adapt themselves so brilliantly to the modern world and to save their heritage for posterity by opening their gates to the *hoi polloi* and creating new pleasure grounds for their enjoyment. Between the Wars pride in their ownership was all that some of the less wealthy families had to keep them going when it was hard to make both ends meet, and even pride had to be sacrificed from time to time together with all the accretions of snobbery belonging to the past. Leisure and idleness were no longer the absolute prerogative of the gentleman. Younger sons were actually encouraged to go into trade or to get jobs in the City, daughters were left to sink or swim in a matrimonial market that was forever widening, for no one could afford to be too fastidious. And although many of the older aristocrats were greatly disturbed in the Twenties by the fear of a Bolshevik revolution, it was not this that really threatened their chances of survival, but the ever increasing, penal taxation of their lawful government which so effectively drew their blood and diminished their power.

Not that lack of money worried the young unduly. They disliked the over-elaborate ritual of Saturday to Monday as the Edwardian week-end had been called, the visits to church on Sunday morning with everyone dressed as if for a gala occasion, the tour of the stables and the kennels in the afternoon, the formal ceremony of going into dinner and sitting down to six or seven

27 *The Earl of Derby at Ascot. He indulged his interest in the turf, but no one was more aware of the responsibilities of the aristocracy towards the whole community. (Central Press Photos Ltd.)*

courses. They preferred running around in sports cars, playing tennis or drinking cocktails on the side in their bedrooms. At Longleat, Lord Weymouth, heir to the Marquess of Bath since his elder brother had been killed in action, had to engineer a dogfight in his room at the top of the house where he was serving cocktails to his young friends to cover the quick removal of the bottles and glasses when his father came upstairs without any warning; and later when he wanted to marry Daphne Vivian, one of the gay young people who danced at the Embassy, he was even more resourceful. He took out a special licence and married her in church under his family name of Henry Thynne, and the secret was so well kept among their friends that when the Marquess of Bath unexpectedly withdrew his opposition to the marriage a year later, they were married a second time with all the expensive trappings of a spectacular society wedding at St Martin's-in-the-Fields. Daphne was by no means so frivolous as the newspapers made out when they wrote up the Bright Young People. She was extremely intelligent and charming, and her romantic marriage lasted more than twenty years.

Christmas at Longleat, as described in her autobiography *Mercury Presides*, followed the traditional pattern of the past with the whole family gathered together, including Lord Bath's three sisters, known collectively as 'the Aunts', one of whom always wore an evening dress like 'a black sack', black woollen stockings and heavy, rustic shoes. She had advanced views on art, which compensated for her being unmarried and accounted for her lack of interest in the opulent clothes of her own generation, besides making her more sympathetic towards the fashions of the young, who by this time had totally rejected the long

28 *The Duchess of Bedford preparing to compete in the Lord Northesk Cup competition for women pilots, 1936. The seventy-year-old Flying Duchess was to disappear during the following year, attempting to clock up 200 hours of solo flying. (Radio Times Hulton Picture Library)*

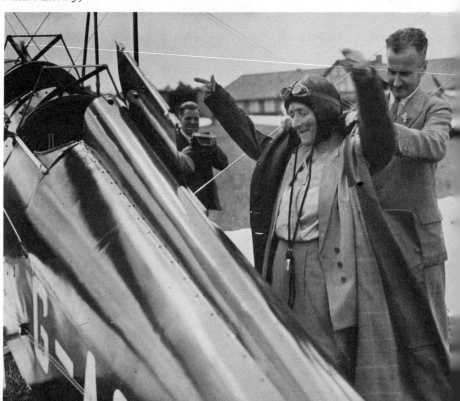

skirts worn by their mothers in the country, the sable trimmings to cloth overcoats, the hats with feathers and the tailored coats and skirts with countless buttons down the front and sometimes down the back as well. They wore instead the casual clothes of their decade, jumper suits, tweed suits and natty little cloche hats, for even if they could not afford to get their clothes from 'Coco' Chanel, they could imitate her style and run something up for themselves at home or buy a hat at Pontings for £1.

The revolution in women's day clothes, sparked off by Chanel, had actually started before the War when, for a joke, she had worn one of her English lover's polo-necked jerseys to go out riding with him. He persuaded her that she looked more attractive in this simple masculine attire than in the elaborate feminine *toilette* of the period, and he also bought his underwear at one of the most exclusive gentleman's haberdashers in Bond Street. The vests were made by a top quality, old-fashioned English firm in Nottingham, woven in the finest silk and wool that folded to nothing in the hand and clung luxuriously to the body. As an experiment, Chanel took one of them and cut the buttons off, trimming the neck with a collar of crêpe-de-chine

29 *Shooting parties were popular with visiting royalty. Alfonso XIII, King of Spain, is pictured on a deer-stalking trip in Scotland in 1928. (Central Press Photos Ltd.)*

and dying the whole thing a pale peach colour to match a pleated crêpe-de-chine skirt. The result was her first 'jumper suit', which made her fortune and for a time the fortune of the old-fashioned firm in Nottingham, besides changing the direction of women's clothes altogether and creating the basic style of the future.

Chanel was a genius in her timing as in everything. She knew what women wanted before they realized it themselves. She emphasized the new freedom of thought and the defiant, forward-looking instinct of the new generation, and she made everyone look young and desirable. She liberated women from the cumbersome trappings of the past and taught them to move more naturally, unhampered by the restrictions of heavy materials, skirts down to their ankles and big sleeves. Yet she never forgot their femininity and to offset the extreme simplicity and boyishness of her new line, she invented costume jewellery, great lumps of real or artificial emeralds, rubies and ropes of pearls, bracelets, brooches and earrings, that by contrast to the austerity of her style had the glamour of a Cleopatra. Her business in the Rue Cambon prospered and so did her love affairs, one with a Russian Grand Duke and one which lasted on and off for twenty years with the Duke of Westminster.

'Bend Or', as the Duke was called by his intimate friends, a nickname given to him as a boy after his grandfather's horse of that name had won the Derby, was said to be the wealthiest man in England. The vast Grosvenor estates he inherited from his grandfather in 1899 when he was twenty years old, comprised a very large chunk of Mayfair and the whole of Belgravia from Hyde Park Corner down to Pimlico, besides three properties in Scotland, 30,000 acres in Cheshire and the enormous, sham Gothic mansion built by his grandfather at Eaton. As a young man he was handsome, wilful, arrogant and very spoilt; no one ever dared to correct him, least of all his gentle mother and his step-father George Wyndham. He had, moreover, an irresistible charm and great panache. During the War he ran his own fleet of Rolls Royce cars mounted with guns and armour in the Libyan desert, harassing the Senussi and rescuing a party of British prisoners hidden by the Germans at Bir Hakim, a small oasis miles deep in the waterless terrain. After the War his first wife divorced him and he married a divorcée, Violet Rowley, thereby incurring the displeasure of King George, who demanded his resignation as Lord Lieutenant of Cheshire. This set him against the Court for ever, while increasing his arrogant opinion of himself and his restless search for the magic elixir of life that constantly eluded him.

Duchess Violet divorced him in 1926 and four years later, after a swift and dramatic courtship, he married Loelia Ponsonby. She was twenty years younger than Bend Or and although she had lived among the gay young people of Mayfair, still romantic enough to be dazzled by him. That she was comparatively poor and he was exceedingly rich had very little to do with it. 'He was a legend, almost a myth . . . He stood for dash, glamour and fast living,' she wrote later in her memoirs, *Grace and Favour*. Everyone danced attendance on him, and it never occurred to Loelia that she might be too inexperienced to deal with anyone of so complex a character, or that she belonged to a younger generation with which he had very little sympathy. She very soon discovered, however, that she had not married 'a partner or a companion, but a formidable and capricious autocrat, a Tsar, a Sultan, a Jove hurling thunderbolts', someone whose 'every passing whim had to be obeyed as if it were a divine command'.

Bend Or had everything. He was the only non-royal personage for whom the station-master at Euston would hold the fast train for Chester if he sauntered onto the platform a few minutes after it was timed to leave. When he went cruising in the Mediterranean in the *Cutty Sark*, a fleet of chauffeur-driven Rolls Royces followed the progress of the yacht by land and was instantly available whenever he came into port. He had three houses in Scotland with fishing and shooting rights stretching as far as the eye could see and beyond; another in Wales; and two hunting lodges in France: one on the Spanish border not far from Biarritz and the other a château at Saint Saens near Rouen, where he entertained large parties for the boar-hunting and once sent a servant off to Paris to buy a tricorne hat for one of the ladies because she was riding side-saddle and he thought she would look nice in it. In Paris, at Deauville and in Monte Carlo and Biarritz, he had a suite of rooms always at his disposal in his favourite hotels there, and at Eaton Hall an army of servants at his command. Yet almost as soon as he had arrived at one or the other of these places, his restlessness and fear of boredom drove him and his retinue off again somewhere else, or if something displeased him he flew into a rage, the hangers-on and yes-men who surrounded him scattering like frightened rabbits. His temper did not improve with age. Denied the favour of the Court because his matrimonial disasters had given offence, and equally hostile to the rebellious instincts of the young, he became increasingly out of touch—a lone wolf, like Hugh Lupus, his Grosvenor ancestor, who invaded England with William the Conqueror and subdued the people of Wales with great ferocity.

As a landlord, the Duke of Westminster was consistent in his endeavour to improve the fortunes of his family, though the death of his only son and heir in 1908 had embittered his whole life. He sold land in Cheshire, much to the dismay of his tenants, to invest in South Africa, Canada and Australia; and apparently with no regrets at all, he sold Grosvenor House to Lord Leverhulme, whose trustees promptly resold it for development, which meant that this grand house on Park Lane built by Cundy in 1842, with its handsome Corinthian colonnade based on Trajan's Forum and its splendid picture gallery, was demolished in 1927. Previously, in 1921, the Duke had created a sensation by selling off some of his finest paintings to Sir Joseph Duveen, the most daring and most brilliant art-dealer in the world.

The newspapers featured the sale in big headlines:

THE 'BLUE BOY' SOLD

Another big picture 'deal' was reported yesterday: the sale by the Duke of Westminster to Sir Joseph Duveen of Duveen brothers of Sir Joshua Reynolds's 'Mrs Siddons as the Tragic Muse', and Gainsborough's famous 'Blue Boy', the price paid being stated to be £200,000.

Asked if it was likely to go to America, Sir Joseph Duveen replied, 'I am not in the habit of buying on commission for someone else. It is not going to America. I have bought it for myself. My wish is that the picture should remain in this country and I shall do all in my power to attain that end.''

In fact, Duveen had already teased one of his richest American clients into falling in love with the *Blue Boy* on board the

30 *Madame Gabrielle ('Coco') Chanel with Lady Abdy, 1929. The now classic
jumper suit was inspired by a gentleman's vest. (Radio Times Hulton Picture Library)*

Aquitania, where a reproduction of it was hanging in the dining-
room of H. E. Huntington's suite. H. E. and his wife, Arabella,
got off the boat at Cherbourg; Duveen went on to Southampton
and, deferring all other engagements, immediately set off for
London, where he called on the Duke of Westminster and in less
than an hour had settled the deal for cash.

The Huntingtons—H. E. was Arabella's third husband and
the nephew of her second husband, Collins Huntington—were
a little disappointed that the actual *Blue Boy* was not as blue as
the reproduction they had seen in their state room on the
Aquitania; but they looked up to Duveen as their guide and
mentor and were reassured when he told them the boy only
needed a wash with soap and water to come up as blue as they
could wish and that for 620,000 dollars they were in possession of
the greatest Gainsborough in the world. He had more difficulty
in persuading them to take *Mrs Siddons as the Tragic Muse*,
because Arabella was profoundly shocked at the idea of hanging

the portrait of an actress—even a dead actress—on the walls of her Californian home, and it was only when Duveen argued that she would be allowing a great masterpiece to fall into the hands of another collector that she submitted.

For good measure Duveen sold the Huntingtons another of the Duke of Westminster's Gainsboroughs, *At the Cottage Door*, an Arcadian rural scene to which no one could take exception. But it was the sale of the *Blue Boy* that caused one of those sudden outbursts of indignation in the British press questioning the propriety of the whole transaction. Was it right for the Duke of Westminster to sell a priceless heirloom to the highest bidder in another country? How many aristocratic family portraits had already found their way into the millionaire households in America? And how many more would continue to be shipped across the Atlantic if something was not done about it? Nothing, of course, was done about it; partly because the English public on the whole was more interested in football than in Gainsborough and partly because some of the aristocratic families found a wad of American dollars very comforting. Besides Duveen was the biggest art Mogul the world had ever seen. To sell him a painting conferred honour on the vendor; to buy a painting from him at the colossal figure he asked was to be granted a concession.

The American millionaires of two generations—Altman, Morgan, Frick, John D. Rockefeller Jr., Mellon and Kress—went to him cap in hand. They bought a 'Duveen', not a Gainsborough, a Titian or a Rembrandt, but a masterpiece that Duveen had judged worthy of their attention, and they bought the eighteenth- and early nineteenth-century English portraits in particular to give themselves a sense of equality with the titled aristocracy they secretly envied and wished to emulate on the other side of the Atlantic. Duveen understood this; and he understood what H. G. Dwight, a director of the Frick Collection, called 'the stormy human equations of collecting, the gnawing obsessions, stealthy pursuits, crushing disappointments and intoxicating triumphs that lie in the backgrounds of the most beautiful things'. Thus to the impoverished English aristocracy he was a God-send and to his American clients a God of the Old Testament, whose word was law.

Yet there was something this Yorkshire-born Dutch Jew

31 *Wedding of the dazzlingly wealthy Duke of Westminster to Loelia Ponsonby, 1930.*
This was the third marriage of the charming but wilful property magnate who seemed to
have everything. (Central Press Photos Ltd.)

wanted for himself that only England could give, and with this
in mind he endowed the Tate Gallery, the British Museum and
the National Gallery in London with money to build new exhibition rooms. He also made friends with Ramsay MacDonald, who
appointed him a Trustee of the National Gallery in 1929 and
four years later recommended him for a peerage. As Lord
Duveen of Millbank, cited on his promotion to the House of
Lords as 'a great benefactor to art', Sir Joseph had achieved his
final apotheosis. Only Osbert Sitwell saw the irony of the
situation, observing that 'as most of the money from Lord
Duveen's munificent gifts to the nation had come from the
English paintings he had shipped across the Atlantic, we now
have the galleries but no paintings to hang in them'.

No one in England could afford any longer to compete with
the Americans or to become a collector on the grand scale. The
great days of aristocratic patronage were over. Yet there were
compensations. With the change in fashion from opulence to

simplicity, many of the younger people looked for a more Bohemian kind of enjoyment in their style of living and the inherent English desire for a country house was expressed in new and individual ways. Cecil Beaton discovered Ashcombe set in a remote valley in Wiltshire in 1930. His work as an artist and a photographer was not yet fully appreciated as the very subtle mirror of his own times that it has since become, reflecting the bright image of a whole generation with all its craziness, glamour and freshness. But he had already emerged from his first experiments with a box Brownie at home, using his sisters, Nancy and Baba, as models against fantastic backgrounds created with bits of wire netting, glass vases and mirrors, and he was already recognized as an exciting new phenomenon, a photographer with a highly individual vision, great originality and a taste for the exotic. He successfully posed Edith Sitwell under a glass dome, in a Chinese dress against a lacquer screen lit with candles and lying on a tomb like a mediaeval saint. Nothing was too bizarre for his imagination, no experiment with lighting, texture and finish too difficult to be tried, for Beaton worked exceedingly hard to achieve perfection and he was much tougher than his rather frail appearance suggested.

In *The Wandering Years* he admits that he was 'a frightful snob' when he came down from Cambridge, but his snobbery belonged to the adolescent feeling that somewhere inside himself he possessed talents which could only flourish in the world of fashion beyond the conventional middle-class background of his family, and his instinct was right. As his confidence increased, he began to conquer the smart world of Mayfair. Society girls, tired of the expensive portrait photographers who made them all look alike, rushed to his improvized studio in Sussex Gardens or begged him to bring his camera to them. He was entertaining and amusing. He made friends with other creative artists—the Sitwells, Rex Whistler, Oliver Messel and Frederick Ashton, the young choreographer of the Sadler's Wells Ballet—and they stimulated his own ideas about decorating Ashcombe, helping him to achieve a marvellous effect on very little money. He foraged for antiques in the junk shops abroad and at home long before it had become the fashion to do so, made his bed out of the carved horses and sugar stick pillars of an old merry-go-round, devised carpets out of the animal baize used to cover pantomime horses, and curtains out of bright materials that gave a strange and fantastic aura to the old rooms, so that 'the small habitation, for so long abandoned to its loneliness, suddenly became alive and took on its own personality'.

Week-end parties were gay and lively with Ashton doing his witty imitations of Sarah Bernhardt and Sir Thomas Beecham, Rex Whistler brilliant and funny at the drawing games of Heads, Bodies and Legs, and the Sitwells reciting poetry or making pungent comments on their friends and their enemies. More ambitious parties, a *fête champêtre* with decorations brought from Milan and Paris and guests arriving from all over the world in fancy dress, were equally successful, and if some of Beaton's improvized effects appeared frivolous, they were none the less devised with great ingenuity and a sense of style. Daphne Weymouth said, 'his parties radiated excitement for weeks before in the neighbourhood of Wiltshire, engendering the sort of atmosphere to be found in a theatre before a first night' and reaching a climax of expectation as the guests converged on the exquisite house and garden isolated in its own romantic and thickly wooded fold of the downs. Yet parties were by no means

32 *The new informality: a house party at Ashcombe. Cecil Beaton (seated, right) and his guests in 1934. (Radio Times Hulton Picture Library)*

the only joy of Ashcombe. Cecil Beaton was just as happy there alone with the gardener and his wife. He loved his 'small habitation' as much as any of the great aristocratic landlords had ever loved their more palatial and luxurious houses in the country and he had one great advantage: he could still enjoy what was to become the rarest commodity in the modern world—privacy.

4 HIGH SOCIETY AND CAFÉ SOCIETY

One of the most civilized men ever to enjoy London society—
Max Beerbohm—shook the dust of Piccadilly off his elegant
shoes in 1926 and went to live in Rapallo. In his opinion London
had been 'vulgarized, democratized, commercialized, standard-
ized' and ruined beyond redemption. He vowed he could no
longer enjoy strolling up St James's Street with the motorized
traffic snarling at his heels like an angry pack of hounds and the
pedestrians on the pavement always in a hurry. He remembered
the hansom cabs and the gas-lamps, the red carpets and striped
awnings outside the houses in the squares in the Season and the
crush of carriages when Lady X or Lady Y was giving a ball.
What was Piccadilly without Devonshire House, or Park Lane
without its private palaces? And *what* were the hideous high
blocks of hotels, offices and flats that displaced them doing to the
homely scale of London?

    In Rapallo, Max often talked of London and his friends there
with nostalgia; but whenever he returned, he could not get away
from it quickly enough, so terrible was the wanton destruction
he observed all around him in the city he loved so much. Year by
year the property speculators were nibbling away at the Georgian
fabric: wolves in the sheep's clothing of 'progress', with big
money behind them and the co-operation of the aristocratic
landlords riddled with the cancer of taxation and afraid of
dying to the detriment of their estates. In Bloomsbury, the Duke
of Bedford was yielding to pressure from the London University;
in Mayfair the Duke of Westminster was pushing up the rents
and looking at site values; in Hanover Square, Cavendish Square
and Portman Square, commercial exploitation of the land so

close to the shopping centres was very tempting when the old and inconvenient Georgian houses fell vacant and servants could no longer be induced to live and work in them. It all seemed inevitable—at least no one lifted a finger to stop it; and the Commissioners of Crown Lands, who should have known better, were inordinately proud of annihilating Nash's Regent Street, this particular piece of vandalism being celebrated in 1927 when King George V and Queen Mary drove down the heavily rebuilt street in a state landau amid cheering spectators, flags and floral decorations.

Yet in spite of the rapacious tide of destruction, there were still some private houses in London that maintained the dignity of the past and continued to be inhabited by their aristocratic owners. While the other mansions in Park Lane were rapidly disappearing in a heap of rubble, Londonderry House stood like a fortress against the flood of post-war commercialization. It occupied the corner block of Park Lane and Hertford Street and was originally two early Georgian houses remodelled and made into one by Benjamin Wyatt for the 3rd Marquess of Londonderry in 1825.

Outside, like so many other London houses, its rather pedestrian neo-Classical façade gave little expectation of the luxury and splendour within. On entering the main hall, however, the visitor was at once impressed by the magnificent staircase ascending in a double flight to the *piano nobile*, its highly wrought balustrade and the surrounding marble columns with festooned Ionic capitals leading the eye up to a clerestory toplight and a coffered roof supported by Atlas figures. Double doors from the balcony at the head of the staircase opened into the ballroom, a long gallery sumptuously decorated in the French Renaissance style revived by Benjamin Wyatt and hung with full length portraits of George IV, the Duke of Wellington, the Tsars of Russia and the 2nd Marquess of Londonderry, better known as Lord Castlereagh, the distinguished British representative at the peace conference in Vienna after the battle of Waterloo. Beyond the ballroom, three splendid drawing-rooms leading one out of the other had painted ceilings and panelled walls of silk damask framed in richly gilded scrollwork, and were filled with handsome furniture, *boulle* cabinets, tables and chairs inlaid with marquetry and ormolu, tall *torchères*, statuary and busts,

33   *Max Beerbohm, by Powys Evans. He left England in 1926 when London was becoming unrecognizable to those who remembered a more leisurely age. (Mary Evans)*

which all added to the opulence of the decor and made Londonderry House a superb setting for the long series of receptions and
entertainments begun there in 1828 by the 3rd Marquess and
continued by his successor one hundred years later.

Charles Stewart Henry Vane-Tempest-Stewart, the 7th
Marquess, Knight of the Garter and Privy Councillor, had the
nonchalant air of an eighteenth-century Irish grandee, who had
strayed into politics by accident and was faintly amused by the
whole business. But behind this careless display of aristocratic
indifference, he was an astute man of the world and together with
his wife, a grand-daughter of the 3rd Duke of Sutherland,
exercised considerable influence on public affairs from behind
the scenes. The receptions they gave on the eve of the new
parliamentary sessions for the Prime Minister and the Government of the day were an outstanding feature of the two decades
after the War and established Lady Londonderry as the ruling
hostess in high society. A tall and stately figure in white satin,
wearing the fabulous Londonderry tiara of diamonds, diamond
earrings, a diamond stomacher and ropes of pearls, she stood
graciously at the head of the staircase receiving her guests, as the
Master of Ceremonies in powdered wig, knee breeches and white
silk stockings called out their names. On the occasions when
fifteen hundred invitations had been sent out, it could take an
hour or more for the guests to move up the staircase and this
could be a frightening experience for those of a nervous disposition. Hazel Lavery, according to her own story, was so overcome
with fright after her husband, the portrait painter, had been
knighted, she could only murmur inaudibly to the flunkey 'Lady
Lavery', whereupon he blushed under his powdered wig and
whispered: 'At the bottom of the staircase, m'lady, and through
the baize door.'

The ascent of the staircase at Londonderry House was, none
the less, an event of the highest importance in the lives of a great
number of people, and even those who found it somewhat
alarming could console themselves with the comfortable feeling
that they had 'arrived' and were 'in' with the top rank of society.
Moreover, at this level the privileged status of the aristocracy
was something still to be reckoned with and their power to

34   *A look of dateless elegance captured by Royal Academician Sir John Lavery,
whose favourite model was his lovely wife Hazel. This portrait was called 'Hazel in
Rose and Gold'.*

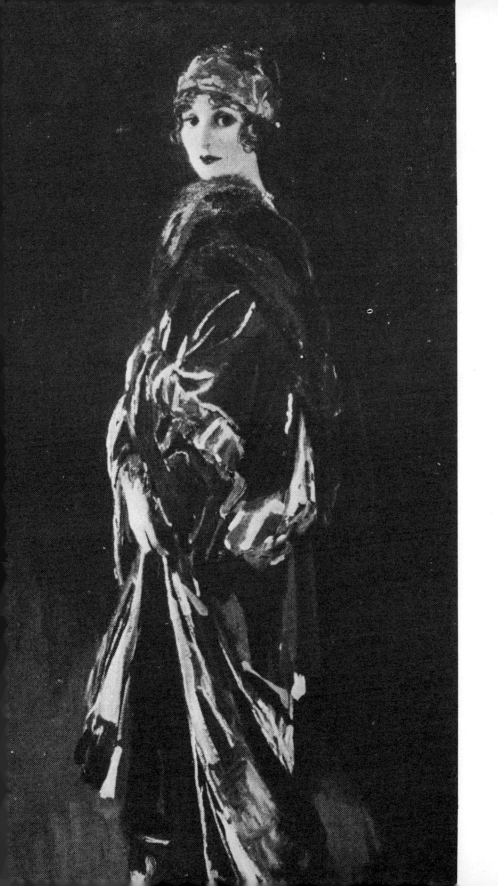

influence events was by no means ineffective. Informal discussion between the eminent men and worldly women assembled in the ballroom could advance or retard the political career of an ambitious Member of Parliament. What was said—or not said—in these gilded surroundings could bring pressure to bear on the policy of the Government as subtle and as insidious as in the days of Gladstone and Disraeli. Ramsay MacDonald, who greatly enjoyed his elevation to this pinnacle of society on becoming Prime Minister, was at first overawed and then so enamoured of the Marchioness that his ardent pursuit of socialism was considerably weakened by his devotion to her, much to the dismay of his cloth-capped colleagues and much to the delight of the aristocracy in general who considered his pink Socialism infinitely preferable to red Bolshevism.

Lady Londonderry had been nicknamed 'Circe' as a child and although she abstained from turning men into swine, she did have a snake tattooed on one of her ankles, which was rather surprising, and she did cast a spell over her admirers. She gave brilliant musical evenings and intimate little supper parties for a select circle of her friends, gathering them into what she called her 'Ark Club'. Her husband, whose dalliance with other women she tactfully accepted, was known as Charlie the Cheetah, Lord Hugh Cecil, the Member of Parliament for Oxford University, as the Lynx and Ramsay MacDonald as the Lion in this private and somewhat exotic bestiary of hers. All the renowned virtuosi of the day—Chaliapin, Rubenstein, Kreisler, Rachmaninoff, Ruth Draper and many other international celebrities, were invited to perform at Londonderry House; and perhaps because she knew her position in London was unassailable, Lady Londonderry did not consider Lady Cunard as a rival, but subscribed generously to all her efforts to promote grand opera at Covent Garden with Sir Thomas Beecham as her Knight in armour.

Lady Cunard is reported to have flung Cecil Beaton's *Book of Beauty* on the fire and to have called him a nasty, common young man because he had described her as a hostess. Later she forgave him and they became great friends. And it was, of course, her rare capacity for entertaining and mixing people together that made her parties in Grosvenor Square unique; for whereas Lady Londonderry dominated the highest and most exclusive ranks of society, by cultivating a wider circle, Maud Cunard

35　*The Marchioness of Londonderry with two of her daughters, Lady Margaret and Lady Helen Vane-Tempest-Stewart, in 1927. The most distinguished hostess of the aristocracy, she wore the Londonderry jewels with pride and dominated high society. (Mansell Collection)*

became the mistress of a salon more akin to what is known as 'café society'.

She was not an aristocrat. She was a lively go-getting American, who had married Sir Bache Cunard, the grandson of the founder of the shipping line, on the rebound from an affair with a Polish prince. Sir Bache was old enough to be her father. He had dark eyes like a spaniel dog and a passion for fox-hunting and was the owner of a large mansion in Northamptonshire, called Nevill Holt. He adored his 'Pocket Venus', for the most part in silence and with diffidence, and was puzzled by her wild and wanton ways. She hated the country and his hunting friends and spent most of her time reading Balzac and Shakespeare, or turning the furniture in the house upside down, ordering new hangings from London, expensive Louis Seize cabinets and *bibelots* from the antique shops and expensive, diaphanous tea-gowns from Poiret and Worth, which were not in the least suitable for Northamptonshire.

After her daughter Nancy was born, she became even more restless, spending more time in London and in Paris and filling Nevill Holt with the friends she had made there while her husband was away hunting and shooting in the neighbouring counties. George Moore worshipped her from the moment she laid her 'fern-like hand' on his arm at a luncheon party in 1894 on her first visit to London before she had married Cunard, to the day of his death forty years later. She did not always treat him very kindly, especially as he grew older and became more tiresome. But she was his goddess, his Primavera, 'more like a sprite than a human being', and he once wrote when he thought he had lost her: 'Thinking of her my senses grow dizzy, a sort of madness creeps up behind the eyes—what an exquisite despair is this—that one shall never possess that beautiful personality again, sweet-scented as the May-time, that I shall never hold that oval face in my hands again, shall look into those beautiful eyes no more . . .' Yet with all his Irish romanticism and his eagerness to act out the fantasy he wove round their relationship,

36/37 *Nancy Cunard (left) and her mother, Lady Emerald Cunard. Beautiful and headstrong in their different ways, mother and daughter were always at odds with each other. Lady Emerald adopted her name because of her love for the jewel. American by birth, she married into society and became an enthusiastic patron of the arts. (Cecil Beaton)*

G. M. was no fool and by no means blind to the faults of his beloved. He admired her courage, her independence and her intellectual audacity and at the same time wrote of her 'cold sensuality, cold because it was divorced from tenderness and passion'. When she suddenly decided in 1926 to change her name and without any explanation wrote to him from Switzerland signing herself Maud Emerald, he was so upset, he sent her a telegram: 'Who is Emerald? Are you married?'—only to discover that, as she was called the Emerald Queen from the jewels she wore, she had adopted Emerald as her christian name.

By this time she had been separated from Sir Bache Cunard for fifteen years after falling in love with Beecham and following him to America in 1911. Young, eloquent and irrepressible, Beecham had already startled London the year before with his season of Russian opera and ballet, revealing the sensational art of Chaliapin, of Diaghilev, Stravinski and Bakst to a public accustomed to the conventional operatic performances at Covent Garden and the bits and pieces of ballet put on at the music halls. A perfectionist behind the mask of a dilettante, he was the most controversial figure in the musical world and though

married with two children, known to be totally undomesticated. Cited as co-respondent in the Foster divorce case, he was quite unrepentant, treating the court to a bravura performance that was extremely impressive and exceedingly funny. No one was ever more of an expert at deflating an opponent. His wit—mischievous, caustic and barbed with malice—was perfectly timed, and even those who accused him of egotism, vanity and a swaggering awareness of his own brilliance, never doubted his magnetism. He could draw exquisite sound from his orchestra with a devastating accuracy and an apparent insouciance, as if his genius were no more than an accidental gift of the gods to make life easy and enjoyable. He could play upon the emotions of his audience with all the wit and glamour of his dandified superiority while discovering the very essence of the music of Mozart, Haydn, Puccini or any other of his favourite composers. Even upon his 'lollipops', the lesser pieces he played for his own enjoyment, he lavished a loving care and all the *joie de vivre* that bubbled up in him. No wonder Lady Cunard found him irresistible.

Her interest in music was genuine. On hearing her first Wagnerian opera at the Metropolitan in New York at the age of twelve, she had been quite overwhelmed, and her meeting with Beecham twenty-five years later was the catalytic moment in her life. Thereafter she bullied, cajoled and enticed everyone she knew into supporting him, sinking vast sums of her own money in the various projects he conceived which so often ended in financial disaster. Indeed, without her persistence it is doubtful whether the international seasons of grand opera at Covent Garden would have survived at all. When the wealthy industrialist, Samuel Courtauld, withdrew his patronage after the death of his wife in 1932, and the Royal Opera House itself was threatened with demolition to improve the traffic flow of Covent Garden market, Lady Cunard came to the rescue by organizing a new company with Sir Thomas Beecham as artistic director. Splendid summer seasons were given with unforgettable performances of Wagner's *Ring* sung by Frida Leider, Lotte Lehmann and Lauritz Melchior, and with the dazzling Spanish *coloratura*, Conchita Supervia, in Rossini's *Cenerentola* and Bizet's *Carmen*. With no subsidy from public funds, it was a singular achievement, due almost entirely to Emerald Cunard's unceasing activity; and if some of the rich subscribers she drummed up went to the opera simply to be seen sitting in a grand tier box, the elegance of the audience attired in full evening dress added to the brilliance of the occasion and enhanced the classic beauty of the auditorium.

Everyone in London knew of Lady Cunard's passion for Beecham, though she was careful to conceal the real depths of her feeling behind a mask of flippancy, always referring to him in public as Sir Thomas and pretending that his infidelities caused her no qualms of jealousy or resentment. Meanwhile the numbers of friends and acquaintances who came to her house in Grosvenor Square continued to increase, and if she had not quite forgotten the earlier rebuffs she had received from the more snobbish members of high society when she had first married Sir Bache, she was now in a position to cock a snook at them and more than capable of doing so.

The luncheon parties and dinner parties she gave round her circular dining-table of lapis lazuli, which reflected the candle-light and the gilt epergne of naked nymphs and naiads standing at the centre of it, were staged with a perfection that enchanted everyone. She was usually late for her own parties, leaving her guests to stand awkwardly about among themselves in the drawing-room until she entered suddenly, 'like a jewelled bird uncaged' all of a flutter, her bright eyes darting among them, her cheeks rouged a vivid carnation pink and her fluffy canary yellow hair aglow. Then in her husky little voice, like a corncrake, she would make some absurd and shrill comment on her own arrival. 'My maid is furious with me—she says I'm not properly dressed and she hasn't had time to straighten my eyelashes'—and immediately her guests would melt into laughter and coalesce into a group of friends, spell-bound by her gaiety and animation. She was the *enfant terrible* among them, the magician with a wand that touched them playfully on the shoulder and trans-formed them into what they desperately wanted to be taken for—witty, talented men and women playing the game of conversa-tion with the ease, the verbal athleticism and the ardour of a first-class tennis match.

'As one switches the radio to a different station,' Lord Kinross wrote, 'she instantly transposed the conversation into a livelier and more volatile rhythm, and with an inspired inconse-quency, a calculated attempt, as it were, to appear scatter-brained, her words flitted brightly round the table, settling here, there and everywhere in the course of their erratic and restless flight.' Ambassadors, cabinet ministers, artists, writers and musicians all felt the life-enhancing quality of her personality, whether she was teasing George Moore or describing the eccentric Lady Sackville sitting up in bed 'eating *pâté de fois gras* with a shoe-horn', or firing off one of her witticisms at the expense of some-one she disliked. They treasured every word she uttered, repeated the gossip she invented about people with a wicked delight and, quite overwhelmed by her fascination, were unaware of the dextrous cunning with which she played on their emotions. To Harold Acton, just down from Oxford and very impressionable, her parties were 'evenings when nothing in the world mattered but the purest art, whose essence was all around us like the fragrance of cassia . . . Lady Cunard had created an ideal setting for a synthesis of the arts. One could only abandon oneself joyfully, inhaling the luxuriance of sight and sound until one was lapped into silence. The pretentiousness that paraded in the other "literary" houses was absent: there was never a false note.'

Yet there was one person with whom Lady Cunard could never strike the right note—and that was her daughter, Nancy. She once said: 'Motherhood is a low thing—the lowest'; and judging from her disastrous lack of sympathy with Nancy, this was no idle remark made to amuse her dinner guests. Like so many upper-class Edwardian mothers she left her sensitive and precocious little girl entirely in the hands of a formidable gover-ness, showing her off on occasions in the drawing-room to her own admirers and then wondering why the child was not more affectionate. George Moore, the only one of her mother's friends whom Nancy felt she could trust, encouraged her intellectual curiosity, but at the age of twelve she shocked him profoundly by declaring in all seriousness—'I don't *like* her Ladyship'; and in spite of anything G.M. could say or do, her hostility towards her mother increased until it developed into a phobia.

Lady Cunard was determined to make a splash with her daughter's first Season in society. Nancy was equally determined not to be bullied into wearing frilly dresses and picture hats like any other debutante. She had grown into a strikingly beautiful young woman, with slanting sapphire blue eyes, hair like beaten gold, a creamy complexion and long, slender legs. She preferred

38 *Ivor Novello, whose romantic songs captured the bubbling atmosphere of the musical stage, is seen here in sombre mood at the funeral of Lady Tree, 1937. (Radio Times Hulton Picture Library)*

leopard skin to fox and sables, turbans and berets to flower-trimmed hats, the garish colours of the Russian ballet to the pastel shades that suited her mother's Marie Laurencin style of prettiness. And she preferred the Eiffel Tower Restaurant in Percy Street, the Café Royal with its artists and writers and the East End pubs where some of them foregathered to drink and smoke and talk all through the night, to the social programme Lady Cunard had arranged for her.

By 1922, having married a Guardsman and left him eighteen

months later, she was on her own in Paris, writing poetry, arguing with Louis Aragon about politics, collecting African bracelets to wear from her wrists to her shoulders, outlining her eyes with kohl and roving from night club to night club in Montparnasse with her *avant garde* friends. Her intelligence and her rebellious spirits combined with her enigmatic beauty, brought her admirers and lovers of both sexes, and her highly individual style made her almost a legendary figure of the Twenties. But as time went on politics began to occupy her mind more than ever. She hated Mussolini and more than once embarrassed Norman Douglas when staying with him in Italy, by treating him to one of her fierce flights of anger against the Fascist regime. Any injustice to the poor and the oppressed sent her into a frenzy and this, allied to her passionate preoccupation with Afro-American art, developed into an obsessive sympathy with the negroes living in Paris, so much so, that she took Henry Crowder, a jazz pianist working in a Montmartre night club, to live with her.

For a time this worked well enough. She rented a peasant's cottage in a Normandy village one hour from Paris by train, filled it with her growing collection of African masks, ivory gods, ornaments and fetishes and started a private printing press with the help of Henry, who was a gentle creature, though not always able to soothe her demoniacal fits of rage with his piano playing. They returned to Paris and then, because Nancy wanted to study Afro-American culture at the British Museum, to London, taking a room above the Eiffel Tower Restaurant.

Nancy's cat-like elegance, her pale ivory skin, gleaming hair and exotic Egyptian eyes were too well known in London to escape detection, even if she had wished to remain *incognito* with Henry Crowder in the background. Possibly she had intended to pursue her researches in the British Museum in peace; if so, she was horribly mistaken. English society was by no means as tolerant as it pretended to be. Most people looked with abhorrence on the association of a white woman with a black man, and Lady Cunard, in spite of her opposition to the conventional ways of the old-established aristocracy, was no exception. She was, however, one of the few people in London who was not aware of her daughter's affair with Henry Crowder until Margot Asquith marched into her drawing-room one day with her tricorne hat at an aggressive angle, and in front of all her guests, asked in a loud voice: 'Well, *Maud*, what's Nancy up to now? Is it dope, drink or niggers?'

The press followed up this appalling confrontation and Lady Cunard found herself in the most embarrassing situation she had ever had to face. Quite unable to comprehend Nancy's feverish obsession with anything so abominable as a *black* man, she reacted blindly, threatening to use her influence to have Henry Crowder deported and hiring a private detective to spy on all her daughter's movements. George Moore alone kept his

39 *Beachwear was nothing if not discreet. Here Lady Louis Mountbatten models a voluminous robe and the type of unflattering bathing-cap of the times. (Radio Times Hulton Picture Library)*

head and persuaded Nancy to leave London; but he, too, was appalled when she retaliated by publishing a vicious pamphlet against her mother, called *Black Man and White Ladyship*, which was so scurrilous even Lady Cunard's enemies found it regrettable. She, herself, behaved with great dignity at this testing moment. 'One can always forgive anyone who is ill,' was her only comment, though it was far too late for mother and daughter ever to understand each other's psyche.

That Lady Cunard was able to survive the scandal Nancy's affair had caused and still go on entertaining her society friends was a measure of her success as a hostess. In fact, she emerged from it with her reputation as bright as ever and ahead of her two most serious rivals, the Hon. Mrs Ronald Greville and Lady Colefax, both of whom she disliked intensely, calling them the Dioscuri of Gloom. Mrs Greville retaliated by calling her the Lollipop or the Yellow Canary, though she had little reason to be jealous, since her own position in society was well established before the War and as Queen Mary often visited Polesden Lacey, her country house near Dorking, she could boast of a royal approval that was strictly withheld from Lady Cunard. The Yellow Canary may have enticed the go-ahead Prince of Wales and his younger brother Prince George into her gilded cage— she often did entertain them—but Mrs Greville lent Polesden Lacey to the Duke and Duchess of York for their honeymoon and became extremely fond of the young couple, continuing to enjoy their friendship after the Duke's accession to the throne as King George VI.

As the only daughter of a Scottish millionaire who was a Privy Councillor and a Liberal Member of Parliament, Mrs Greville had the virtue of never attempting to conceal the fact that her wealth had its origin in beer. She was proud of her father's business acumen and had inherited much of his ability, being a woman of discernment and a shrewd judge of character. Although she collected Chinese porcelain and bought a number of paintings for Polesden Lacey, she was more interested in politics than in art; and since she was capable of summing people up at a glance, she developed strong likes and dislikes, working indefatigably behind the scenes to promote the cause of anyone she considered worthy of her support. She knew what was going on at the centre of things and people of importance came to her for advice, recognizing the value of her perspicacity and her clear understanding of the most complex situation. She could, however, be very malicious about the intervention of any other lady on the political front, as in her remarks about Lady Austen Chamberlain who went to Rome to visit Mussolini to further the cause of Anglo-Italian friendship. '*Dear* Ivy Chamberlain,' she said, 'how good of her! It would not be the first time Rome had been saved by a goose.'

Meanwhile, she filled Polesden Lacey and her town house in Charles Street with foreign royalty, ambassadors, eminent statesmen and a few of their wives; and as time went on with a sprinkling of the young people whose courage and audacity she admired. Like Byron's Lady Melbourne, the famous Whig hostess of the Regency, she had more use for men than for women and to those of her own sex who tried to ingratiate themselves with her, she could be a formidable opponent, leaving them in no doubt of what she thought of them. Painted in 1891 in a sable wrap down to her ankles by the fashionable Parisian portrait painter, Carolus-Duran, she remained until her death in 1942 a powerful personality, her houses possessing 'a kind of unobtrusive luxury of life and background' that Osbert Sitwell said he had never encountered elsewhere. Her generosity was unobtrusive also. She insisted on remaining anonymous when she gave any money away to charity, declaring that she did not wish to resemble 'Lord X, who blows a trumpet every time he puts a shilling in the collection bag'. Nor did she care if people mistook her canny Scots instinct for meanness, for she took a great delight in raising the expectations of some do-gooders she had no patience with and then letting them down with a thud.

Lady Colefax, a much younger woman, had a different kind of personality, less dominating, more gentle and more erratic. She was small and neat with dark hair and a slight stoop, bright beady eyes and a silvery speaking voice. Neither very rich nor an aristocrat, she had a quick brain and was genuinely interested in people, especially in those who possessed artistic and intellectual originality. Max Beerbohm, Bernard Shaw, Somerset Maugham, Arnold Bennett and Bernard Berenson were among the friends she entertained at her parties and knew well enough to call by their christian names; and as she was also a keen playgoer, her dining-room at Argyll House in Chelsea sometimes resembled

95

a stage set, the leading actors and actresses of the West End theatre playing their off-stage star rôles for the benefit of her and her guests.

Osbert Sitwell wickedly re-christened Argyll House, 'Lion's Corner House', and Lord Berners made fun of Sybil Colefax when he said he had not been able to sleep in Rome in the room next to hers because 'she never stopped climbing all night'. Yet she did not concentrate exclusively on the best-known celebrities. She had a marvellous flair for spotting talent in the young, going off to the little Everyman Theatre in Hampstead to see Noel Coward in *The Vortex* and inviting him to supper almost before anyone else had heard of him. She also drew into her net the young John Gielgud, Ivor Novello, Harold Nicolson, Cecil Beaton, Rex Whistler and Beverley Nichols, before they had made a reputation for themselves, her sincere enthusiasm for their gifts and her kindness—a very rare quality in society—setting her apart from the more predatory lion hunters of the day.

Her Georgian house in the King's Road was delightful. It had a paved courtyard in the front and a large garden at the back, and even the people who made fun of Sybil Colefax behind her back admired her impeccable taste. Nothing fussy or ornamental was allowed to break the muted and restful colour scheme she introduced of pale almond green and grey with a touch of yellow, the hangings and the upholstery blending with the furniture into a synthesis of charm and elegance which enhanced the eighteenth-century proportions of the rooms. Later, when her husband died and she was in financial difficulties, she had to move to a smaller house in Westminster and decided to start an interior decorating business with a young man, called John Fowler, creating a new fashion for the Regency style of striped satin materials, ebony chairs and Madame Récamier sofas, which helped to kill the mania for the 'all-white' decor made popular by Mrs Syrie Maugham.

Perhaps there was some ulterior motive in this. Lady Colefax and Mrs Maugham, whose marriage had foundered on the rocks of her husband's infatuation with a young man called Gerald Haxton, had lived next door to each other in Chelsea and as they belonged to much the same social world, there was a good deal of rivalry between them. Soignée, elegant and very astute,

40 *The evergreen Savoy Hotel was the centre of after-theatre entertainment – cabaret
of stars and dancing to the Savoy Orpheans. (Radio Times Hulton Picture Library)*

Mrs Maugham started by revamping the interior of her own
house. She stripped the dark Georgian panelling in the hall and
had it pickled, and completely redecorated her drawing-room in
all white—white walls, a white rug, white brocaded curtains and
upholstery and a white lacquer screen. Even every flower in the
house had to be white: camellias, lilies, gardenias, stocks, lilac
and chrysanthemums in season; and the effect produced, according to Cecil Beaton, 'a strange and marvellous surprise'. Numer-
ous upper-class drawing-rooms in Mayfair caught the virus of
this very modern, non-colour scheme, sometimes successful in
its pristine freshness and sometimes very bleak and clinical. For
white distempered walls, white fur rugs, shiny white satin
couches and white metal and glass furniture were hardly conducive to friendliness and warmth; and when it came to stripping
and bleaching antique Louis Seize commodes and bureaux to
match their dead white surroundings, the epidemic went too far
and a reaction set in. Syrie Maugham herself introduced Venetian
blackamoor figures bearing gilded torches or brightly lacquered

trays as an exotic note into her own drawing-room and was clever enough to recognize the need for more colour in her advice to her clients.

Like Lady Mendl, the former Elsie de Wolfe, who pioneered the trail of interior decorating in America, Mrs Maugham made a great success of her business and combined this with a very busy social life, often giving a party on the same day as Lady Colefax. This led to a certain amount of spying from one house to the other, Beverley Nichols telling the story of how Syrie Maugham made him climb onto a wheelbarrow to look over the garden wall to see whether Sybil Colefax had succeeded in luring Charlie Chaplin to lunch or not. It was all rather childish and silly, the sort of tittle-tattle that everyone found amusing, especially if it carried overtones of bitchiness between one hostess and another.

As lion hunters, however, neither Lady Colefax nor Mrs Syrie Maugham had the wealth, the energy and the sheer determination of Mrs Laura Corrigan, whose conquest of London society in the Twenties was achieved by a brilliant series of manoeuvres worthy of a commander in the field of battle. She came from Cleveland, Ohio, and is said to have started life as a telephone operator, whose voice over the wire sounded so desirable she made a blind date with a multi-millionaire steel magnate and got him to the altar the next morning. James Corrigan died six months later, leaving his widow 80,000,000 dollars in steel shares which she sold for cash and brought to England, having failed to make herself a social success in her home town.

On her arrival in London she rented the splendid house in Grosvenor Street belonging to the last and most discreet of King Edward VII's lady friends, Mrs George Keppel, with the proviso that Mrs Keppel should include her guest list as part of the lease. Mrs Keppel agreed—at a price, which was no hardship for Laura Corrigan. She had the money—plenty of it—and the list of everyone in high society. She was presented at Court by the wife of the American Ambassador and like Cinderella at the ball, stared in wonder and surmise at all the dukes and duchesses she wanted so much to know. The list, however, was not quite enough, except for identification purposes, and the invitations she sent out for her first party were politely declined. The aristocracy was otherwise engaged. Who *was* Mrs Corrigan? She had a vulgar American accent. She was small and sprightly; she painted her face and wore a wig. She looked common and she made absurd remarks, though some of these Malapropisms *were* quite funny, as when she called her house in Grosvenor Street 'my little *ventre-à-terre*' and commented on some cathedral she had seen having 'magnificent flying buttocks'. *Was* she, perhaps, rather amusing after all? A few of the young people in search of a gay time began to think so, but that was not quite enough for Laura Corrigan either.

She hired a social secretary who had worked for Lady Londonderry and knew how things should be done, and with an astute eye for business, she realized that the favours of the aristocracy could be bought if the bribery was subtle enough not to be obvious. So on the invitation cards for her next party, she announced that there would be a cabaret from Paris and a tombola with prizes for the guests. The prizes consisted of gold cigarette cases from Cartier, gold sock suspenders and braces with gold tabs for the men, gold vanity bags and tortoise-shell combs inlaid with gold for the women—and the odd thing was that the lucky ones in the raffle happened every time to be the highest-ranking members of the nobility who had accepted her invitation, the dukes and duchesses in the strict order of precedence winning the most valuable gold objects and the other guests silver pencils and trinkets of a lesser price.

It took a little time for the guests to realize that the tombola was always rigged, but by then Laura Corrigan had hooked them and everyone who was anyone wanted to be asked to her parties. She *was* amusing and she *was* gay, the kind of rich outsider the post-war world of society was willing to accept. And apart from the fact that she really enjoyed entertaining people, she artfully built up her reputation as a 'character' by deliberately coming out with her nonsensical remarks on every possible occasion. When someone asked her if she had seen the Dardanelles while cruising in the Aegean, she replied that she did have a letter of introduction to them but had not used it, and when Lady Mendl showed her the indirect lighting she had installed in her villa at Versailles, Mrs Corrigan said: 'How nice—I just love this confused lighting.'

At several of her stunt parties for the Bright Young People

she encouraged her guests to make their own fun, issuing a long and facetious programme of the performance with such items as Lady Louis Mountbatten in a ukelele turn described as 'B Natural (always am)' and Lord Ashley as 'B Sharp (in business)' Lady Plunket, who was Fanny Ward's daughter, did an exhibition dance and Daphne Vivien, Lord Weymouth, Lady Lettice Lygon and Lord Brecknock did a tandem cycle act. Then Laura Corrigan herself danced the Charleston in a top hat and red-heeled shoes in a number called 'On with the dance, let joy be unrefined', and to a rolling of the drums, as a final dramatic gesture, stood on her head, having first tied a scarf round her skirt for the sake of her modesty.

Her success was sensational. Everyone had a story about Laura Corrigan, what she had said or done or would do next. Even her bright auburn wig became a topic of conversation, which she did nothing to discourage. Some accident in her obscure childhood had left her totally bald, but not content with one wig to cover up this unhappy condition, she had a whole series to suit every occasion: one perfectly groomed or 'just back from the hairdressers'; one dishevelled—'must go to the hairdressers, my dear'; another windswept for the country and yet another attached to a bathing-cap, which came off once when she dived into Lord Dudley's swimming-pool at Himley, keeping her underwater for quite a time until she had retrieved it. She then gamely went indoors as if nothing had happened, appearing half an hour late for dinner with the explanation that she had been 'drying her hair'. Everyone gallantly kept up the fiction—it was so amusing; though Lady Cunard on another occasion when Laura Corrigan asked her if she was going to wear a tiara for a gala night at Covent Garden, maliciously replied: 'No, dear, just a small emerald bandeau and my own hair.'

Mrs Corrigan's giant wig box, called 'Laura's wigwam' by her friends, travelled everywhere with her. She was perhaps aware that some of the people she entertained ridiculed her behind her back, though they continued to accept her hospitality and to flatter her vanity. She may even have enjoyed the fun herself in a back-handed way as part of her triumph, for she never quite forgot that the telephone girl from Cleveland, Ohio, had once been the Cinderella among the coronetted lords and ladies who now cultivated her society so assiduously, and as her wealth kept the stroke of midnight at bay, she had nothing to fear.

In the summer of 1931 she rented the Palazzo Mocenigo in Venice, where Byron had once indulged in his orgies of pleasure —or, as Lady Diana put it: 'She married the Adriatic and seemed to be holding the palaces in fee.' A wilder season had not been seen in Venice before. 'Lured into the maelstrom of loyal and disloyal guests' and without Duff Cooper who had returned to England, Diana wrote: 'We all look filthily rapacious, but I don't feel so at all and probably no one does. Laura really has the world's happiness at heart.' She gave wonderful presents to all her guests and there were notices in every bedroom telling them not to tip the servants, never to buy stamps or cigarettes for themselves, and not to pay for their washing and cleaning or the drinks they had at the Grand Hotel and the Lido Bar.

Visitors arriving from all the playgrounds of Europe to feed off the honey provided by the little woman with a lot of wigs brought life and gaiety to the faded Palazzo, and Venice enthralled them. There were luncheon parties on board the flat-bottomed

41   *Animated conversation coupled with good food and wine at a party given by the*
Duchess of Sutherland. On the right, with glass raised, is the then Lord Blandford.
Seated next to him is the Countess de Flairieu. (Radio Times Hulton Picture Library)

fishing boats moored off the Lido; speed-boat trips and water-bicycles; long hours of sunbathing, swimming and gossipping; and from midnight into the early morning masked balls and fancy dress parties, moonlight bathing and fishing, or the pleasures of lying in a gondola and drifting in ecstasy through the decaying glory of the most glamorous city in the world. Laura herself went fishing and caught two royal fish in her net, Prince and Princess Christopher of Greece, though she was bitterly disappointed when they arrived without a retinue of servants, having rented another floor of the Palazzo Mocenigo to house them. 'Why, ma'am!' she exclaimed, curtseying on both knees to the Princess, 'I have two body-maids and Mr Corrigan never crossed the Atlantic without two body-men'—but as Mr Corrigan had long since crossed the Styx leaving his dollars behind him, this statement·could have been yet another of her serio-comic remarks designed to emphasize her 'character'. She was not as foolish as she pretended to be and she had courage. She was in Paris in 1940 when Hitler rolled his tanks across Europe and refused to budge; and by selling her fabulous jewellery bit by bit, she helped to feed the French prisoners of war held by the Nazis. Though she no longer stood on her head for fun and her stunt parties were over, her good-hearted generosity never wavered.

Equally famous for her freak parties, though a very different kind of character from Laura Corrigan, another American burst upon London in the Twenties and soon had everyone talking about her. Noel Coward met her first in Oxford at a house party arranged by Lady Colefax and described her as 'a very unfamiliar personality indeed'. Of her arrival, he wrote: 'The elms shuddered a little when a large car drew up at the door and disgorged, amid raucous laughter, the bouncing, Michelin figure of Elsa Maxwell . . . She at once proceeded to whistle through the house like a cyclone, strumming the piano, talking and striking the rose-white youth of England present into a coma of dumb bewilderment.'

Everything about Elsa was large, ebullient and overwhelming: her voice, her laughter, her bumptious egotism, her zest and her thick-skinned way of never taking 'no' for an answer. Born in San Francisco, her origins were obscure. She had toured with a theatrical company in the States, had played the piano in honky-tonks, singing a bit and boasting a lot, and by giving charity shows had gradually got her foot on the ladder leading to the higher reaches of New York society. At a party in Washington Square given by Mrs Bridgit Guinness she met Cole Porter, and later in Paris, when she had pushed her way into the rich, post-war international set, she promoted his songs and encouraged his marriage to the wealthy and beautiful American divorcée, Mrs Linda Lee Thomas.

Cole wrote a song for her, which she belted out on every possible occasion:

> I met a friend of mine a week or two ago
> And he was all togged out.
> I said, 'Excuse me but I'd really like to know
> What this is all about.
> You're over-dressed, you're absurd!
> He answered, 'Haven't you heard?
>
> I'm dining with Elsa, with Elsa supreme
> I'm going to meet Princesses
> Wearing Coco Chanel dresses,
> Going wild over strawberries and cream.
> I've got Bromo Seltzer
> To take when dinner ends,
> For I'm dining with Elsa
> And her ninety-nine most intimate friends!'

Cole was fond of her and very generous. He forgave all her mischief-making and persuaded his beautiful wife to do the same, though Linda was by no means so keen when she discovered Elsa, who was always penniless, flaunting a roll of bank notes she said she had 'won' from Cole after 'teaching' him how to play mah-jongg.

It was, however, impossible to snub Elsa Maxwell—she simply bounced back like a rubber ninepin; and the more outrageous she became, the more the gay-timers with money to burn danced to her tune. Cecil Beaton said: 'Her real ambition was never satisfied until she had made the most distinguished people look undistinguished. To this purpose she invented many clever 'stunt' parties at which members of the aristocracy in Italy, France and England, together with politicians and statesmen were knocked off their pedestals . . . and since she had much more character and intelligence than most of her victims, she succeeded in making them appear wonderfully foolish.' One of her parties was a farm-yard affair with an artificial cow yielding champagne when it was milked. Another was the 'Murder Party' she organized in London for Lady Ribblesdale, an absurdly complex crime involving Zita Jungman and the Duke of Marlborough, with two actors impersonating the police and an elaborate trail of clues planted beforehand to make the whole spoof performance appear real—at least until the dead Zita, in a nightgown stained with tomato juice, sat up in bed and roared with laughter.

All this put Elsa exactly where she wanted to be—in the limelight. But as Noel Coward said: 'She curdled her own personality with too much *crème de la crème*', and got more obstreperous as time went on, borrowing money off so many friends on the strength of her mother being ill, it was suggested to Cole Porter that they all ought to belong to the 'Burying Elsa's Mother Club'. Yet Cole never lost his affection for her, and Elsa's bouncing self-importance never evaporated. Having worked through the Russian grand dukes, the exiled royalty and the smart international set of the Twenties and the Thirties, she went blithely on to the new jet set of Greek shipowners, opera singers and American presidents in the Fifties and the Sixties, cracking her whip like an ageing ring-master long after the fun of the circus was over.

5 STAGE AND SCREEN

With the wireless in its infancy and television unknown, the theatre in the Twenties, in spite of the challenge from the cinema, was still pre-eminent as a form of entertainment. Not only first nights which had a special glamour of their own, but ordinary nights in the West End drew a fashionable audience dressed for the occasion, the men in white ties and tails and the ladies wrapped in furs and wearing their jewellery, much to the delight of the humbler people who had queued outside the doors of the pit and the gallery and were adept at spotting their favourite society beauties and theatrical personalities. A spontaneous outburst of applause often greeted a celebrity entering the stalls, adding to the air of expectation and excitement before the curtain went up; and if many of the plays did not require much intellectual effort, they were none the less very well acted and for the people in the stalls, filled the hours between dinner at the Savoy or Boulestin and supper at the Embassy or Ciro's very pleasantly.

'The stage was very much a part of our life,' Barbara Cartland wrote. 'We went to every new show, we discussed it, criticized it and were absorbed by it'—and of the leading actors and actresses: 'They were very real to us. We copied them and tried to look like them.' They had only to enter a public restaurant for a frisson of pleasurable curiosity to run through the room, for all eyes to be turned discreetly towards them and for the head waiter to glide immediately to their assistance. They dressed as well off the stage as on the stage; the best tailors of Savile Row looked after Owen Nares and Gerald du Maurier, and the couture houses vied with each other to enhance the beauty of Gladys

Cooper, Margaret Bannerman and Gertie Lawrence. They were never ordinary. The mystique of the footlights surrounded them, and it was not yet the fashion for actors and actresses to look scruffy or to be photographed doing the chores in a crumpled shirt and old trousers. Even the chorus girls dolled themselves up in the hope of following in the footsteps of the Edwardian Gaiety Girls, who had so often found husbands or lovers among the sons of the aristocracy. If Rosie Boote could become Marchioness of Headfort, Gertie Millar Countess of Dudley, and Zena Dare the daughter-in-law of Lord Esher, there was always a chance for Mr Cochran's glamorous Young Ladies. *The Maid of the Mountains*, the most successful of all musical comedies, threw Jose Collins, the brilliant daughter of 'Ta-ra-ra-Boom-de-ay' Lottie Collins, into the arms of Lord Robert Innes-Ker in 1920, and the *avant garde* producer Basil Dean reversed the process by marrying the Countess of Warwick's daughter, who went on the stage under the assumed name of Nancie Parsons, provoking Mrs Patrick Campbell to comment incorrectly: 'I hear Basil Dean has *left* the stage to join the aristocracy.'

Mrs Patrick Campbell herself, as much at home in society as in the theatre, was a glorious hangover from the past and as such fascinating to the younger generation. Eccentric, witty and devastatingly unpredictable, with her lustrous dark eyes and her figure gone to seed—'I look like a burst paper bag, my dear!'—she still had an aura of magnificence, the brilliance of Paula Tanqueray, the earthiness of Eliza Doolittle and the grandeur of an arch-duchess. She trimmed the tattered edge of her huge black velvet hats with nail-scissors, and the tired black velvet dresses she wore were speckled with little white hairs from Moonbeam, the pekingese she hugged perpetually to her ample bosom; but at parties, she sailed up the stairs to make her entrance with superb theatrical aplomb and her voice with its thrilling range and power hypnotized everyone in the room. She could be a devil or a sucking dove, utterly impossible one minute and all sweetness the next, her outrageous temperament the despair of every theatrical producer in the West End. Indeed, long before the War the most eminent actor managers had given up trying to cope with her; and after her marriage to Lady Randolph Church-

42　*Clara Bow, the original 'It' girl and dazzling star of the silent screen.*
(Popperfoto)

ill's second husband, Captain Cornwallis-West, had disintegrated, she was reduced to tagging round the provinces until 1929, when she reappeared in London in *The Matriarch* and once more held her audience spell-bound. But this was the last display of her magnificent eloquence, never to be forgotten and never to be seen again. The post-war theatre in the West End pointed in a different direction, away from the grand manner towards a more modern style of acting.

Gerald du Maurier, knighted in 1922, stood at the head of the profession in the dual capacity of actor and producer. An old-Harrovian, he had many friends among the upper classes and could have been mistaken for any gentleman strolling from the St James's Theatre to Boodle's or White's Club just round the corner; and while he continued to uphold the traditions of the eminent actor managers of the Edwardian era with whom he had started his career, he had already supplanted them before the War by sweeping away the flamboyant ham acting of the past with his naturalistic style of expression. Deliberately casual and apparently careless, he never seemed to raise his voice or to make a grand histrionic gesture, behaving on the stage with the subdued elegance of an English gentleman dressed in a dark suit for formal occasions, impeccable evening clothes and well cut, never too new-looking tweeds for the country. That all this could only be achieved by the art that conceals art and the gradual development of a superb technique was only apparent to the audience when some of his imitators failed to create the same effect with what looked like the same means, the flick of a wrist, the sudden caress of a woman's cheek, or the lighting of a cigarette. He was, indeed, sometimes accused of 'walking through his parts' and of always being Gerald du Maurier, both accusations a compliment to the ease with which he strolled across the stage with an air of amused and worldly tolerance as Lord Arthur Dilling in *The Last of Mrs Cheyney*, or, with the same self-assurance, entertained his friends in his own drawing-room at Cannon Hall in Hampstead.

Yet behind the mask of unruffled calm, du Maurier suffered from the general disequilibrium of the post-war decade. He had one foot in the old world of Sir Herbert Tree and Sir George Alexander, actor managers of the highest integrity who commanded respect and devotion from their colleagues, and one

43 *Sir Gerald du Maurier, originator of the new naturalistic style of acting. Yet even his relaxed manner was not proof against the increasing pressures of everyday life. (Radio Times Hulton Picture Library)*

foot in the new world, where the theatre was as vulnerable as everything else to the collapse of the old standards and the uncertainties of the future. Big money was injected into it by speculators concerned more with the box office than the quality of achievement; actors and actresses went more into society and society amateurs invaded the profession, crowding back-stage to chatter and laugh with their friends, calling everyone 'darling' and lavishing praise with a total lack of discrimination on those they hoped would give them a touch of reflected glory. To maintain the dignity of the profession in these circumstances without becoming old-fashioned and alienated was none too easy and du Maurier found himself in a dilemma, one minute deploring the vulgarity of the new age and the publicity given to the theatre by the gossip writers, and the next deliberately creating gossip by giving parts to his society friends or by lunching at the actors' favourite restaurant, the Ivy, with a pretty young *ingénue* for three or four days in succession. Gladys Cooper was about the only woman who approached him in a direct way without flattery, as a good comrade, and would stand no nonsense from him. Others fluttered round him like blow flies, drinking his whisky, borrowing his money and upsetting his nerves. And as time went on, in spite of all his devoted wife and daughters did to keep him amused, he became hopelessly dependent on having people round him: people to dispel the boredom, the gloom and the sour taste of not being quite modern enough, people whose insincerity in the end failed to satisfy the actor's incessant need to be admired.

Du Maurier was not alone in being obsessed with the fear of boredom and in trying to cure it by surrounding himself with gay people. It was a symptom of the age and Freddy Lonsdale, the author of *The Last of Mrs Cheyney* and half a dozen other brilliant drawing-room comedies, was another victim. Born in Jersey of very humble and respectable parents—his father kept a small shop in St Helier—Freddy was the black sheep of the family: a vagrant, undisciplined child, always getting into mischief and refusing every attempt made to send him to school, yet emerging from this background with the cultured accent of a young man from Eton and Oxford and with a charm that enabled him to get his own way with people all through his life. He had no money in the world when he captured Miss Hoggan, a retired colonel's daughter who was engaged to marry a rich man with a house in Scotland, but he had imagination and faith in his own future; so he carried Miss Hoggan off, still in the muslin dress she was wearing when she escaped from her fiancé's home, and took her to Weymouth, where he borrowed the money to pay for a special marriage licence from the vicar who joined them together. Moving from one lodging to another, with only his charm to placate the irate landladies whose bills he ignored, he wrote two upper-class drawing-room comedies and two romantic musical plays, which were accepted by Frank Curzon and produced between 1908 and 1910.

From then on, one success followed another for Lonsdale. *The Maid of the Mountains*, for which he wrote the book, made him a fortune. *Aren't We All?, Spring Cleaning, The Last of Mrs Cheyney* and *On Approval*, all produced in the Twenties, put him in the front rank as a playwright and brought him what he wanted most from life, recognition from the top people in the theatre, membership of the Garrick Club and the entrée into society. Here he moved as if he had been born a member of the upper classes, with a natural ease and self-confidence that in someone so totally uneducated was, perhaps, his greatest triumph. Unlike Somerset Maugham, who affected to despise the hand that fed him, Freddy enjoyed his success enormously. And he was not a snob. The bland superiority of the aristocracy, which he pin-pointed with such skill and originality in his comedies, was something he admired with his whole being, and in seeking to shine in society he was following the example of Vanbrugh, Sheridan and Wilde, whose gifts had thrown them into the company of the most amusing and distinguished people of their day. As with them, his own personality—witty, worldly and gay— matched his achievement in the theatre, his white socks and the

44   *Gladys Cooper (Lady Neville Pearson) and her daughter Joan at the Lawn Tennis Exhibition Matches at West Hill, Highgate, 1932. Gladys Cooper typified beauty and British womanhood of the period. (Radio Times Hulton Picture Library)*

white muffler he always wore adding an exotic note of eccentricity to his appearance which appealed to his friends and made him still more lovable in their eyes.

On Broadway, Lonsdale's comedies created a sensation. Their mocking, airy view of the English aristocracy stimulated the love-hate relationship of the American smart set for the titled nobility on the other side of the Atlantic. Freddy was fêted in New York, travelling *de luxe* on the *Mauretania* backwards and forwards across the ocean and staying at the best hotels, but as the years went on, he became more capricious in his movements, more exigent in his demands, less and less able to find the company he kept amusing enough to hold boredom at bay. Even success was boring in the end, and what was worse, the theatre was moving on and leaving him behind. In 1937, Hugh Beaumont put a play of his into rehearsal and it was suddenly withdrawn. Apparently someone in the star cast had been heard to say that it was 'old-fashioned', a word Freddy would not accept from anyone and could not forgive. He cancelled his contract and left for America, dismayed by the idea of growing old and out of date, and although he went on living until 1954, his day was over.

But Freddy had been lucky in one way. No other time, with its conflict between the old and the new standards of behaviour, its questioning of the whole image of the aristocracy and its light-hearted, self-indulgent pursuit of frivolity and fun, could have been more rewarding for the development of his particular talent. And he was lucky again in the actors and actresses who interpreted his upper-class characters without caricaturing them. A. E. Matthews, Ellis Jeffries and Ronald Squire knew exactly how to carry his frothy dialogue at a pace which involved the audience in the stalls and made them feel this was how they spoke and behaved in the brilliance of their own drawing-rooms. Arrogance and egotism, even stupidity if it was funny enough, could be forgiven; the only enemy on or off the stage was dullness, and Freddy's plays were never dull.

For stronger intellectual meat, the more adventurous members of the fashionable audience had to look to the small and brilliant company organized at the St Martin's Theatre in the early Twenties by Basil Dean and then to his other ventures, which included such controversial plays as *A Bill of Divorcement*, with Meggie Albanesi, the grand spectacle of *Hassan* at His

45   *Mrs Patrick Campbell and 'Moonbeam'.*

Majesty's Theatre, *R.U.R.*, the Robot play, *The Constant Nymph* and *Young Woodley*. Far in advance of any other producer in his choice of plays and ever willing to take a risk for something he believed in, whether it met with public approval or not, Basil Dean fought hard for the more serious aspects of the drama at a time when the theatre was given over to more frivolous entertainment, with *No, No Nanette* filling the Palace and *Charlot's Revue* playing to packed houses. The elaborate staging of James Elroy Flecker's verse drama *Hassan*, with Henry Ainley looking extremely handsome on the Golden Road to Samarkand and music by Frederick Delius, occupied him for months in advance of the first night, which caused a furore and became the talk of Mayfair, everyone at cocktail parties discussing the tragic fate of the lovers, even though the heroine's choice of death rather than dishonour was no longer the accepted standard of feminine morality.

Outside the West End at the Old Vic, the redoubtable Lilian Baylis, on nothing but endless cups of tea brewed up in her office and the certain faith that God would send her some good actors cheap in answer to her prayers, was giving Shakespeare to the mob and to anyone discerning enough to cross over the river to the Waterloo Road, adding Sadler's Wells to her shoe string in 1931 to provide opera and ballet at reasonable prices. Down at Hammersmith at the little Lyric Theatre, affectionately called 'the Blood and Flea Pit' by the West End playgoers who quickly found their way to it, Nigel Playfair revived *The Beggar's Opera* with designs by Lovat Fraser, and then *The Way of the World* with a very young Edith Evans as the most tantalizing Millamant ever to be seen in Congreve's high comedy of fashion and sexual finesse. The Lord Chamberlain refrained from censoring Shakespeare and Congreve, evidently believing that the bawdiness of the past was less damaging to the morals of the audience than the scarifying wit of Shaw, whose plays were rarely performed in London, except on Sundays for members of the Stage Society— or not until 1924 when *St Joan* was staged at the New Theatre with Sybil Thorndike as the Maid and Ernest Thesiger as the Dauphin. This was the theatrical event of the year. Everyone was raving about Sybil Thorndike's inspired performance and arguing about the astonishing last act of the play; not to have seen it was almost equal to committing a social solecism.

Then suddenly, six months later, everyone was talking about a new play at the little Everyman Theatre in Hampstead—*The Vortex*—and for two weeks the ex-drill hall with coconut matting on the floor and hard chairs instead of comfortable red plush *fauteuils*, was packed every night with the *cognoscenti* of the smart world. Noel Coward had arrived. The play moved into the West End and ran for over two hundred nights. It startled and shocked the public, the final, highly emotional confrontation between Lilian Braithwaite as the foolish, amorous mother and Coward himself as her neurotic, drug-addicted son, a modern Hamlet and Queen Gertrude, sounding an authentic note of desperation behind the brittle gaiety of the younger generation and the bewildered uneasiness of the old.

Noel Coward was not quite twenty-five. The press took him up in a big way. He was photographed in a Chinese silk dressing-gown, in and out of bed, smoking through a long cigarette-holder, standing or sitting with a cocktail glass in his hand, while airing his views on life and the world and the modern young woman— all of which amused him enormously though it aggravated the jealousy of some of his less successful colleagues and encouraged his admirers to overpraise his perspicacity. People who had merely nodded to him in the past and people who did not know him at all now claimed his acquaintance, invading his dressing-room after the performance and smothering him with super-latives. Society hostesses tumbled over each other to lure him to their parties; but although he enjoyed all the fuss and had always intended to become a celebrity, he was not taken in by the effusiveness of all the people who ran after him or much

46 *Noel Coward and Lilian Braithwaite in* The Vortex, *a resounding success for Coward as author and actor.*

deceived by the superficial glamour of the social merry-go-round. 'I went to a lot of lunch parties in the most charming houses, which, in retrospect, appear all to be exactly the same,' he wrote later in his autobiography *Present Indicative*. 'This may be a trick that time has played upon me . . . The conversation I am sure was distinguished, but that too has become lost in transit . . . I only remember that I felt happy and confident and very pleased to be eating such nice food with such nice people . . . I loved noting that fleeting look of pleased surprise in people's eyes when it was suddenly brought to their attention that, in spite of theatrical success and excessive publicity, I was really quite pleasant and unaffected . . . or at least no more affected than anyone else . . . I think possibly what surprised them was that I could play the game as well as they could, but then, after all I had learnt many different parts by heart long before I had ever met them.'

How many parts he had learnt since his first appearance at the age of ten as Prince Mussel in a fairy play at the Court Theatre, was only known to his devoted mother and to a few of his intimate friends in the theatre like Gladys Calthrop, Madge Titheradge and Gertie Lawrence. To everyone else, unaware of his long struggle to emerge from the rather seedy gentility of Ebury Street into the neon lights of Shaftesbury Avenue, or of his courage in the face of obstacles, disappointments and lack of money, he was known only as the author of two flimsy comedies and some of the sketches and musical numbers in Charlot's revue, *London Calling*, in which he danced not very well and sang in a slightly cracked voice. *The Vortex* could have been a fluke. To impertinent questioners he attributed his success to luck, deliberately encouraging the image of the idle, decadent playboy when, in fact, with his phenomenal powers of concentration, he was poised to take advantage of every opportunity that opened in front of him and already on the way to becoming what he remained for the rest of his life, one of the most versatile men in the whole history of the English theatre.

Still acting in *The Vortex*, he wrote the sketches, the lyrics and most of the music for Cochran's revue, *On With the Dance*, and in his 'Poor Little Rich Girl' revealed his mocking insight into the feverish impulse behind the frivolity of his own generation. *Fallen Angels* with Tallulah Bankhead and Edna Best went farther still. The press, mistaking satire for permissiveness,

47 *Charles B. Cochran arrives from New York aboard the 'Berengaria'. With him are his wife, Noel Coward and three of his Young Ladies. His revues represented all the gaiety and sparkle of the age. (Radio Times Hulton Picture Library)*

howled at the idea of two young women being depicted on the stage in a drinking scene. It was described as 'vulgar, obscene and degenerate'; but the chic audience went to see themselves— and Tallulah, looking marvellous with her heavy-lidded eyes and her smouldering sexuality in a play so daring and amusing it was the talk of the town.

Undaunted by rude letters threatening to horse-whip the life out of him from ex-colonels living in the country who had never seen the play, Noel sailed blithely on to direct Marie Tempest in *Hay Fever*, the most brilliant light comedy he had written so far. Terrified of Marie Tempest's reputation for being difficult, he found her exquisitely reasonable and helpful, and his own image in the theatre was enhanced by the glittering success of the play. In New York, then in the throes of prohibition and the all-time high of big money, bad whisky and hectic parties, *Hay Fever* was a flop, but *The Vortex* whirled him into an orbit of exhilarating—and exhausting—stardom. Back in London his performance as Lewis Dodd in *The Constant Nymph* and his Ruritanian comedy, *The Queen was in the Parlour*, superbly acted by Madge Titheradge, brought him further praise and adulation. Could it last? He was still only twenty-six, 'burning the candle at both ends and in the middle as well', when the nervous strain began to tell and suddenly his whole future looked bleak.

No one analysed Coward so acutely as Coward himself; his self-knowledge was devastating. Isolated on a ranch in Honolulu after a severe breakdown, he slowly recovered his equilibrium. People, he came to the conclusion, were the danger. 'If you gave them the chance they would steal unscrupulously the heart and soul out of you without really meaning to. A little extra personality; a publicized name; a little entertainment value above the average and there they were, snatching and grabbing, clamorous in their demands, draining your strength to add a little fuel to their social bonfires. Then when the time came and you were no longer quite so resilient, you were pushed back into the shadows . . . and left to moulder in the box-room like a once smart hat that is no longer fashionable.' Two failures in New York had taught him things about 'the chinchilla wraps and *piqué* evening shirts', which he was never to forget. And in London in 1927 the public suddenly turned against him on the first night of *Sirocco*. The gallery gave Ivor Novello and Francis Doble the bird and booed Coward when he took his call, and the critics the next morning, with a spiteful exhibition of malice, accused him of superficiality, cynicism and conceit, some of them writing him off as a complete failure.

This set-back, however, was brief. Coward's friends in the theatre stood by him and before long the critics were eating their words and the fashionable first night audience at his new revue for Cochran, *This Year of Grace*, was as enthusiastic as ever. It could not very well be otherwise; for Coward's talent to amuse was inexhaustible and his influence without parallel. He both reflected and created the style of his own generation with a subtle and extraordinary sensitivity. His songs, 'Dance Little Lady', 'Room with a View', 'Mad Dogs and Englishmen' and

'Don't Put your Daughter on the Stage, Mrs Worthington' had vigour, romance, irony and wit. His fast, snip-snap dialogue, apparently flippant, trivial and nonsensical, was entirely new. Mrs Patrick Campbell said his characters talked 'like type-writing', and very soon the people of Mayfair were talking like them, abandoning their aristocratic drawl for the clipped speech of a Noel Coward comedy, trying to imitate the urbane elegance of his wit. Yet he was the master and they were his material. He knew before they did how to capture and enhance their mood of the moment. He gave them romance and nostalgia with *Bitter Sweet* in 1929, sincere, sentimental and moving patriotism with *Cavalcade* in 1931 and between these two, *Private Lives*, a

48   *Noel Coward wrote the comedy* Private Lives, *especially for himself and Gertrude Lawrence. They are seen here in a still from the play. (Radio Times Hulton Picture Library)*

comic masterpiece in the high tradition of the English stage. His Elyot and Amanda, both very rich, very elegant and very sophisticated, quarrelling, loving, hating and hiding their romanticism behind an incomparable flippancy, were of their time when disillusion with the mad gaiety of the Twenties had set in and the colour of the post-war world was growing darker; but they belonged also to the immortals, to the battle of wits between Millamant and Mirabell and the never-ending human comedy of the sexes.

Coward had written *Private Lives* for himself and Gertrude Lawrence, the little Cockney girl from Clapham he had first encountered at Italia Conti's School of Dancing in 1913. Of her performance, he said: 'Everything she had been in my mind when I first conceived the idea in Tokio came to life on the stage; the witty, quick-silver delivery of the lines; the romantic quality, tender and alluring; the swift, brittle rages; even the white Molyneux dress.' There was no other Amanda for Noel, no other woman of her time—on or off the stage—with such glamour; and her rags to riches story added a romantic aura to the mercurial fascination of her personality. She was not beautiful as a child or in adolescence. Her features were irregular, her nose an impertinent blob and her mouth merely pretty when she smiled. But by the time she had reached her early twenties, she had acquired with no apparent effort at all the ravishing loveliness of moonlight and May-time that stayed with her for ever. Her eyes and her hands were marvellous and she moved with an exquisite grace, was captivating, seductive, enigmatic and mischievous, her mood changing as quickly as the sky in April and without any affectation. She could be world weary and disillusioned, wide-eyed with wonder like a child, wickedly funny, superbly at ease in the highest society and down to earth in her job.

Like Coward, the job meant more to Gertie Lawrence than anything else in the world and the fury of her struggle to become a star had taken her from one greasy theatrical lodging to another in the provinces, singing, dancing and acting in blowsy little companies that often folded at the end of the week. On one occasion when this happened and she had no money for the train fare back to London, she took a job as a barmaid in the Lion Hotel at Shrewsbury and was so good at it, the landlord wanted to keep her on. But soon afterwards André Charlot took her into the

49 *Beatrice Lillie with Lew Cody and John Gilbert. Gertie Lawrence and Bea Lillie took Broadway by storm in the mid-twenties, in Charlot's Revue. (Radio Times Hulton Picture Library)*

chorus of his war-time revue *Some*, starring Beatrice Lillie; and a year later, married by then and about to have a baby, she went on as Bea Lillie's understudy and made her first big hit. One revue followed another after the Armistice and by 1921 Gertie had become a star, leaving Clapham, her feckless husband and the provincial landladies with iron curlers in their hair a long way behind. There were mobs of people at the stage door of the Vaudeville Theatre, bundles of flowers, orchids, roses and camellias, presents from Cartier and Boucheron, boxes of chocolates and dashing young Guardsman off duty, fluttering £5 notes under the nose of the door-keeper. Philip Astley, a Captain in the Household Cavalry, fell in love with her and brought the Prince of Wales and Prince George up the alley by the Vaudeville to the emergency exit where the stage door-keeper was waiting to let them in; then off they would all go to a private room at Rule's in Maiden Lane or back to St James's Palace to laugh and sing and enjoy themselves dancing all night to the gramophone.

Gertie was in her element: cossetted, adored and spoilt, with a natural goodness that could not be spoilt at all. She took stardom in her elegant stride. Other women envied her, copied her, tried to look like her and never came within a mile of her. Molyneux dressed her exclusively and for nothing, on condition that she did not buy any clothes anywhere else, though she often did. Money poured out of her hands the moment she earnt it. She did not buy a Bentley—she had one built for her; and her flat in Portland Place was decorated by Sybil Colefax with a white dining-room and silver sequin curtains, while at Staines, where she had settled her mother, her step-father, her daughter and her grandmother in a house by the river, she would suddenly descend after the show with Philip Astley or Ned Lathom and a party of friends bringing hampers of cold chicken, caviar and champagne to picnic in the garden, the wheels of their fast motorcars crunching the gravel long after midnight had come and gone.

Life was gay in New York, too, where *Charlot's Revue* on Broadway, starring Gertie and Bea Lillie together with Jack Buchanan, was a wild success. Bea Lillie had a cool, slick kind of humour, a marvellous idiocy that was sophisticated, very modern and inimitable. She had only to flick an eyebrow in mockery, or to point her index finger at the audience, to get her feet tangled up in her skirt or to pause significantly in a number, to have the whole theatre rocking with laughter. With her boyish dark hair closely cropped and the needle in her eye, she was a perfect foil to Gertie's feminine fascination, and the two of them were inseparable. The apartment they shared on West 54th Street quickly became a rendezvous for all the brightest and most talented composers, lyric writers, newspapermen and theatre-goers of the smart, mixed society of New York. George and Ira Gershwin wrote songs for them; Jerome Kern, Irene Castle, Irving Berlin, Laurette Taylor, Oscar Hammerstein, Dorothy Parker and Jules Glaenzer, the Maecenas of Park Avenue, were in and out of their living-room, laughing, talking and playing the piano at all hours of the day and night. Alexander Woolcott, who adored them, said that no two girls from overseas had ever been

50   *Tallulah Bankhead in* Let Us Be Gay, *1930. Spectacular on and off stage, she had a wild following wherever she went. (Radio Times Hulton Picture Library)*

fêted like it; though what really amazed their new friends most was that they were never jealous of each other, or, as stars in the same show, given to temperamental outbursts of bitchiness—an idea so preposterous to them both, they found it irresistibly funny.

The Gertie Lawrence-Bea Lillie conquest of New York society in 1924 was only equalled on the English side of the Atlantic by the success of Tallulah Bankhead with the smart set in London. She was not much of an actress when she arrived in 1923 to take up a part in *The Dancers* with Gerald du Maurier, who turned her down at their first interview; but when he saw her without a hat and her radiant hair falling to her shoulders, he thought she was the most beautiful young woman he had ever beheld and promptly engaged her. A Senator's daughter from Alabama, she had an exotic, sultry quality; an outrageous, uninhibited egotism quite different from even the most daringly modern English girl; a husky voice with a southern drawl that was sexually exciting and an extravagant idea of her own importance. Besides this, she was determined to succeed, and her vitality, whipped up even then by sniffs of cocaine, was frenetic.

She already knew and was in love with Napier Alington, an attractive, epicene young English lord with an apartment in New York known as Naps Flat, an estate of some 18,000 acres in Dorset and a leaning towards the Bohemian pleasures of the Bright Young People. He introduced her to Olga Lynn, the opera singer *manquée*, who excelled as a professional organizer of society parties, and at once Tallulah became the most sought-after young woman in London. She was so amusing, so wild and wilful, shouting out loud rude things that had never been said before, doing her cartwheels across the room—not in her silk pyjamas, either; stripping to her flimsy underclothes, mimicking people, chain smoking, experimenting with drugs and revelling in champagne, brandy and whisky. She appeared not to mind *what* people said so long as they talked about her, and she could not resist shocking them by spreading scandalous stories about herself, her sexual conquests and the intimate cocktail parties she gave while taking her bath. Yet her exhibitionism was the outcome of her passionate individuality, stimulated by the undisciplined fire in her nature and exaggerated by the unbalanced freedom she found in the merry-go-round of Mayfair.

After *Fallen Angels* she appeared in the dramatized version of Michael Arlen's notorious novel *The Green Hat*, identifying herself completely with the bold, *déclassée* heroine, whose melodramatic suicide, driving her yellow Hispano-Suiza into an oak tree at 70 miles an hour, ostentatiously presumed to expose the hypocrisy and the rottenness of the high society that had cast her out. Gladys Cooper had turned the part down. Tallulah triumphed—by being Tallulah, according to the dramatic critic, Hannen Swaffer, who wrote: 'She is almost the most modern actress we have. She belongs to the semi-exclusive set of whom

51 *Gladys Cooper in one of her most famous rôles, in* Flies in the Sun *at the Playhouse, 1933. (Radio Times Hulton Picture Library)*

Michael Arlen writes. She has beauty and a shimmering sense of the theatre. So she makes Iris Storm a most fascinating study . . . and has succeeded in a part about which even Gladys Cooper felt nervous.' And it was not only the fashionable audience in the stalls who raved about Tallulah. The girls in the gallery went mad about her. They swooned with joy the moment she appeared, cheered hysterically, shouted 'Tallulah! Hallelujah!' and rushed the stage door in a wild stampede to catch a glimpse of their goddess—all of which flattered Tallulah enormously, without improving her hit or miss technique as an actress or helping her much to maintain her rather tenuous foothold in society.

At Farm Street, where she found a cosy little mews cottage and spent thousands of pounds on having it decorated by Mrs Syrie Maugham, she gave more and more extravagant parties, which went on from one night to the next and ended in orgiastic scenes of insobriety, all her 'dahlings' lying flat out on the floor. Yet her friends loved her and it was only gradually that the law of diminishing returns began to catch up on her with too much insistence on the febrile aspects of her character at the expense of her genuine good qualities. Cecil Beaton saw her at the Eiffel Tower Restaurant and commented in his *Diary*: 'Tallulah arrived late, went to every table and was quick-witted at each. She has developed her personality to such an extent that she always seems natural, but is only acting.' Society, in fact, was beginning to get a little tired of her outrageous behaviour—it was no longer quite so amusing as it had been. Even Count Bosdari, the ubiquitous Italian Renaissance nobleman she picked up in Brighton, backed away after giving her a white Rolls Royce and a diamond necklace he was unable to pay for; and in 1930, she waved good-bye to England with tears in her eyes and went back to the U.S.A. with a lucrative offer from Paramount Pictures in her pocket, though Hollywood did not find Tallulah as exciting or as attractive as Marlene Dietrich, Paramount's number one star, whose film *Shanghai Express* made a gross profit of 4,000,000 dollars.

In England the stars of the silent films had far less influence on society than the actors and actresses in the theatre. For one thing the film première had not yet reached the status of a fashionable first night in the West End. For another the cinema was cheaper and the rivers of spectacular and sentimental cellu-

52 *Greta Garbo—a totally new female image, soft and natural in looks, casual and mysterious in her movements, and inimitable. (Radio Times Hulton Picture Library)*

loid that gushed out of Hollywood were aimed at the suburban middle classes, who found the sight of Lillian Gish turned out in the snow in her nightie very good value for a seat costing 6d. or 1s. There were exceptions, of course. Women of all classes adored Rudolph Valentino, the handsome, smooth-skinned, languorous-eyed lover of *Blood and Sand*, whose uninhibited warmth suggested a Latin sexuality that excited all his female admirers to indulge in the vicarious delight of harbouring an illicit passion for him; so much so that when he died suddenly in 1926, still in his prime, there were unparalleled scenes of hysterical mourning all round the world. Debonair Douglas Fairbanks, a shining example of healthy American virility, and Mary Pickford, the image of kittenish youth and prettiness, travelled in great state across the Atlantic and were invited to meet the Prince of Wales at a party given in their honour by the Hon. Mrs Richard Norton. And there was Charlie Chaplin, no longer just a funny little Cockney from Kennington in baggy trousers with a battered bowler and a stick, but 'the King of the Silver Screen', earning £150,000 a year, and a symbol of the gay spirit of laughter in a cruel and crazy world. Crowds followed him in the street when he came back to London, and society hostesses tried every stunt they knew short of kidnapping to catch him in their net.

The arrival in 1927 of synchronized sound pictures, or 'the talkies' as they were called, seemed to offer a more serious challenge to the popularity of the theatre. Vast new cinemas of florid architectural design—the Capitol, the Stoll and the Tivoli —were built in the West End as well as in the suburbs to attract a new audience. They had large organs capable of imitating every kind of sound from the squeak of a mouse to the reverberations of the last trump, comfortable plush seats and spacious bars and refreshment rooms with gilded Art-Deco lattice work climbing up the walls. But even so the upper classes continued to look on the films as an inferior entertainment to the theatre and they did not dress to go to the cinema in the evenings.

For a time it was quite fashionable to imitate the latest American slang and to look like the 'It' girl, Clara Bow, a dazzling, sexy redhead who ousted the vamp made popular by Theda Bara and Gloria Swanson in the silent pictures; and in the Thirties, while Fred Astaire and Ginger Rogers were dancing their way through endless glossy ballrooms, Jean Harlow started an epidemic of blondes. But the English got more fun out of visiting Hollywood than by watching the products of the studios. They loved being entertained by the stars in a luxury that surpassed anything they could afford at home, seeing the swimming-pools, the patios and the expensive houses on Beverly Hills with their wrought-iron balconies, Moorish pillars, Spanish mosaics, Italian marble halls and bathrooms with gold lions' heads spouting water. And it was all quite reassuring in a way, because it was so vulgar and not quite real and might well melt away like the ice tinkling at the bottom of the tumblers of orange juice mixed with champagne that all the stars and their guests never stopped drinking. Marlene Dietrich, Garbo, Clark Gable, Gary Cooper, Joan Crawford, Constance and Joan Bennett—their names and the gossip about them, their love affairs, their tantrums and their exorbitant demands, rang like a carillon of bells in a ridiculous Disneyland that encouraged more than it diminished the inbred feeling of superiority that still belonged to the English. They might not be so rich or much good at making films themselves—they were not—but most of the stuff that came out of Hollywood was laughable.

Only one figure stood out among the rest with a personality big enough to influence the whole trend of fashion on both sides of the Atlantic in the Thirties and that was Garbo, the most elusive, most sensitive and strangely inhibited woman of her generation. Her passionate desire for privacy and her constant withdrawal into her own skin stimulated curiosity about her private life. When the cameras off the set caught her in a turtleneck sweater and a pair of slacks, or in a raincoat with a large hat jammed firmly down over her eyes, every woman modelled her clothes on the same casual style without achieving at all the same effect of a startled fawn about to take flight into the forest. Garbo killed the synthetic, tarted up image of the film star with platinum blonde wavy hair, red lips and a pink and white doll's complexion, revealing instead the dark line of her eyelashes, the enigmatic paleness of her skin and the marvellous mobility of her features. Hauntingly beautiful, with the sad gaiety of a clown suddenly aware of the tragic significance of life, she seemed to hug the secret wisdom of the Sphinx to her soul and to reflect in her tantalizing smile all the desires of the feminine psyche since the world began.

'Imitations are always a far cry from the original, and especially in the case of Garbo,' Cecil Beaton wrote. 'The carbon copies often looked more decadent than sensitive.' None the less Garbo created a new pattern of beauty that caught the imagination of the chic women of the Thirties. Their brief flirtation with short skirts and cloche hats, the doll-like boy-cum-girl look, was over, dying a natural death with the loss of innocence in their revolt against the conventional mores of the past. They had dared and won their battle and it was only a Pyrrhic victory after all, for the Bright Young People were growing up and already looking back with nostalgia to their salad days. Coward's

'Children of the Ritz' in 1932 was more satirical, more bitter and more disillusioned than 'Dance, Dance, Little Lady'; the beat of the rhythm was more jaded. The days of *No, No Nanette* and 'I Want to be Happy' were over. Gaiety and folly had turned to dissipation and the fun was less spontaneous as the drinking, chain-smoking, sleepless nights began to rob youth of its freshness and vitality. Yet society went on seeking entertainment like a clockwork toy wound up, and the expensive restaurants and clubs were full.

Cabaret had developed into an art of its own since the *Midnight Follies* had been put on at the Hotel Metropole as the first 'floor show' to be seen in London. Individual artists were now paid huge sums of money to appear at the Café de Paris, Ciro's or the Savoy, and they had to be good to survive. They were out on their own with no support except from a pianist or the drums, in front of the most sybaritic audience in the world; right on top of them, too, at such close quarters that a woman drinking a cup of coffee or a man lighting a cigar could throw an inexperienced singer off his beat. Even Delysia, who had made her first appearance at the old Moulin Rouge in Paris at the age of fourteen, confessed to an agony of nerves every time she descended the staircase at the Café de Paris; yet no artiste ever had more poise and although her songs were 'naughty' by the standards of the time, she combined the allure of a *grande cocotte* with the air of a well-bred foreign princess.

Scores of cabaret turns became a cult. Hutch, the talented negro performer, had a doting public of debutantes and not so young duchesses, who demanded their favourite tunes and showered him with gifts. Florence Desmond perfected her brilliant imitations of Tallulah Bankhead, Lilian Braithwaite and Gladys Cooper without any props at all, simply by rearranging her hair, changing her voice and assuming the mannerisms of her victims. Douglas Byng, the queen of female impersonators, did his Millie, the Mermaid and his Flora MacDonald night after night to the delight of an audience consisting of royalty and all the élite of London.

Like Coward and Gertie Lawrence, Douggie Byng came up the hard way from seaside concert parties through pantomime to the Charlot and Cochran revues. In the early Twenties he had an interest in the Kinde Dragon, one of the small night clubs which, like Elsa Lanchester's club in Seven Dials, the Ham Bone and the Blue Lantern, proliferated in the yards and alleys behind St Martin's Lane and were popular with the smart set. Elizabeth Ponsonby, a cousin of Loelia's, took her crowd of Bright Young People to the Blue Lantern; actors and actresses, writers and artists and people on the Bohemian fringe of society went to the Ham Bone; and at the Kinde Dragon, Douggie Byng tried out many of his best numbers before moving upwards, first to the Café Anglais in Leicester Square and then to the Café de Paris and Monseigneur. 'My songs were considered very daring in those days,' he has since written in his book *As You Were*. 'The only way you could be risqué was with *double entendre* and innuendo. Now with four letter words accepted,

53   *Douglas Byng in* Willie the Mermaid *at the Monseigneur, 1931. His cabaret act and impersonations of female dowagers were famous. (Radio Times Hulton Picture Library)*

anything is permitted . . . and my songs are really only suitable for children.' But he was a past master at suggesting the improper in a song that was apparently innocuous on paper and his subtlety inspired Coward to comment that his was 'the most refined vulgarity in London'.

Douglas Byng's name as an attraction to the charity balls of the Season sold more tickets than anyone else's and since he was wonderfully generous in giving his services for nothing, society paid court to him, though without ever making him conceited or snobbish. He was too good a trooper for that and his sense of humour saved many an entertainment from disaster, for these events were a gorgeous opportunity for society amateurs to appear among the professional stars of the stage and the screen and to be photographed with them for the next issue of the *Tatler* or the *Sketch*. They spent immense sums of money on their dresses, so much so that Lady Bridgit Poulett admitted she had no money left for anything else and even Barbara Cartland wondered whether a direct donation to Queen Charlotte's Maternity Hospital would not have been more profitable than the ball at the Dorchester for which she arranged a very expensive pageant of lovelies dressed up as oysters and champagne. Byng appeared as Narcissus in a gathering of Greek gods and goddesses organized by Olga Lynn at Claridges and said: 'There were more people in the pageant than in the audience, as all London society seemed to want to take part.' Perhaps the new sense of guilt beginning to nibble at the conscience of society had something to do with it. The plight of the unemployed and the poverty in the depressed areas of Britain could not be swept under the carpet for ever, and a five guinea ticket for a ball, a champagne supper and Douggie Byng was bound to benefit someone somewhere.

6 LITERATURE AND ART

Several writers in the Twenties and the Thirties succeeded, like Freddy Lonsdale, in enhancing their social status through their work and the prosperity it brought them. There was nothing new in this, of course. Shakespeare was granted a coat of arms by the College of Heralds and bought the largest house in Stratford-on-Avon. Congreve and Vanbrugh were elected to the exclusive Kit-Cat Club organized by members of the rich Whig aristocracy; Pope consorted with the Earl of Burlington, Lord Bathurst and Lady Mary Wortley Montagu; and even in the nineteenth century, when it was no longer necessary for writers to beg for the patronage of the aristocracy, there was much to be said for the kind of success that brought recognition from the élite. Thackeray, Dickens and Carlyle, the ill-tempered sage of Chelsea, all climbed into the higher ranks of Victorian acceptability. Oscar Wilde conquered London society in the Nineties and Henry James, who found England more compatible than America, was an honoured guest at Edwardian country house parties, while some of the younger authors—Galsworthy, Arnold Bennett, H. G. Wells and Somerset Maugham—who made a reputation before the War and maintained their position for some time after it was over, were by no means averse to being fêted in the London drawing-rooms.

John Galsworthy had no need to push his way into society. He was educated at Harrow and Oxford and a member of the Athenaeum. Dressed with impeccable precision in dark suits from Savile Row and the white spats belonging to his class—how D. H. Lawrence hated those spats—he had the sedate air of a respectable lawyer or a high-ranking civil servant. Yet the plays that made his name—*The Silver Box* in 1906, *Strife* in 1909 and *Justice* in 1910—were considered very *avant garde* in the sympathy they showed for the injustices suffered by the lower classes at the hands of their masters; and again in 1920 with *The Skin Game*, he appeared as a serious dramatist deeply concerned with social problems. The publication two years later of *The Forsyte Saga*, in which he so faithfully depicted the pre-war world of upper middle-class family life, made him one of the most successful authors of the day; though when he continued the *Saga* with *A Modern Comedy*, it became painfully obvious that he was altogether out of touch with modern life and in spite of the honours heaped upon him—the Order of Merit in 1929 and the Nobel Prize for Literature in 1932—the younger generation found him out of date and rather stuffy.

Arnold Bennett, born in the same year as Galsworthy, emerged from a very different background, his father at the time of his birth being a pawnbroker in Burslem, one of the gloomiest and most neglected industrial towns in the Potteries, where the smoking chimneys left a pall of vapour in the sky that soiled and shrivelled the surrounding country and drenched the rows and rows of sombre little Victorian houses in a layer of black dust. Enoch Bennett was a harsh, autocratic parent, who seemed to take pleasure in humiliating his son and especially in taunting him most cruelly about the unfortunate impediment in his speech; so it was not surprising that Arnold made up his mind to leave home. 'I am going to get out of this,' he told a friend—and get out he did, though when he first arrived in London at the age of twenty-one to take a job as a junior clerk in a solicitor's office, he was just another raw provincial with a broad midland accent and nothing to recommend him except his audacity.

His first contribution to *Tit-Bits*, which earned him one guinea, turned his attention to the possibilities of journalism; his first short story in *The Yellow Book* convinced him that he could write, and on May 15, 1896, 'at noon precisely', he finished his first novel, *A Man from the North*. Again after the cost of having it typed his profit amounted to a guinea, but he was already obsessed with the number of words he could write at a stretch, noting them down in his *Journal* at the end of each day, and already determined on his future. As the Editor of *T.P.'s Weekly* said of him: 'He knew his powers and how to apply them. He

54   *W. Somerset Maugham by Powys Evans. His own experience of contemporary life in London and abroad was used as the basis for a . . wide range of short stories and novels. (Mary Evans)*

built his career as methodically as a man builds a house and developed himself according to plan.'

The process required guts and extraordinary self-discipline considering the chronic disadvantages from which he suffered. Yet his capacity for working on two levels at the same time never deserted him and he insisted that his journalism and his pot-boilers, motivated by the strong desire to escape from the poverty of his uncongenial early surroundings, gave him the financial independence he needed 'to manufacture a dazzling reputation'. This he achieved in 1909 with the publication of *The Old Wives' Tale* and with *Clayhanger* in 1910, following up his success as a major novelist with *Milestones*, a play written in collaboration with Edward Knoblock. At forty he had married a Frenchwoman, Marguerite Soulie, and was living in Paris; at forty-five he was a person to be reckoned with on the London literary scene—a friend of Shaw and Wells, Conrad and Somerset Maugham and a member of the Reform Club, dining with Winston Churchill and Lord Birkenhead; affluent, gregarious and firmly established in the world he had dreamed of conquering. It was not, however, until after his war-time service as Director of Propaganda in the Ministry of Information that he finally reached his apotheosis as a celebrity and was recognized everywhere he went, applauded when he came into the theatre, stopped by strangers in the street and invited by all the London hostesses to their parties.

By then he lived in 'a rather noble thing in houses' in Cadogan Square and 'just to show those rich chaps that an author can make money too', had bought a private yacht which he sailed with a captain and a crew of five, entertaining his guests on board with great splendour. Yet there was nothing offensive in his display of self-satisfaction, for he remained quite objective about his own success and was not in the least ashamed of his own vanity. His well-known appearance was a work of art, the up-standing quiff of hair an inspiration which turned an ugly face into an interesting one. It balanced the heavy-lidded eyes of an insomniac, just as the moustache balanced the flabby lower lip and the deeply indented chin. And the face was set off by the clothes he wore with deliberate ostentation—the frilled evening shirts from Sulka of Bond Street, the boots made by Lobb of St James's Street, the carnation in his button-hole and the gold fobs

55 *Arnold Bennet by David Low. Will-power and determination brought him success as an author and respect as an observer of his age. (The New Statesman, Witt Library)*

hanging from his waistcoat, which H. G. Wells maliciously called 'Arnold's gastric jewellery', his derision mixed with no little envy. For Enoch Arnold Bennett, the young lout from Burslem, by turning his deficiencies into assets, had become Arnold Bennett, the sophisticated man about town, the rich and successful author whose opinions on current affairs, books and art had a great influence. Even the horrors of his speech impediment became a token of his individuality, the long pauses and explosive words uttered beyond them adding significance to what he said.

None the less there was a high price to be paid for all this. He was fifty-one at the end of the War and putting on weight, which he kept in check by doing Hornibrook exercises and learning to dance. After his marriage with Marguerite had broken down in 1921, he became involved with an actress young enough to be his daughter and when their child was born, she changed her name to Dorothy Cheston Bennett because he was trapped in the terms of his over-generous separation from Marguerite and could not get a divorce. Arnold persuaded himself that his friends in society would accept Dorothy as his 'second wife', and some of them did; but the situation frayed his nerves and worried the Methodist conscience he thought he had buried long ago, besides requiring a greater effort than ever to make enough money to support himself and Dorothy and his ex-wife as well. Just when his reputation as serious novelist was beginning to sag, he produced *Riceyman Steps* and *Lord Raingo*, a high society political novel that caused a great stir. But Somerset Maugham considered that social success had ruined him by cutting him off from the original sources of his inspiration. 'He never knew anything intimately but the life of the Five Towns,' he wrote, 'and it was only when he dealt with this that his work had character. When success brought him into the society of rich men and smart women, and he sought to deal with them, his work was worthless.'

It was, however, with smart women and rich men that he mixed for his remaining years, working himself to a point of utter exhaustion to keep up with the world he had conquered and the way of life he could not now do without. His weekly articles in the *Evening Standard* on Books and Persons brought him £300 a month and the friendship of Lord Beaverbrook, and one year he noted with satisfaction in his *Journal* that he had earned £20,000. But it was not enough; and if he could write as he did in *These Twain*, 'most folk are nobodies, but I am somebody', the life he had chosen was increasingly self-destructive. His *Journals* report the torment he suffered from neuralgia and insomnia and the hectic pace of the Twenties, dining late and dancing late, revelling at the Gargoyle, the Kit-Cat and Ciro's, lunching at the Ritz and the Savoy, then off to dinner with Lady Colefax or the Sitwells and giving his time and energy in between to helping young authors and trying to arrange some order out of the chaos of his domestic affairs. The servants, he noted, were more censorious of his equivocal relationship with Dorothy than his worldly upper-class friends. The nurse gave in her notice because the other nurses in Kensington Gardens got to hear that the child was ille-

56 *George Bernard Shaw's garden party at Malvern, August 1932. With him are Sir Edward Elgar (left) and Mrs Claude Beddington. (Radio Times Hulton Picture Library)*

gitimate and the cook took umbrage when the butcher-boy winked at the goings-on upstairs—all of which proved that lower-class prejudice had not changed at all in spite of the more tolerant attitude of modern society.

But Noel Coward came to see him and Ivor Novello called. T. S. Eliot came to ask his advice and stayed too long. There were dinner parties when the cook was in a good humour and lunch parties at Cadogan Square, and holidays on the Continent staying in the best hotels in Rome and Paris and on the Riviera, travelling on the European *trains-de-luxe* and cruising on the Duke of Westminster's yacht in the Mediterranean. Then suddenly in 1931 he caught typhoid from drinking a glass of water in a French café, and with no reserve strength and not much money in the bank either, his heart failed.

Punch wrote that Arnold Bennett was 'a connoisseur of living'. His old friend H. G. Wells was not so kind and in a fit of ill-tempered jealousy wrote disparagingly of his social success after his death. Yet they had been friendly rivals all their lives and Wells, with an equally humble background—his mother was a housekeeper and his father a failed shop-keeper turned cricket professional—was not without his own social prowess. Intelligent women found him fascinating in spite of his not very attractive appearance, his moth-eaten moustache and the middle-aged paunch he developed, his Cockney accent and his exasperating inconsistencies . . . The thought-provoking ideas that poured out of him on religion, science, sex and politics, and his fantastic imagination, forever probing the future, swayed the minds of his contemporaries. They hailed him as a prophet, a master of science fiction and as a man with advanced views on free love. But his own private life was permanently beset with turbulent, amorous adventures, which he entered into with boundless energy and enthusiasm and emerged from rather the worse for wear. 'I want a healthy woman handy to steady my nerves and leave my mind ready for real things,' he wrote to his wife in explanation of one of his affairs, not realizing that he could not always have his cake and eat it and that when this desirable situation failed to materialize, his nerves went to pieces and he became an impossible companion.

'With no personal advantage but a bright eye, he made everyone else in the room seem a dull dog', according to Rebecca West; yet even his best friends found H.G. infuriating and his messianic faith in his own theories verged on paranoia, so that in the end he quarrelled with almost everyone except Bennett. Before the War he quarrelled with Shaw and the Fabians and after the War when his reputation stood at its height, with his publishers, his agents, the Authors' Society and the young women who fell for his inexplicable charms. Then as his vision of a new world darkened, his prophecies became more depressing. *The Way the World is Going* in 1928 was followed by *What Are We To Do with Our Lives?* in 1931 and soon he believed that 'the human species was on its way through a succession of disasters to extinction'—a dreary forecast that appealed to those who thought they saw another war coming but failed to convince the unconverted.

Wells's pessimism and his declining influence turned him sour. Bernard Shaw, who also spent his life castigating *Homo sapiens* for his stupidity and incompetence, never lost his Irish sense of humour in the process. In the Twenties he was still the *enfant terrible* of society, incalculable, irrepressible, fighting on all fronts in a suit of Jaeger underwear and darting away like a trout in a stream when anyone with a baited hook tried to catch him. 'One day he will eat a steak,' Mrs Patrick Campbell said, 'and then *where* shall all we poor women be!' Yet with all his fads and fancies, his maddening inconsequence and his love of arguing for the sake of argument, Shaw was a great hirsute giant among the lilliputians of his day. Of his purpose as a playwright, he declared: 'I am no ordinary playwright. I am a specialist in immoral and heretical plays. My reputation was gained by my persistent struggle to force the public to reconsider its morals'— and it was this facet of his genius, so brilliantly disguised by his wit, that appealed to the post-war generation in its search for

57   *The novelist Christopher Isherwood and the poet W. H. Auden. The Thirties marked the beginning of political commitment in literature. (Radio Times Hulton Picture Library)*

more freedom in the structure of society.

Shaw made mince-meat of the stultifying prejudices of the late Victorians and the Edwardians. He preached freedom of thought, new ideas on sex and a new concept of good and evil, his passion for justice working like the fermentation in a vat of wine. He refused the Order of Merit and the peerage Ramsay MacDonald offered him in 1924, preferring to retain his independence as the arch debunker of pretentiousness, conformity and woolly thinking. Five years later, his political extravaganza, *The Apple Cart*, written at the age of seventy-three, startled everyone by its freshness and vitality. Once again he gaily turned the world upside down. 'The conflict,' he wrote, 'is not really between royalty and democracy. It is between both and plutocracy . . . Money talks; money prints; money broadcasts; money reigns; and kings and labour leaders alike have to register its decrees, and even by a strange paradox, to finance its enterprises and guarantee its profits.' This was strong, controversial stuff, anticipating what some intelligent people, disillusioned with orthodox Socialism, were beginning to feel; and since the play was as witty as ever and superbly produced, Shaw's popularity increased at a time when most men in their seventies were being written off by the younger generation as a spent force.

Debunking—a word adopted from America—was all the rage among the young and, if not the actual motive of Lytton Strachey in his *Eminent Victorians*, the aspect of his subtle and incisive art that suddenly made him famous in the Twenties. A strange, spidery looking creature with long legs and limp hands, owlish eyes and a pale, El Greco countenance, elongated by a tawny red beard, Strachey had an enigmatic, complex character, aggravated by constant ill-health and conditioned by his strong homosexual inclinations. He was shy and sensitive, yet sharp as a needle, his feminine sensibility combined with a mocking irreverance for all that was pompous or hypocritical, and a teasing, ironic perception of the absurdities inherent in the people he examined with such microscopic intensity.

He brought a new approach to the art of biography, utterly remote from what he himself described as 'those two fat volumes with which it is our custom to commemorate the dead . . . with their ill-digested masses of material, their slipshod style, their tone of tedious panegyric . . . as familiar as the cortège of the

58 *Augustus John at his easel. He was one of the decade's foremost portrait painters, but is also remembered for his vivid paintings of Romany life. (Radio Times Hulton Picture Library)*

undertaker'; and the result was exhilarating, as if a gust of bright, cool air had blown open the windows of the fusty Victorian rooms occupied by Cardinal Manning, Florence Nightingale, Dr Arnold and General Gordon. Here was the heroic Lady of the Lamp, sanctified and sentimentalized by her previous biographers, revealed with a merciless clarity as a ruthless, indomitable woman. Here was the much honoured headmaster, Thomas Arnold, moulding the pattern of the public school system with the tyrannical, self-obsessed authority of Jehovah, so that 'the Rugby schoolboy walked in holy dread of some sudden manifestation of the sweeping gown, the majestic tone, the piercing glance of Dr Arnold.' No one before had dared to attack the validity of Dr Arnold's system or to hold the man himself up to ridicule, and by doing so Strachey at once achieved a conspicuous reputation among the moderns while giving great offence to Sir Edmund Gosse, the dons and bishops and men of letters belonging to the established hierarchy.

He was quite unrepentant. He enjoyed being denounced as a bearded Mephistopheles with a mind full of cunning and depravity, bent on destroying all that should be held sacred in society. It gave him confidence and stimulated his ironic sense of humour. He was forty; old enough to have known the rigours of a Victorian upbringing in a large family dominated by his mother, the widow of General Sir Richard Strachey, and to have found relief from his dissatisfaction in the Bloomsbury Group of artists and writers consisting of the two daughters of Sir Leslie Stephen, Virginia Woolf and Vanessa Bell, Clive Bell, Duncan Grant, J. M. Keynes, Roger Fry, E. M. Forster and some other forward-looking undergraduates down from Cambridge.

As rebels against the inhibitions of upper-class family life, the Bloomsburies had deliberately set out to create their own values of intelligence and taste and of love and friendship on a basis of absolute sincerity and freedom from prudery, resolving to conduct their lives without the evasions and concealments that the previous segregation of the sexes had imposed. Art was their *modus vivendi*; contempt for philistinism, brutalism and vulgarity, and a desire for complete self-expression, their avowed faith. They dressed in unconventional clothes—some woven at the Omega Workshop of Roger Fry—and talked endlessly in a superior tone of voice that was entirely their own, high-pitched and animated, discussing openly and with some indecency the sexual deviations among themselves, while nibbling the rather dry little buns they bought at a shop round the corner near the British Museum. The ladies wore beads and the men went in for beards, cloaks and sombreros; neither could be mistaken for the *bourgeoisie* they so heartily despised. And considering the bitchiness with which they quarrelled from time to time, swapping partners according to their homosexual or heterosexual

, 59 *Augustus John's portrait of Lady Ottoline Morrell, whose parties at Garsington Manor brought together many outstanding writers of the day. She was used by at least two of the circle as a model for characters in their books. (Private Collection)*

instincts and making hay out of their three- and four-cornered love affairs, it was remarkable how well they survived the tormenting and tormented quagmire of their emotions to emerge into middle-age after the War as the élite of the upper-class intelligentsia.

Virginia Woolf was as sensitive to atmosphere as a piece of litmus paper. To her intimate friends she was very beautiful, with a noble beauty of bone and form distilled in the high forehead, aquiline nose and deepset eyes of her long, aristocratic face and in the graceful line of her etiolated body. To the uninitiated she seemed aloof and alarming; her long silences were unnerving and her voice when it came at last swooped down on her victims like the flickering tongue of a snake. There was malice and mischief-making in her wit and high tension in the movement of her tapering hands. But her integrity as an artist and her quality as a writer were never in doubt.

Like Strachey, she was modern: incomprehensible to the old-fashioned reader looking for a straightforward, realistic story; life-enhancing and fascinating to those who believed in the infinite possibilities of the subconscious mind acting and reacting on the imagination and the visible surface of things. In *Mrs Dalloway* in 1925 and *To the Lighthouse* in 1927, she smashed the conventional novel like a looking-glass and from the broken pieces put together a kaleidescopic pattern which reflected the inner frustrations, desires and complex humanity of her characters with a marvellous unexpectedness. Writing and rewriting her novels increased her irritability and brought on exhausting headaches that reminded her of her previous mental breakdown, and for years she was haunted by the fear of going mad; yet she remained the high priestess of Bloomsbury and with her husband, Leonard Woolf, at the Hogarth Press, did much to help the younger writers of the Twenties and the Thirties.

It was, indeed, a feather in the cap of any writer to be taken up by the Bloomsburies, though D. H. Lawrence, preaching his own gospel of the primitive sexual urge between a submissive woman and a strong-loined man, found them anaemic and thought they talked too much, while they, after their first enthusiasm for his fiery genius, considered him rather common and secretly despised his fierce involvement with phallic symbols of fecundity, Mexican fetishes and Madame Blavatsky's confused theosophical arguments. His avowed belief 'in the blood, the flesh, as being wiser than the intellect' was totally at variance with their kind of cerebral rope-dancing; but having erupted from his working-class provincial background into the high society of the intelligentsia, he was fascinated by it and enough of a snob to enjoy the friendship of the Bloomsburies even when the fire of the dark religion burning within him set him against them and drove him to seek his Utopia abroad.

Before he left England for good after the War, Lawrence was a frequent visitor to Garsington, the Elizabethan manor house in Oxfordshire, where Lady Ottoline Morrell entertained all the Bloomsburies and was surrounded by a court of sponging admirers. Augustus John painted her in 1926 in a peacock-green velvet gown with a peacock's feather in the large black hat sailing on top of her massive, mahogany-coloured hair. He penetrated to the veiled uncertainty behind the bold, enquiring gaze of her glacial, peacock-green eyes and emphasized her aristocratic features, the high, rouged cheekbones, the long, patrician nose and jaw and the open, talkative red lips. Her booming voice, it was said, could be intimidating or insinuating and seductive; and like the huge ropes of pearls cascading down her bosom, she was altogether larger than life—a Borgia or a Medici, whose majestic appearance, with a touch of the decadent 1890s, somewhat belied her true qualities of generosity and perception.

A half-sister of the 6th Duke of Portland, she had escaped from the hunting and shooting routine of a rich aristocratic family be marrying Philip Morrell, a Liberal Member of Parliament with a modest disposition which acted as a foil to her more spectacular temperament; and from her first rather timid contact with the Bloomsbury Group she had blossomed into a woman of great consequence, capable of friendship with a wide and varied circle of writers and artists, in whose talents her submerged creative instincts and her Bohemian curiosity found compensation. Lytton Strachey saw her salon in Bedford Square and her drawing-room at Garsington as a re-creation of Madame du Deffand's distinguished entertainments at Sceaux, but the civilized manners of the eighteenth century could not be so easily invoked in the unrestrained and disturbed atmosphere of the Twenties. Lady Ottoline was too farouche in her likes and dislikes and too fond of intrigue to become another Madame du

Deffand. She had very little tact, and her possessiveness and love of power tended to embroil everyone sooner or later in a bedlam of conflicting emotions. She also had an embarrassing habit of 'loudly sucking and crunching between her prominent equine teeth a succession of bull's-eye peppermints', while subjecting some of the shyer and more inarticulate poets and painters she gathered round her to a cross examination on their work and their love affairs. If they resented her curiosity, she was upset, and if they revolted—as some of them did—she failed to understand why.

None the less, Garsington was the mecca of two generations of artists and writers and even those like Lytton Strachey, who made cruel fun of Lady Ottoline behind her back, continued to accept her hospitality. Young undergraduates from Oxford like John Rothenstein, Edward Sackville-West, Peter Quennell, L. P. Hartley and David Cecil were invited to tea on the lawn under the ilex trees with Strachey, Duncan Grant and Aldous Huxley, or entertained in the scarlet drawing-room which, however ill-suited to an old Tudor manor house, was consistent with Lady Ottoline's flamboyant personality. Silk hangings, rich Persian carpets, pouffes and cushions, Chinese lacquer screens, bowls of pot-pourri and jars of incense steaming perfume in the air, were incoherently mixed up with the drawings and paintings of Augustus John, Henry Lamb and Mark Gertler; and in this somewhat overpowering ambience of quasi-oriental luxury, Lady Ottoline's several and not very well-behaved pug dogs snuffled behind the trailing velvet skirts of their mistress. No wonder Garsington was an experience never to be forgotten. No wonder Virginia Woolf, querying whether anything, even the sunlight, was ever normal there, said: 'I think even the sky at Garsington is done up in pale yellow silk, and certainly the cabbages are scented.'

D. H. Lawrence ill repaid Lady Ottoline's eccentric generosity by caricaturing her as Hermione Roddice in *Women in Love*. Aldous Huxley paid her the same backhanded compliment in his first novel *Crome Yellow*, which amused the *cognoscenti* enormously and with its blend of disillusion, fantasy and farce was the first of his satires to reveal the underlying dissonances of the post-war world of society. Still under thirty, Aldous had inherited great talents from his distinguished family, his own

60 *Aldous Huxley in 1931. His cleverness and the vast range of his writing won him great acclaim. (Bassano and Vandyk Studios)*

intellectual qualities humanized by a brilliant sense of comedy and a sharp perception of the people around him. Garsington, he said, was 'an education', not only for the intelligent conversation to be found there, but in its atmosphere of uninhibited emotional freedom and sexual sophistication, though this was painful to Maria, the Belgian girl Lady Ottoline took in as a refugee during the War and treated with more cruelty than kindness. Inevitably Aldous felt sorry for her and she was attracted by his gentleness in such alien surroundings, admitting afterwards that the other men and women at Garsington had so squashed her, she had been terrified of them. Difficulties of all kinds were put in the way of their courtship, but happily surmounted when they had waited two years for each other, Maria proving to be the most sympathetic wife Aldous could ever have chosen, her marvellous care of him surviving his serious love affair with Nancy Cunard and his minor infidelities without ever diminishing in strength.

After the publication of *Crome Yellow* he was acclaimed as 'the brightest of the younger writers', though his satirical view of the half crazy intellectual characters he depicted with such skill in his next novel, *Antic Hay*, was mistaken by some critics for approval of their cynical disenchantment, and he was accused of encouraging the debauchery and the decadence of his own class of society. Nothing could have been farther from the truth for, like Swift and Daniel Defoe, he was fundamentally a serious student of mankind and a creative thinker. Osbert Sitwell found his conversation fascinating. 'Versed in every modern theory of science, politics, painting, literature and psychology, he was qualified by his disposition to deal in ideas and play with them. Nor would gossip or any matter of the day be beneath his notice: though even these lesser things would be treated as a philosopher with detachment and an utter want of prejudice . . . He would speak with obvious enjoyment in a voice of great charm, unhurried . . . and utterly indifferent to any sensation he was making; and then fall into silence, drooping into a trance-like state of meditation.' It was no surprise to his friends that Huxley developed into a mystic as he grew older, his work becoming more and more concerned with the contrasting forces of illusion and reality.

The Sitwells themselves—Edith, Osbert and Sacheverell— were doughty fighters against the philistinism of the upper-class world which had bred them and the creeping mediocrity of the new democratic society they viewed with the utmost distaste. In the public mind the one sister and two brothers seemed more akin to the three weird sisters in *Macbeth* after their first highly controversial performance of *Façade*. Never before had such strange incantations been heard in the genteel surroundings of the Aeolian Hall and what was worse, they issued from a gigantic mask set in a painted curtain, were amplified into a fearsome boom by a special type of megaphone and accompanied by a discordant background of a-tonal music composed by a young man named William Walton. The Sitwells' aim was to emphasize the parallel dance rhythms, mocking gaiety and tenderness of the poems with an equal volume of sound in the music, to match the spoken word with the sextet of musical instruments and to give the whole entertainment a new dimension by performing it in an abstract setting. Time has proved the unique quality of *Façade*. But in 1923, Walton's music was a cacophony on the ear and Edith Sitwell's

Said King Pompey, the Emperor's Ape,
Shuddering black in his temporal cape
Of dust: 'The dust is everything—'

sounded like nonsense. The public thought it was having its leg
pulled and resented it bitterly. The Sitwells thought the public
and the press were conspiring against them and redoubled their
furious polemical energy for denouncing their critics. They took
themselves very seriously as artists, even if no one else did; and
when Coward put a frivolous skit on them into *London Calling* as
the Whittlebots, they took it very badly indeed.

Yet there was something very touching—almost heroic—in
the way the three Sitwells stood together. At Renishaw they had
often found themselves in league against their parents' persistent
habit of belittling their youthful aspirations, and it was years

61   *Edith and Osbert Sitwell who, with their brother Sacheverell, formed a sparkling
trio outstanding in their originality. (Radio Times Hulton Picture Library)*

before Edith had begun to emerge from the painful chrysalis of shyness this had induced. Neither the eccentric Sir George nor the frivolous Lady Ida Sitwell could understand this palefaced, lanky-haired daughter of theirs being more interested in poetry and music than in finding a suitable husband; and it was only with the collapse of the rigid Edwardian code of behaviour after the War that she was able to escape from her aristocratic prison into the freer, more Bohemian society cultivated by her brothers. Osbert and Sacheverell had faith in her talents. They encouraged her to trust her own imagination and her wit, and to make a virtue out of the strange, elongated Gothic features she had inherited from her Plantagenet ancestors, so that her appearance assumed a highly individual quality of beauty, as of a mediaeval saint in a stained glass window.

At the house Osbert and Sacheverell shared in Chelsea there was a constant coming and going of young musicians, artists and writers from abroad, for the Sitwells' pursuit of what was new and exciting in the arts had a cosmopolitan background. The sudden, vivid revelation of the Diaghilev Ballet in the seasons before the War had whetted Osbert's appetite for the music of Stravinski and the brilliant stage designs of Bakst, Benois and Picasso, while the various movements in painting and sculpture which continued to develop after the War towards a more and more abstract idea of art, stimulated his imagination and increased his antipathy towards the aesthetic ignorance of the English upper classes. His attempt to promote the work of Modigliani, Derain and Utrillo at an exhibition in London met with so much abuse, he became more than ever convinced that the Anglo-Saxon attitude to art was irredeemably obtuse, when not actually conditioned by 'that deliberate malice which the stupid always have in reserve for the creative'.

There was some truth in this arrogant assumption, for London was always some ten years or so behind the Continent in its acceptance of the *avant garde* artists working in Paris. But never before had one movement in art followed another with such bewildering anarchy. After Post-Impressionism, there was Cubism, Futurism and Expressionism, yielding to 'the violent storms of emotion beating up from the unconscious mind'. Then came Dadaism, 'art's scornful denial of art', and the Surrealism of Salvador Dali with its obscene overtones of sexual aberration

62 *Jacob Epstein whose sculpture invariably aroused public comment and whose 'Genesis' caused a general furore. (Press Association)*

and morbid fantasy. It was not surprising if the press and the public in general failed to understand what was going on, or that a wide gulf separated them from the critics like Roger Fry, Clive Bell, Wyndham Lewis and Herbert Read, who preached the gospel of the moderns in such esoteric terms, few people were any the wiser. Picasso, Braque, Matisse, Kandinski, Derain and their followers challenged the most basic conceptions about art and only the most high-brow members of the intelligentsia could cope with the new images they created. The rest of society turned its back on them or decided they must be joking.

None the less there were periodical outbursts of indignation and fury from those who wrote letters to the *Times* and set themselves up in judgement on the modern art which came to their notice. The sculpture of Jacob Epstein never failed to raise the hackles of the philistines and when his memorial to W.H. Hudson was unveiled in the Bird Sanctuary in Hyde Park in 1925, it was immediately defaced by resentful art lovers who had expected something pretty and were given instead a vigorous representation of Rima that they considered 'foul and repulsive, and an outrage on the divinely formed goddess' of Hudson's romantic fantasy, *Green Mansions*. Epstein retaliated by recalling that in Renaissance Italy it had been necessary to protect Michelangelo's statue of David in Florence with iron bars to prevent the mob from mutilating it; but it was a long time before the controversy died down, only to erupt again with still greater animosity when his large stone carving of Genesis was put on view at the Leicester Galleries six years later. This pregnant figure was described as 'gross and obscene' and gave rise to a cartoon in which one woman spectator was saying to another: 'If that's what Guinness's does for you, give me Watney's.' The exhibition, however, drew crowds of people with a prurient curiosity, and it was only for the power and vitality of his magnificent portrait busts in bronze that Epstein was given some credit as a sculptor.

Fashionable society in general preferred the safer shores of art at the Royal Academy. The private view of the Summer Exhibition was still an event of the London Season, attended by cabinet ministers, bishops in their gaiters, dowagers and debutantes in summer hats and summer dresses and a sprinkling of the artists themselves with their wives or their mistresses and their models. Augustus John, Sickert, McEvoy and some of the other rebels of the New English Art Club had by now been gathered rather reluctantly into the academic fold and they succeeded in livening up the august and ponderous galleries at Burlington House with a few outstanding paintings in the midst of what Wyndham Lewis described as 'a large and stagnant mass of mediocrity', consisting of airless landscapes, pretty flower pieces and superficial portraits.

Sir William Orpen and Sir John Lavery had been given the royal accolade for their work as official war artists, and as portrait painters were both very rich and very successful. For portraiture, or 'phiz-painting' as Hogarth had derisively called it, was still the only lucrative form of art in England. Upper-class vanity had not changed very much and if the aristocracy no longer had the money to commission so many family portraits, the *nouveau riche* press lords and profiteers could well afford to have themselves painted—in hunting pink if they had acquired horses and land in their upward climb—and their wives in the full bejewelled

63   *The famous portrait-painter, Sir John Lavery, and his wife. (Witt Library. Photograph by Hoppé)*

splendour of an expensive evening gown. Photography had in no way diminished the status symbol of a glossy portrait in a gold frame hung upon the wall, and if it had first been 'on the line' at Burlington House so much the better; snobbery was twice satisfied, for then the parvenu could also be seen in the rôle of patron of the arts.

Sir John Lavery's beautiful Chicago-born wife, Hazel, held a high position in London society. 'She looked,' according to Cecil Beaton, 'like a Luini Madonna—skin of alabaster, hair aflame, eyes huge as a hare's,' and was invariably to be seen wearing mauve Cattleya orchids or Parma violets pinned to the clouds of tulle and ostrich feathers she continued to favour as an adornment to her person long after a more simple style of dress had begun to prevail. Her drawing-room reflected the same femininity and fuss with silk hangings, soft lighting, tasselled cushions and heavily scented floral decorations. Yet there was nothing feather-brained or foolish about her. She had an extensive knowledge of public affairs and men like Winston Churchill and Lord Londonderry admired her worldly wisdom. 'She really whistled to men,' Shane Leslie wrote of her, 'and they obeyed as if it were a whip fashioned of her eyelashes.' Women— naturally—were less obliging. They resented her high-handed assertion that as most men were never at their best in front of their wives, it was more fun to ask them to separate parties. But Lavery never grew tired of painting her and year after year his latest portrait of her appeared at the Royal Academy under various romantic titles—Hazel in Rose and Gold, Portrait of Hazel in a Mirror and even Hazel Looking at an Aeroplane.

Other portrait painters—McEvoy, a sensitive observer of the *beau monde*, Philip de Laszlo, Oswald Birley, Gerald Kelly and the Zinkeisen sisters—were in great demand in fashionable circles. Augustus John, who surpassed them all, was a law unto himself, equally at home among the gipsies in a hayfield or among the society beauties and eminent men in the drawing-rooms of Mayfair. His bold and brilliant portraits were painted with a superb panache, a richness of texture and a grandeur and radiance of vision that challenged the great masters of the past and yet was modern in its acute psychological perception. He never kotowed to his sitters—he would fail rather than flatter them; and his integrity of purpose joined to the inexhaustible

64 *Art was appreciated by the* cognoscenti *in society. Here the author Evelyn Waugh (centre) is seen at an exhibition with Lord Berners and Lady Rosebery, wife of the Jockey Club doyen. (Radio Times Hulton Picture Library)*

vigour of his genius made him a dauntless opponent of dullness and conventionality in life as in art, his vivid personality dominating any society he chose to mix with, whether in the *fin de siècle* atmosphere of the Café Royal with its marble topped tables, gilt mirrors and red plush, or at the Eiffel Tower Restaurant in Percy Street where Stulik, the stout proprietor, kept a special bottle of brandy for him.

Stulik came from Central Europe and had a friendly disposition. His restaurant was unique in London, its informal atmosphere attracting a wide variety of people: stars of the theatre who were able to relax more freely there than they ever could at the Ivy or Boulestin, writers and artists from Bloomsbury and Chelsea and some of the Bright Young People in search of Bohemian gossip and fun. Among them Evelyn Waugh could often be seen getting drunk on someone else's money, his adolescent blue eyes protruding like angry marbles in the face of a faun flushed with wine, his aggressive temper liable to veer out of control over the inattention of waiters or at the slightest whiff of condescension from any of his friends, whose superior upper-class background was a constant thorn in his side.

Oxford in the early Twenties had been the turning-point in his life, for it was there that he fell in with the rich smart set of undergraduates from Eton—Hugh Lygon, Patrick Balfour, Brian Howard, the Earl of Rosse, the Plunkett-Greens and the Ponsonbys—and realized how dull and distasteful his own middle-class milieu in Golders Green was by contrast to the high-flying glamour of their cosmopolitan taste, their amoral self-indulgence leading to the sexual deviations among them, and their easy assumption of a nonchalant superiority. Their deliberately shocking behaviour, which often went far beyond the ordinary daring of youthful high spirits, had an irresistible fascination for him, even when it repelled him and made him feel inferior. He did not really belong to their world and he had no money of his own. But he was clever and amusing and by emulating the extravagance, the boozing and the bravura of their attitude to life, he kept up with their social dissipations in Mayfair, revelling with the Bright Young People at their parties, adopting their private language—'too, too sick-making'—and in between dreary school-mastering jobs, acquiring a reputation for the smartness of his wit.

By the end of the Twenties, with the publication of *Decline and Fall* and *Vile Bodies*, he finally emerged from his almost pathological condition of insolvency, insobriety and insecurity into the character of a brilliantly successful young man, whose dissection of the crazy modern world of post-war society rivalled Huxley's in perception. There were differences between them. Huxley's satire had the flavour of a dry white wine; he was more objective and more aloof. *Vile Bodies*, with its sequence of fantastic and grotesquely funny scenes, suddenly explodes with the author's own disgust and helplessness in front of the negative decadence of a world without standards of belief or judgement. 'D'you know,' Agatha Runcible says, 'all the time I was dotty I had the most terrible dreams. I thought I was driving round and round in a motor race and none of us could stop, and there was an enormous audience composed entirely of gossip writers and gate crashers and Archie Schwert and people like that, all shouting at us at once to go faster, and car after car kept crashing until I was left all alone driving and driving—and then I used to crash and wake up.' But the waking up was no better than the nightmare. The delirium went on with Agatha's friends holding a macabre cocktail party at her bedside in the nursing home in a feverish attempt to cheer her up.

And Evelyn Waugh himself was heading for a crash. Having married a grand-daughter of the Earl of Carnarvon in 1928, he returned to London a year later after spending three weeks in the country finishing his novel, to discover she had fallen in love with an old-Etonian, John Heygate. His humiliation was appalling. Had he not emerged after all from Golders Green? With a paranoic feeling of betrayal, he believed everyone was laughing at him and he became vindictive, more assertive and more of a snob than ever. The upper-class world had failed him; all he wanted was to be revenged. He would not do what was expected of a gentleman—hire a room in a hotel and take a woman there so that his wife could divorce him; he would do things his own way, take proceedings against her as the guilty party, show her up, break her if need be. So with a bitter fury he carried the divorce through in 1930 and a few months later was received into the Roman Catholic Church. The first post-war decade of thoughtless gaiety, freedom and fun was over.

One of the writers to realize this was Michael Arlen, whose best selling novel *The Green Hat* had made him not only very rich, but the vogue in smart society. The book, published in 1924, high-lighted the spirit of independence in the younger generation. It was romantic, melodramatic and very daring. The glamorous, oversexed heroine, Iris Storm, with her seductive sensuality, her impetuosity and her courage to face the unforgiving attitude of conventional society, sacrificed herself in the end by sending the man she had truly loved back to his wife and driving her car head-on into a tree. It was over-written, lush and preposterous. Yet it said shocking things that had not been said before—it even mentioned syphilis—and its setting in the expensive night clubs of Mayfair and the world of fast motor-cars, decaying country houses and a remote French nursing home where the heroine nearly dies after an abortion, was very striking and all the more remarkable because Michael Arlen himself had not yet had much experience of the smart world he depicted with such verve.

His real name was Dikran Kouyounidjan. He was born in Bulgaria of refugee parents, who had escaped from Armenia at the time of the first Turkish massacres and later settled in Manchester, where their son grew up and went to school. After a short spell at Edinburgh University studying to be a doctor, he came to London to try his luck as a journalist, living alone in a small room over a shop in Shepherd Market. He had no money and no friends, but was fiercely ambitious and acutely aware of being a stranger and a foreigner in London, unacceptable to the people he saw around him unless he could startle them. He admired Arnold Bennett and H. G. Wells and tried to write like them, until D. H. Lawrence persuaded him that his real gift lay in the exoticism of his romantic imagination and in the very elements of his Levantine character that made him so different from everyone else.

He worked hard and was taken up by Heinemann, who published a collection of his stories, *The London Venture*, under the name of Michael Arlen, one reviewer suggesting that this was perhaps a pseudonym for George Moore. Other volumes followed one on top of another, short stories and novels portraying marvellous girls and upper-class young men who drank champagne in the morning and threatened to horsewhip anyone doubting their honour as gentlemen or their chivalry towards women. The writing was mannered, yet full of wit and elaboration, a modern kind of *Arabian Nights* revealing the garish fantasies of the Twenties and the disequilibrium of Mayfair society in a stylized language that was entirely his own. People began to talk about him and to notice him in a restaurant or walking down the street. Then he disappeared for a time, returning to his parents' home in Manchester where he spent two months writing *The Green Hat*, his facility and his imagination working at high speed under pressure from the nervous tension of his private need to excel.

When the book sold out in the first two weeks and Heinemann ordered a massive reprint, his triumph was complete. Suddenly he was rich and famous, written up in all the news-

65   *Michael Arlen, whose best-seller,* The Green Hat, *published in 1924, caused a sensation in the social world with its theme of changing sexual mores among the élite. (Press Association Ltd.)*

papers with an explosive publicity that few authors had ever known, courted by fashionable society and seen here, there and everywhere in 'the best company' as a regular first-nighter with a table reserved at the Embassy, a sleek Rolls Royce painted canary yellow and a beautiful Greek Countess for a wife, his Levantine good looks and impeccable manners an enormous asset at parties. Envious people said his talent was 'brilliantine— not brilliant' and accused him of being ostentatious, cynical and decadent. But he was none of these things. He loved the luxury of success, the publicity, the people who flattered him at luncheon and dinner parties, yet he was curiously detached from the aura of his own celebrity. And he was very generous. He had been poor himself and now he was rich. When Noel Coward desperately wanted money at the last minute to back *The Vortex*, he went to Michael Arlen, who immediately wrote a cheque for £200 'without making any cautious stipulations about repayment'.

The Green Hat was made into a film and a play. Katherine Cornell played the heroine on Broadway, Tallulah Bankhead in London; Garbo and John Gilbert did the film, and the money kept on rolling in. There was really no need for Michael Arlen to write anything else, though he did, of course; he wrote a number of books which no one liked as much, for the glittering world of *The Green Hat* was fading into the grey depression of the Thirties and he was no longer a sensation. Whatever disappointment he may have felt he disguised behind the urbane mask of a gay man of the world and a good talker, declaring that it had always been his intention to retire when he had made X amount of money, not like 'poor Willie Maugham' to go on grinding out book after book. 'And as things turned out,' he airily said, 'I eventually had X amount of money. And retired. And lived happily ever after,' adding: 'I have the affection of my wife, the tolerance of my children and the friendship of head waiters. What more do I need?' Not cynical, but shrewd, he faced the decline in his popularity with an elegant fatalism and was wise enough not to tamper with the legend of Michael Arlen, the best-selling author of the Twenties.

7 THE AWAKENING CONSCIENCE

The landslide from the mad, irresponsible mood of the Twenties began in America in 1929. Ramsay MacDonald, newly elected in June and for the second time Prime Minister of Great Britain, sailed in the Cunard liner *Berengaria* for New York at the beginning of October, with his daughter, Ishbel, and a staff of high-ranking civil servants on a friendly visit to President Hoover. As the first British Prime Minister in office ever to visit the U.S.A. he was making history, a fact which enhanced the idea he held of his own dramatic destiny as a saviour of mankind, besides stimulating his high-minded good intentions towards the Americans, the world in general and his own country in particular. A romantic idealist, he took the view that no problems of international greed, selfishness or bellicose discontent could fail to be solved by men of good will sitting down together like the lion and the lamb, provided, of course, that he was cast in the rôle of the lion. Like Bottom, he could 'roar as gently as any sucking dove' in his eloquent, heart-throbbing Scottish voice and was a master at filling his audience top-full of lush rhetoric that stirred their emotions.

Thus, the moment he set foot in the City Hall after driving with the Mayor of New York through a ticker-tape welcome from the American citizens, he at once addressed the assembled company with all the authority of a prophet called to witness the truth in a strange land. 'I have come on a Mission of Peace,' he declared. 'I think I can say this morning Nation speaks to Nation. Looking forward into the future we must be inspired by a new faith in fraternity, with a new courage to follow large, inspiring moral aims and to supplement out material achievements by things that belong to the spiritual excellences of the peoples of the wurr-r-ld.' The applause rang out. Diplomats, bankers, businessmen and their ladies gathered at the special luncheon in honour of the Prime Minister, raised their non-alcoholic glasses to these noble sentiments and were suitably impressed. The date was October 4. No one apparently had any idea that the fabulous post-war prosperity of America was on the verge of collapse or that spiritual excellences and inspiring moral aims, however large, would be quite unable to give material support to the almighty dollar in exactly twenty days time.

Speculation on Wall Street had been rising at a fantastic rate over the years. In 1927 it was reckoned that the amount of money loaned to brokers to carry margin accounts was in the region of four billion dollars. And it was not only the rich of Park Avenue, Newport and Long Island, the filmstars of Hollywood and the Chicago and Detroit millionaires who cashed in on the big bull market; thousands of small-timers speculated—and won—without the slightest knowledge of the stocks they were gambling in or any idea that the bits of paper they held could become worthless. They knew better on Thursday, October 24, the day Wall Street went berserk and billions of paper profits disappeared in the panic on the floor of the Stock Exchange. Five days later, on the day known as Black Tuesday, 400 banks failed and the rush to get out of the stock market developed into a stampede.

The effect on the small-timers and on the American economy was devastating. Whole families in the towns and cities and away on the farms in the Middle-West were ruined without knowing quite what had hit them. The numbers of unemployed mounted astronomically, reaching 14,000,000 in 1930, when another 1,300 banks went broke. Thousands of boys and girls leaving school were unable to find jobs and entered what were called the 'Hobo jungles' by the railroad tracks, where they lived in semi-savage, criminal conditions. Gangsters hogged the streets and fought their way out of the mess with machine guns, protection rackets and bribery. Suicides were a commonplace among the rich and the poor, tumbling headlong out of skyscraper windows or quietly fixing themselves an overdose of aspirin. And President Hoover seemed utterly helpless. The Great Depression had engulfed his administration as surely as it had swept over the

6   Ramsay MacDonald speaking during the election campaign which ended in his forming the Coalition Government, and alienating many of his fellow socialists. (Keystone Press Agency Ltd.)

heads of the unsuspecting American people; and what was worse, there seemed no way of emerging from the flood, no Mount Ararat for the homeless and the unemployed, only the shanty towns bitterly called 'Hoovervilles' and a sour popular song, 'Brother Can You Spare a Dime?', which swept the country from coast to coast.

Naturally the rich suffered less from sheer physical deprivation than the poor. Yet for them the Depression was also the end of an era and a psychological shock from which they never really recovered. Material prosperity and the security of the dollar had been their guiding light ever since the War, and the country from 1920 onwards had enjoyed the biggest boom in history. Far more than in England where the monarchy and the old established aristocracy still gave some stability to the whole structure of society, in America success could only be measured by money. Scott Fitzgerald in *The Great Gatsby* saw the rich as a race apart, their existence somehow more beautiful and more intense than that of ordinary mortals—almost like royalty, breeding an aristocracy of wealth through intermarriage, family settlements, art collections and property. He saw himself as 'a poor boy in a rich town; a poor boy in a rich boy's school; a poor boy in a rich man's club at Princeton', adding: 'I have never been able to forgive the rich for being rich, and it has coloured my entire life and works.'

The Great Gatsby was published in 1925 when Fitzgerald's blend of flippancy, charm and brashness, which had made him a hero to the younger generation in revolt against their elders, had matured into something more compassionate and real. But Scott's dilemma remained. Money was a terrible necessity. He needed money to live the American dream of youth and early success with his ravishing young wife Zelda, and to write as an artist was not enough. So he turned out story after story for the *Saturday Evening Post* to double and treble his income, and the money leaked away in bootlegger's gin, diamonds for Zelda, which she sometimes threw away in a fit of rage, and all-night parties with their exhausting hangover lasting for days on end. They egged each other on, like naughty children surrendering to the gay impulse of the moment, never counting the cost of their idiocy until the golden Twenties melted into the leaden Thirties and an alcoholic haze began to dim Scott's perceptions, though not to diminish his torment over Zelda's increasingly obvious

67 *Soup kitchens were the symbol of depression. They provided contemporary 'do-gooders' with opportunities to give practical help. (Radio Times Hulton Picture Library)*

mental instability. Yet he had realized even in 1926 when he returned from Europe the way things were going in New York. 'The restlessness approached hysteria,' he wrote. 'The parties were bigger . . . The pace was faster . . . the shows broader, the buildings were higher, the morals were lower and the liquor was cheaper; but all these benefits did not really minister to much delight . . . Most of my friends drank too much—the more they were in tune with the times, the more they drank . . . The city was bloated, glutted, stupid with cakes and circuses, and a new expression "Oh yeah?" summed up all the enthusiasm evoked by the announcement of the last super-skyscapers.' The big American dream was losing its lustre. By 1929 it had become a nightmare.

It was, however, some time before the effects of the Great Depression were felt in Britain. The *Illustrated London News* for

October 24 carried a two-page paeon of praise on the skyscrapers in New York, illustrated with photographs and drawings—it did not mention Wall Street. Ramsay MacDonald returned to England in high fettle and went to visit Lady Londonderry, knowing he could play the lion in her boudoir with impunity. Fear of the Labour Government had by now diminished in English society. It was realized that MacDonald, Snowden, Thomas and even Henderson, the new Foreign Secretary, in spite of the revolutionary and violent things they had said in the past, were no more 'Bolshie' than anyone else, even if there were no old-Etonians in the Cabinet and the number of peers in office had been reduced to four, all of them—Lords Parmoor, Sankey, Passfield and Thomson—newly elevated to the House of Lords as Labour supporters. Only the ex-Fabian Sydney Webb, now Lord Passfield, made any mark on the public mind and that because his obstinate lady insisted on still being known as Mrs Sydney Webb, thereby causing some confusion at government receptions and gaining a perverse notoriety for herself and her lord which she would not otherwise have achieved.

The Government had no clear majority in the House of Commons and was dependent on the Liberal Party, still under the titular leadership of their fallen Lucifer, Lloyd George, whose dynamic energy had once saved the nation but was now mistrusted by everyone. Yet it might have been his economic programme of spending instead of saving that could have solved some of the problems clouding the sky above MacDonald's new Government. The Conservative Party at the election had not had much to offer beyond posters of Mr Baldwin's rather uninspiring features under the caption 'Safety First', which may have appealed to some of the ladies and gentlemen in the shires but did not enthral anyone else or give the Conservatives as the leading party in opposition a very cogent policy to act upon. In these circumstances the Government drifted complacently on, while the unemployment figures spiralled upwards. Arthur Henderson went off to Geneva to preside over the endless discussions on disarmament at the League of Nations; George Lansbury, the fire-eating revolutionary leader of the Left, opened a mixed bathing pool on the Serpentine, called the Lido; and Winston Churchill, championing the cause of the Indian princes and the imperial splendour of the British Raj, attacked everyone in favour of Indian nationalism, resigning in a fury from the Shadow Cabinet and thereby casting himself into the wilderness for the rest of the decade.

Meanwhile London society outside the arena of the politically ambitious still took very little notice of what was going on. The areas of mass unemployment lay a long way from the capital in the coalfields of South Wales and the shipyards of Jarrow. The statistics that looked so dreadful on paper seemed strangely irrelevant, both to the idle men standing about in the silent manufacturing towns and to the busy debutantes ordering their coming-out trousseaux at the fashionable court dressmakers. Some of their parents worried rather more than usual about the expense and, remembering the opulent society of their own youth, believed the country really was going to the dogs. Some justified themselves by saying they were giving employment to the caterers who organized their dances and parties, to the dress-

68   *Beatrice and Sydney Webb at home. They were in the forefront of the socialist movement and among the few supporters of the emerging Soviet Union. (Radio Times Hulton Picture Library)*

making trade, the florists, the milliners and the servants, who should by rights have been more plentiful again and yet were not. The more arrogant and least imaginative of the rich believed from this last assumption and from what they read in the *Morning Post* and the *Times* that the unemployed themselves were somehow to blame for their plight. They did not want to work; they preferred the dole and drifting along on the tax-payers' money. Something ought to be done about it—but what?

It was a renegade from their own class who came up with a plan—Sir Oswald Mosley, the 6th baronet, educated at Winchester and Sandhurst, ex-Lancers and Royal Flying Corps, married in the Chapel Royal to Lord Curzon's eldest daughter in 1920 and at that time the most promising young Conservative in the House of Commons, with what appeared to be the most dazzling future. Mosley had brains and was a brilliant orator, but he was impatient of fools, arrogant and domineering. He quarrelled with the Conservatives and went over to Labour and was appointed by MacDonald with J.H. Thomas and George Lansbury to investigate the problem of the unemployed. In fact, he was the only one of this very odd triumvirate to produce any constructive ideas on the subject, advocating a system of controlled expansion so unorthodox that it frightened his timid colleagues and failed to win the approval of the Cabinet. MacDonald and Snowden did not trust him—he was far too clever—and the rank and file of the Labour Party resented him as a rich, upper-class outsider. So he resigned abruptly and formed his own party in 1931, consisting of himself and his wife and four other Members of Parliament who had been expelled from the Labour Party. The New Party, as it was called, rapidly disintegrated in spite of Mosley's personal magnetism, and a year later he founded the British Union of Fascists, dedicated to 'Action' and supported for a time by Lord Rothermere of the *Daily Mail*. Rothermere admired Mussolini and thought he saw in Mosley, who also wore a black shirt, an energetic young man capable of injecting new vitality into the British people and of leading them forward with vigour and spirit. He soon, however, came to realize that he was backing a very dark horse and withdrew

69 *It was not all polo and dancing for the Prince of Wales. His involvement with the people is clearly shown in this picture taken in 1929 as he visited miner's homes.*
(Popperfoto)

rather hastily when a rival newspaper, the *News Chronicle*, exposed a private letter from Mosley instructing his henchmen to lure the *Daily Mail* into believing that Fascism had more support from the public than was actually the case.

Both Rothermere and Beaverbrook, as peers of the realm and wealthy newspaper proprietors, attempted to exert an influence on politics from behind the scenes, sometimes in opposition to each other and sometimes in a collaboration that was rather uneasy. Beaverbrook's panacea for the economic troubles of the Depression was the Empire Crusade he launched in the *Daily Express* in 1930. It was something this bumptious Canadian millionaire and restless dreamer of dreams really believed in; but behind it was the more sinister motive he entertained of removing Stanley Baldwin, whom he detested, from the leadership of the Conservative Party and putting the more amenable Neville Chamberlain in his place with himself as the manipulator of the puppet strings. He did not succeed; no one ever did succeed in dislodging Baldwin, who remained as immovable as a barnacle stuck to the bottom of a boat and was a far more dangerous opponent than he appeared to be. On this occasion he hit back at a meeting of the Conservative Party. 'The papers conducted by Lord Rothermere and Lord Beaverbrook,' he said, 'are engines of propaganda for the constantly changing policies, desires, personal wishes and personal likes and dislikes of two men. Their methods are direct falsehood, misrepresentation, half truths . . . suppression and editorial criticism of speeches which are not reported in the paper. What the proprietorship is aiming at . . . is power, but power without responsibility—the prerogative of the harlot through the ages.'

Baldwin, it seems, had borrowed this last sentence from his cousin, Rudyard Kipling, and it went down very well. There was nothing much the press lords could do about it. Rothermere minded rather less than Beaverbrook, whose constantly frustrated ambition to shine as a political force continued at this time to blight his otherwise successful career as a go-ahead adventurer in society and the owner of three national newspapers with the biggest circulation in the world. At Stornoway House in London and at Cherkley, his country residence, he was surrounded by a court of beautiful women, clever men, rising politicians and pushing journalists, who flattered him to his face though they

70 *Sir Oswald Mosley was one of the most controversial figures of the times. His Black Shirt movement was involved in many street clashes as well as in political agitation.* (*Radio Times Hulton Picture Library*)

often belittled him behind his back. And if readers of the *Sunday Express* paid more attention to the 'Londoner's Log' than to the Empire Crusade he had only himself to blame. He knew that nothing boosted the circulation of a newspaper more than a gossip column and by a stroke of genius had invited an eccentric Irish nobleman, Viscount Castlerosse, to write a weekly feature on high life in society.

A bon viveur with a passion for squandering money, for eating and drinking and the society of beautiful women, Valentine Castlerosse wielded a quite extraordinary power in his day. Hostesses and head-waiters treated him with obsequious deference. Society beauties and social climbers vied for his attention. Beaverbrook nursed him, paid his debts time and again, and kept him as his boon companion for life. 'Everyone in the social world snatched the *Sunday Express* and read Castlerosse before they even looked at the headlines,' according to Barbara Cartland. 'His page was clever, witty, indiscreet and full of names we all knew.' And it appealed to a still wider public curious to know how upper-class society amused itself in Mayfair, at Deauville and Cannes, in the casinos and at the races. Pictures of the most talked-of and glamorous women of the day appeared at the top of the page with comments that were sometimes impudent and shameless, though seldom malicious and never downright cruel. For Castlerosse himself was not just a *voyeur* with one ear for gossip or a wit with a nose for scandal; he had a truly magnificent lust for the extravagant pleasures of life and his flamboyant personality radiated a genuine human warmth which permeated his writing and made him worth his elephantine weight in gold.

Against the sober advice of every friend he possessed and his own inclination for the untrammelled life of a bachelor, he married Doris Delavigne, a beautiful blonde with a reputation in Mayfair for bewitching every man who came near her. Rosa Lewis, the shrewd old girl who kept the Cavendish Hotel in Jermyn Street and had known the ins and outs of Edwardian high society, once said of her: 'Young Doris may go far on those legs of hers, but mark my words she doesn't know how to make a man comfortable.' And it was true. She had gone far; she had a house in Deanery Street, a Rolls Royce and a chauffeur, and after one of her trips abroad, she brought home 250 pairs of Italian shoes because she thought it was 'idiotic' for a well-dressed woman to wear the same pair of shoes more than two or three times. Rich men paid for her wildly extravagant exploits—and Castlerosse was not a rich man. He could not pay his own debts—£330 for cigars and £250 for shirts—let alone find the money to pay hers. Yet he was captivated by Doris and obsessed with her. He fancied he could not live without her and neither could he live with her in any sort of harmony after their marriage.

Doris had a violent temper and the tongue of a virago. Though intelligent, quick-witted and fascinating, she had no idea of how to make her husband 'comfortable' and no intention of giving up her other admirers—perhaps, no option; and this roused Valentine to a pitch of jealousy that drove him insane with fury. There were scenes in private and noisy scenes in public that titillated the cynical appetite for scandal in society even more than the weekly gossip column their jester provided for them. Tony Wysard, the young cartoonist, depicted Castlerosse as an immensely swollen dandy on tiny, elegant feet, and

71   *Lord Beaverbrook as he was in 1921. It was the start of the heyday of the newspaper barons, fierce competition between papers, and the creation of the opinion-making media. (Press Association Ltd.)*

Doris in a sumptuous fur coat with rows of real pearls round her neck and a fringe of false eyelashes stuck to her eyelids. But the tragi-comical extravaganza of their marriage was much more than a joke. Apart from being a disaster for them both, it was a wildly improbable exposure of the wide gap between the high jinks going on in Mayfair and the sombre misery of Middlesborough, Newcastle and Stockport. For there were, of course, more serious matters reported in the *Sunday Express* and readers of the 'Londoner's Log' could not always dismiss the headlines.

The financial crisis of 1931 blew up suddenly like the General Strike of 1926, though it had a totally different effect on the nation. It gave the upper classes no opportunity to show their mettle and the working classes very little feeling of solidarity, and was only indirectly concerned with the problem of unemployment. All through the summer the banks in Central Europe had been failing and by repudiating their debts, they owed vast sums of money to the British bankers, who in turn were unable to discharge their liabilities elsewhere. Confidence in the pound was shaken and confidence in the Government at a low ebb. None the less, London emptied out at the end of the Season, Parliament rose and ministers went off on holiday, Ramsay MacDonald to Lossiemouth and the King to Balmoral. Only Montagu Norman, Governor of the Bank of England and the grey eminence behind the scenes, remained incarcerated in the City and ordered ration books to be printed in case the currency collapsed and the country had to revert to barter.

On August 11 he delivered an ultimatum to MacDonald, who came scurrying back from Scotland and was told that disaster was imminent unless confidence in H.M. Government could be restored without delay. Not only must the budget which had fallen into deficit be balanced, but 'waste' must be eliminated from all public expenditure and in particular from the ever increasing amount of subsistence paid to the unemployed. Mac-Donald and his colleagues failed to reach agreement after wrangling for five days and on the evening of August 22 the King took the unprecedented step of interrupting his ordered routine at Balmoral to travel back to London on the night train. According to the *Illustrated London News* it was 'the King's own initiative which determined him after consultation with the Prime Minister to bring together the leaders of the three parties with a view to forming a National Government. When Ramsay MacDonald was disposed to resign, the King persuaded him to sleep on the question.'

Press photographers caught the King in Highland dress at Ballater Station and in bowler hat and black overcoat as he drove to Buckingham Palace. His intervention was decisive. Ramsay MacDonald, after sleeping on the idea, decided to take up the burden of office again and was seen striding briskly through St James's Park; Mr Baldwin, wearing a pussy-cat expression, was snapped arriving at No. 10 Downing Street and Sir Herbert Samuel, leader of the National Liberals, got into the picture too. The pound recovered briefly on the international exchange and Montagu Norman pigeon-holed his ration books. A genuine sigh of relief went up on the grouse moors in Yorkshire and in Scotland, among the smart holiday-makers sunning themselves at Cap d'Antibes or gambling in the casino at Deauville. England was safe again—her enemies had been routed. But her peril was by no means over. Snowden's severe budget in September, raising income-tax to 5s in the pound and cutting the dole by 10%, failed to prevent a second and more serious run on the pound, which led to Britain abandoning the Gold Standard, though without the dire and awful consequences that had been predicted if this step should ever have to be taken.

Patriotic feeling was stirred at the General Election in October when the National Government asked for a 'Doctor's Mandate', which seemed to offer a cure-all for the country as a whole. Polling took place on the 27th and resulted in an overwhelming victory for the National candidates; and the following evening King George and Queen Mary with the Prince of Wales and the Duke and Duchess of York went to Drury Lane to see *Cavalcade*, Noel Coward's spectacular evocation of England's

72 *Viscount Castlerosse, vast in size and imagination, was one of the foremost gossip writers on society, politics and life in general. He is pictured here by Tony Wysard, accompanied by his bird-like wife. (Osbert Lancaster)*

greatness in the past. Those who expected cynicism from Coward suggested that he must have written *Cavalcade* with his tongue in his cheek; those who criticized his brittle gaiety and thought him decadent were startled by the sincerity of his feeling and deeply moved by his final toast to the future of England. Once again he had caught the mood of the people and put it into focus.

Class distinction and political squabbling had apparently been overcome by national unity and the English could pride themselves on riding the storm without losing their presence of mind, unlike their American cousins across the ocean. There was no panic, but a general feeling that retrenchment was necessary. The King set an example by accepting a cut in the civil list, and the aristocratic landowners, though they saw their power and privilege as the governing class being whittled away by democracy, were willing to make sacrifices.

National unity, however, was not quite what it seemed. Ramsay MacDonald, in putting country before party, woke up to find the rank and file of his Socialist supporters snapping and snarling at his heels like a pack of hounds and was bewildered when they flung the word 'traitor' at him. James Maxton, the fiery disciple of Karl Marx and leader of the Independent Labour Party, aware of the Prime Minister's attachment to Lady Londonderry, asked in the House of Commons whether the 'Red Flag' or the 'Londonderry Air' was now the anthem of the Labour Party, and if others did not go quite so far as this, there was a distinct anti-capitalist move towards the Left in the remnant of the Labour Party led by Arthur Henderson against their former chief.

Besides this the social conscience of the young was beginning to awaken, especially among the intellectuals at the Universities. Ashamed of the continuing poverty amidst plenty in what they believed to be the decaying structure of society, militant students and dons met the Hunger Marchers passing through Oxford and Cambridge on their way to London in 1932 and took up their cause. For whereas sex and the pursuit of pleasure had been the main preoccupation of the gilded youth of Evelyn Waugh's time at Oxford, now, only a few years later, all the talk was of politics and the rebellious instincts of the young were directed towards the hard-faced men who, in their opinion, so complacently and ineptly conducted the affairs of the nation at the expense of the workers. Experience of Communism in the Berlin of the Weimar Republic where sexual freedom and social anarchy had apparently defeated the standards of the bourgeoisie for good, and ignorant of what was really going on in Stalinist Russia, the Oxford and Cambridge undergraduates were drawn towards the Marxist doctrine like flies round a jam-pot. The Bright Young People and their amusements had no charms for them, frivolity and fun no place in their new involvement; and even art and aesthetics were only valid if they were concerned with the truth. 'No book written *at the present time* can be "good" unless it is written from a Marxist or near-Marxist viewpoint,' Edward Upward asserted in a little volume called *The Mind in Chains*. 'No modern book can be true to life unless it recognises . . . both the decadence of present-day society and the inevitability of revolution.'

This was the theme of Wystan Auden, son of a devout Anglo-Catholic mother, whose poem *The Orators* was published in 1932, and of the other Left-wing poets, Stephen Spender, Louis MacNeice and Cecil Day Lewis: all of them public schoolboys brought up in the discipline of a classical education with its tradition of service to the community in a world that had now changed beyond recognition. MacNeice and Day Lewis were the sons of clergymen, Spender came from an old-fashioned Liberal family; but neither the Christian faith of their fathers nor the antiquated radicalism of the Liberals seemed to offer an effective instrument to solve the problems of the new decade—or, as Cecil Day Lewis wrote later: 'I daily felt the need of a faith which would fill the void left by the taking away of traditional religion, would make some sense of our troubled times and make real demands on me. Marxism appeared to fit the bill.' Marxism was the fashion, too. J. M. Keynes applauded the new generation of Communists, comparing them with 'the English gentlemen who went to the Crusades, made the Reformation, fought the Great Rebellion, won us our civil rights and religious liberties and humanized the working classes in the 19th century'.

Soon, out of sympathy with the unemployed and the doctrine of anti-capitalism, it became apparent to the intellectuals that a world revolution of the proletariat was the only hope for Europe if it was to survive the growing dangers of nationalism. In Italy Mussolini had liquidated the Communist Party and by doing so was regarded by most of the English upper classes as a saviour.

73 *The years of the Depression saw the hunger-marchers. In 1932 they converged on London in their thousands to make clear the plight of the unemployed and their hungry families. (Central Press Photo Ltd.)*

Doubts about his gangster methods of eliminating all opposition were set aside and it was pointed out by travellers returning from Rome that the Fascist leader was loyal to his King and had made the Italian railway trains run to time. Judging by the enthusiastic crowds outside the Palazzo Venezia when he appeared on the balcony, the Italian people were quite happy with the new regime, which was their concern anyway and no business of anyone else's, though it was sometimes wiser for English travellers referring to Il Duce to call him Mr Smith or Mr Brown. Rome was being modernized and there were splendid new roads and new buildings everywhere. The new Stadium at Bologna was dignified with a colossal statue of Mussolini riding a horse nineteen feet long in the heroic tradition of the Roman Emperors and no one could say he lacked vigour in the direction of Italian affairs, while it was generally thought that he had the best intentions towards the rest of the world. He was a signatory of the Kellogg Pact of 1928, which renounced war as an instru-

74 *It was the beginning of mass hysteria in Germany. Hitler's Youth movement was the nucleus of the Nazi armies which dominated Europe after the Long Party. (Central Press Photos Ltd.)*

ment of national policy, and a member of the League of Nations —strong enough in 1932 to threaten the withdrawal of the Italian delegation at the Disarmament Conference unless the Italian navy was given parity with the French.

Germany had also become a member of the League of Nations, her past misdemeanours forgotten or glossed over, the injustices of the Treaty of Versailles open to discussion if not actually smoothed away; and when Hitler came to power in January 1933 it seemed that his conciliatory attitude might help the Disarmament Conference instead of hindering it. But who was this funny little man with a splodge of hair and a Charlie Chaplin moustache, always dressed in a crumpled-looking rain-coat with a swastika armband? It was difficult for the English, especially among the higher ranks of society, to take a common house painter and ex-Corporal of the German army seriously, even when the *Illustrated London News* published a picture of 75,000 Nazis saluting him with outstretched arms at Brunswick.

And it was even more difficult to realize that the Germans actually believed in him and liked marching about in brown shirts, even the youngest boys and girls rushing to join the Youth Movement and hiking through the Black Forest like a miniature army on the move. The discipline was good for them, no doubt, and their fitness quite extraordinary; and if England had Baden-Powell and his Boy Scouts, why should Germany not have Adolf Hitler and his rosy cheeked *Jugende*, chanting *Sieg Heil!*?

Connoisseurs of opera visiting Richard Wagner's holy shrine at Bayreuth were delighted to discover that the Nazi leader was a passionate admirer of the great German composer's music and was indeed obsessed with its mythology of gods and goddesses squabbling over a nugget of gold at the bottom of the Rhine. He was also a close friend of Frau Winifred Wagner, who had sheltered him when he came out of prison in 1924, and as a

75 *Communist procession in the East End of London following riots, 1936. (Radio Times Hulton Picture Library)*

frequent guest at Wahnfried was extremely kind to the whole family, for he loved little children and playing games with them. Jewish musicians resident in Germany had rather a different story to tell of the arrogant decrees issuing from Hitler's Chancellery designed to purge the nation of its non-Aryan citizens. Toscanini, the greatest conductor in the world, refused to return to Bayreuth in 1933 as a protest against the persecution of his colleagues and many of them sought refuge in England or America, bringing home to the society they mixed with in these two freedom-loving countries the underlying brutality of the Nazi regime.

Jewish doctors, professors and writers also fled from Germany, causing some embarrassment to the British authorities. No one, except the followers of Sir Oswald Mosley, wanted to appear anti-Semitic, but Sir John Simon, the Foreign Secretary in the

76   *Uniformed Nazis marched twelve-deep at the end of the Nazi Congress of 1933.* *(Central Press Photo Ltd.)*

National Government, found it necessary to explain that he was really a Welshman with a surname that sounded Hebraic, and there was a hard core of feeling in the country that the Jews had come out on top since the War and perhaps Hitler was not so wrong in trying to thin them out even if his methods were rather drastic. National Socialism still seemed a better alternative to most people than Communism, and Britain had no desire anyway to become involved in the ideological warfare on the Continent. Ramsay MacDonald was more concerned with disarmament and Stanley Baldwin preferred smoking his pipe in comfort to investigating the inflammable situation in Europe. Too much obvious support of the Jews in their tribulation might well endanger the precarious balance of power at the League of Nations, so a compromise was achieved by giving the most distinguished writers and professors academic posts at the Universities and by setting up charitable funds to help some of the others; and although every single refugee in his long dark overcoat and worn felt hat was a silent witness to the horrors of Nazism, sympathy for the plight of these unhappy victims of Hitler's cruelty was mixed with caution, except among the Left-wing intellectuals who became more and more convinced that Communism was the only true faith.

Nazism and Facism they argued would inevitably lead to conflict between the nations, whereas the peoples of the world wanted peace and it was only the armament kings in the capitalist countries and the one-eyed autocrats of the armed forces who were in favour of war. At Oxford in 1933, the Union Debating Society caused a furore when it resolved by 275 votes to 153 that 'this House would in no circumstances fight for King and Country'. Ex-colonels in the shires and bald-headed gentlemen in the Cavalry Club, at Boodle's and the In and Out felt ashamed of the youth of England and thought the principal speaker in favour of the resolution, C. E. M. Joad, ought to be shot as a traitor. But a spate of war books in the late Twenties—Richard Aldington's *Death of a Hero,* Robert Graves's *Goodbye to All That* Siegfried Sassoon's *Memoirs of an Infantry Officer* and *The Good Soldier Schweik* by a Czech writer, Jaroslav Hasek—all exposing the horrors and the insanity of modern war, had effectively inoculated the young against heroism and patriotism and even those who had no violent political feelings believed passionately

77 *Mussolini, for once out of uniform, as he was in the early days, before rising to the dictatorship of Italy. (Barnaby's Picture Library)*

in pacifism.

Beverley Nichols, as ardent as any of the Left-wing poets, wrote a sentimental and rather hysterical book on the subject, *Cry Havoc!*, which was a best seller and changed his image overnight from a frivolous society gossip into an earnest seeker after the truth. He declared that he would only fight in an international army for an international cause under some commander appointed by the League of Nations, and he was voicing the opinion of a large section of the public. There was much talk of 'putting teeth into the Covenant of the League' by organizing an international police force—and no action; just as there was much debate at the Disarmament Conference with Hitler promising total disarmament if the French would do the same and withdrawing behind a smoke screen of indignation when the French demurred.

Active pacifism continued to grow, either inspired by the genuine spirit of Christianity as in the Peace Pledge Union organized by Canon Dick Sheppard, the vicar of St Martin's-in-the-Fields, or by the Left-wing agitators in society. It filtered down to the public schools, where Giles and Esmond Romilly, nephews of Winston Churchill and grandsons of the Earl of Airlie, refused to join the O.T.C. at Wellington and founded a magazine called *Out of Bounds* 'to champion the forces of progress against the forces of reaction on every front, from compulsory military training to propagandist teaching'. The *Daily Mail* took the story up with banner headlines: RED MENACE IN PUBLIC SCHOOLS! MOSCOW ATTEMPTS TO CORRUPT BOYS. OFFICER'S SON SPONSORS EXTREMIST JOURNAL. Esmond ran away from Wellington and issued the magazine from a Left-wing bookshop in Bloomsbury, its circulation reaching 3,000 copies in spite of being officially banned in all the leading public schools, and the bookshop became an underground meeting place for other dissident boys who had absconded or been expelled from school. Both Giles and Esmond were heroes to their friends and their activity could not be dismissed by their families as a schoolboy frolic; it was too serious for that, too alarming and bewildering to those of the older generation who had fought for their country in 1914 and had known a different world where the sons of gentlemen simply did not behave like that or would have been horse-whipped if they had.

Meanwhile, the London Season continued. Debutantes curtseyed to Their Majesties in the red and gold Throne Room, dances and parties went on and fashions changed. Some of the debutantes were changing, too. They were no longer quite so innocent, quite so tractable or so dependent on what their mothers decided was best for them. The Mitford sisters, daughters of Lord and Lady Redesdale, were presented in strict order of seniority: Nancy, the eldest, in 1922 and the other five as they reached the coming-out age of eighteen, each of them reflecting the changing attitudes of the Twenties and the Thirties with a quite extraordinary fidelity.

All of them were brought up surrounded by servants and a series of inept governesses in the family mansion in the Cotswolds, called Swinbrook House, and forbidden to mix with other children even of their own class unless they were cousins from the various families connected with them. Lord Redesdale dominated the household and was portrayed as a comic figure by Nancy in her first novel and later as Uncle Matthew in *The Pursuit of Love*. But at Swinbrook his violent temper, his eccentric aloofness and his positive loathing of anyone in the least intellectual or artistic could not always be seen in a comic light. There were continuous rows and explosions, tears and sulky silences as Nancy, dark-haired, green-eyed, debonair and witty, battled to get her own way and to win her freedom from the monotonous routine of upper-class family life with its horses and dogs and local Conservative rallies and fund-raising garden fêtes.

Not long after she had been presented at Court, she announced that she wanted to live in London and study at the Slade School of Art. She cut her hair off and used a lipstick, played the ukulele reclining on a divan in pyjama trousers, and sometimes was bold enough to invite her aesthetic friends from Oxford to stay at Swinbrook. These languid, mocking young men despised the conventional mores of the older generation and disapproved of hunting and shooting on the grounds that these hallowed blood sports were sadistic and cruel. Lord Redesdale burst into paroxysms of fury at the sight of them and Lady Redesdale exclaimed in horror: '*What* a set!', though there was nothing much she could do about it, for Nancy was determined to lead her own life and pointed the way of escape for her younger sisters.

Pam, the next in age, was content with a quiet country life and passionately interested in horses, and Tom, their only brother, took his own line of independence somewhere between the two of them. But Diana, the third sister and the blonde beauty of the family, got engaged to Bryan Guinness during her first London Season and brought a terrifying storm of parental wrath upon her head, which only receded after she had spent an entire winter at Swinbrook deliberately sulking and pining away. Her marriage was the most spectacular society wedding of the year with crowds of excited people standing in the street to watch the bride arriving on the arm of her father. The Redesdales' huge town house in Rutland Gate was *en fête* for the occasion and even Lady Redesdale, once called the 'penny pinching peeress' by a *Daily Mail* reporter who discovered she had been trying to save money on the laundry at Swinbrook, took no account of the expense in buying the elaborate trousseau and the bride's dress, the brand new pigskin luggage for the honeymoon and the outsize wedding-cake crowned with emblems of happiness in pink and white icing sugar.

Bryan Guinness was exceedingly rich on the money his family had made out of beer and he belonged to the smart set of Bright Young People, neither of which really recommended him to his parents-in-law. He and Diana were in on most of the mad parties in Mayfair and they once put on an exhibition of *avant garde* paintings at a fashionable West End art gallery by an artist called Bruno Hat, who was actually one of their bright young friends, Brian Howard, heavily disguised by a beard and sitting in a wheel-chair at the private view—a hoax that was so successful, quite a few of the art critics were fooled into believing a new genius had been discovered. Diana posed for the photographers as a society beauty and was very beautiful indeed, with huge limpid eyes, pale gold hair and a far away look that gave her a romantic kind of modernism. She and Bryan were to be seen on the Lido in the summer, at Kitzbühel in the winter, in Paris and at Deauville. But the marriage did not last, and soon after her divorce Diana became an ardent admirer of Sir Oswald Mosley, introducing him to her younger sister, Unity, who had been presented at Court in 1932.

Unity Valkyrie Mitford—christened with such a strangely prophetic notion of her future—was very tall and very big with a thick mane of blonde hair and the sombre, brooding expression of a warrior maiden. As a debutante she was a failure, a smouldering volcano of resentment, bored with the fork luncheons, the dances and dinners and the smooth-faced, eligible young men in white ties and tails. She tried shocking her mother by wearing loud evening dresses and false jewellery, though this only served to convince everyone that she was rather eccentric, like her father, if in a different, more enigmatic way. No one knew what she wanted—and she did not know either, until she met Mosley at Diana's house and became utterly absorbed in his doctrine. She bought a black shirt and covered the room she shared at Swinbrook with her fifteen-year-old sister, Jessica, with photographs of Mosley and Mussolini and the Fascist insignia of a bundle of sticks tied with cord, before long adding to these exciting emblems of her devotion the new swastika of the Nazis. Her

78 *Unity Mitford, controversial and self-willed friend of Hitler, photographed during one of her meetings with the Führer. (Popperfoto)*

parents took very little notice of what was going on, but Jessica, by then already an enthusiastic believer in the Communist cause, retaliated by decorating her side of the room with a huge home-made hammer and sickle. There were terrible fights between them. 'The endless school-room talk of "What are we going to do when we grow up", changed in tone,' Jessica wrote later in *Hons and Rebels*. Unity declared that she was going to Germany to meet Adolf Hitler and Jessica that she was going to run away and be a Communist—which was exactly what they both did.

Unity, having persuaded her parents to send her to Germany 'to further her education', practised the technique she had used at home for getting her own way. Night after night she sat at the same table in the restaurant patronized by Hitler, staring at him until he noticed her and sent one of his aides across the room to find out who she was. On learning that she was an English *fraülein* with a fervent admiration for him, he invited her to drink coffee with him, and after this she was constantly in his company with Himmler, Goering and Goebbels in Munich and elsewhere

—rarely returning home to the Cotswolds and when she did, only to startle everyone in the village by giving the Nazi salute and shouting 'Heil Hitler!' instead of shaking hands or saying 'Good morning'. It could have been funny—the kind of idiosyncrasy of character the English aristocracy had always indulged in —but it was not funny at all. Unity introduced her sister Diana to Hitler's inner circle and he declared that they were both perfect specimens of Aryan womanhood'. She even induced her parents to visit Germany, where they were fêted like royalty and came home with a strong feeling that the Führer should be vigorously supported.

Jessica argued in vain, poring over all the Communist literature she could lay hands on, not enjoying her first Season as a debutante at all. Her cousin, Esmond Romilly, though she had not seen him since he was a child, was her god. But he was again in trouble with his family, and, when the Spanish Civil War broke out in 1936, was one of the first of the young upper-class Englishmen to join the International Brigade. That Spain itself was a dark morass of political corruption, backward mediaevalism and ruthless religious persecution made little difference to the fair Anglo-Saxon crusaders, whose idealism had flowered so sweetly in the cool courtyards of Oxford and Cambridge. The bugle had sounded, shattering the rarified air of pacifism with a blast of ideological frenzy. The official British Government attitude of non-intervention was a disgusting betrayal. Auden, Spender, MacNeice, George Orwell, Roy Campbell and hundreds of others took up the arms supplied by the Soviet Union and went into battle against the Nazi and Fascist bombers supporting General Franco.

At home Jessica Mitford hunted through the newspapers for reports of their progress and was rewarded by a despatch from Esmond Romilly himself describing the battle outside Madrid. Shortly afterwards she heard that he was back in England recovering from an illness, and the miracle she had longed for occurred. She met him at the house of an elderly cousin, the only member of the Romilly, Churchill and Redesdale clan still willing to receive the renegade under her roof; and from there the two of them plotted their escape to Spain. The family commotion when their flight was discovered rose to the highest level. Telegrams signed by Anthony Eden, the Foreign Secretary,

79　*The Spanish Civil War sealed the fate of the League of Nations. Civilians, as shown here, manned the barricades in what proved to be a hopeless attempt to stem Franco's ascendancy. (Central Press Photo Ltd.)*

were despatched to the British Consul in Madrid and a destroyer was sent to Bilbao to fetch Jessica home. But to argue her out of her faith in Esmond and the Communists was a total impossibility and she found living a hand to mouth existence with no money in seedy continental lodgings infinitely more romantic and exciting than anything that had ever happened at Swinbrook.

Perhaps it was useless to argue with any of the Mitfords, so closely were they identified with the hectic years in which they grew up. Only Deborah, the youngest sister, remained contentedly at home dreaming that one day she would marry a duke —which she did in 1941; though Andrew Cavendish did not inherit the near-feudal estate of Chatsworth and the Dukedom of Devonshire until nine years later, to demonstrate with his beautiful Duchess that the English aristocracy could still contribute dignity and grace to the modern world.

8 THE ENGLISH ABROAD

Ever since the Grand Tour of the English Milords on the Continent in the eighteenth century, travelling abroad had been the pleasure and the prerogative of the aristocracy, interrupted now and again by wars and revolutions, only to be resumed as soon as possible after the conflict was over. Thus in 1920 the Ladies' Page of the *Illustrated London News* wrote of looking forward to travelling again and recommended a new set of suitcases from Waring & Gillow 'made of the finest real cowhide, finished in a nut-brown colour and fitted with the best nickel-plated locks', adding: 'By their luggage you shall know whether they be well-born folk or not.' Anything so common as imitation leather was unthinkable. Not only trunks and suitcases, but dressing-cases filled with silver-topped bottles, hat-boxes, jewel-cases and the ubiquitous hold-all for umbrellas, rugs, parasols and pillows had to look good. Dignity was of more importance than weight—and why not? There had always been porters everywhere to handle the baggage, maids and valets to pack and unpack and hotel servants to run to the assistance of the fortunate visitors arriving at their appointed destination.

Travelling by the trans-continental *trains-de-luxe* to Vienna, Montreux or the Côte d'Azur had its own ritual that the post-war world was eager to recover. The continental platform at Victoria Station was called 'the gateway to the world' and the dark blue pullman-cars speeding across Europe with their *wagon-lit* and dining-car attendants cossetting the first class passengers, had a splendid aura of opulence. There were changes, of course. No one now wanted to go to Bad Homburg or to Potsdam, and St Petersburg had been denuded of its splendour in the hideous tumult of the Red Revolution, even rechristened Leningrad. Vienna had lost the Hapsburgs and according to Prince Tassilo Fürstenberg most of its pretty *cocottes* as well with the collapse of the Austro–Hungarian army and the death or dispersal of its handsome officers. None the less English society returned after the War to the seasonal migrations of the past, travelling south in the winter in search of a warmer climate.

Cultured people went to Rome and Florence or farther south to Naples and sometimes to Egypt after the sensational discovery of Tutankhamun's tomb; smart people to Monte Carlo and Cannes, where the hotels were large, luxurious and very exclusive. The Carlton at Cannes with its twin domes said to have been modelled on the breasts of a famous nineteenth-century *femme du monde*, dominated the Croisette like a huge baroque wedding-cake. Its list of eminent guests had included kings and princes, Russian grand dukes, rich Americans and the titled nobility of the world. The *haute cuisine* and the ingratiating service in the lofty white and gold rooms with their French Renaissance decor, had given it the highest reputation of any hotel on the Riviera. And although by 1920 the Russian grand dukes were living on tick and many of the kings and princes were exiled from their homes, the aristocratic English with their nut-brown cowhide luggage began to return like a purposeful flock of geese.

Nothing seemed to have changed very much on the Croisette—or was it not quite so high-class, not quite so select? When Mr Gordon Selfridge, the keeper of the American department store in London, brought the Dolly Sisters over from Monte Carlo, they were seen to be loaded from their neck to their feet with jewellery and their vulgarity struck a discordant note. What was acceptable in Monte Carlo with its more exotic atmosphere and its eccentric inhabitants dedicated to gambling at the Casino was not quite the thing at the Carlton in Cannes, and whereas the *grandes amoureuses* of the past, the Russian ex-ballerinas and French actresses living in style along the coast had often succeeded in overcoming their lack of breeding, the Dolly Sisters and Mr Selfridge were quite a different story. They were brash in a new and disconcerting way, very modern and indiscreet and quite unbearably *nouveau riche*—all of which made the well-bred English visitors returning home at the end of the season in March wonder sadly whether the Riviera was not becoming rather overrun by undesirable visitors.

The hotels on the Côte d'Azur were closed from the late spring all through the summer. No one—not even the French *bourgeoisie*—ever thought of taking a holiday on the Mediterranean in August, and the villas of the rich were shuttered and empty. In the summer of 1922, however, two wealthy and cultured expatriate Americans, Gerald and Sara Murphy, who had moved to Europe after the War, rented a whole floor of the Grand Hôtel du Cap at Cap d'Antibes for themselves and their friends. As there was no beach in front of the hotel, they made one by removing the seaweed from the Plage de la Garoupe and revealing the sand underneath, much to the amusement of the local inhabitants who thought their habit of dowsing themselves in banana oil and exposing their bodies to the sun very peculiar indeed. But the Murphys enjoyed themselves so much swimming and sunbathing they decided to build a villa at Antibes, and since they had a large circle of amusing and interesting friends, the proprietor of the Grand Hôtel du Cap soon found it paid him to keep open in the summer to entertain the overflow of their guests. Scott and Zelda Fitzgerald, still at the height of their popularity in smart society, were visitors there in 1925 with Rudolph Valentino, Mistinguette and a number of other gay and decorative people, including some English friends of the Murphys who soon acquired a taste for sunbathing on the plage and for dining out of doors among the orange and lemon trees in the warm night air.

Within a few years the whole character of the Riviera had changed completely. In the winter the sable wraps and elaborate gowns of the older generation of visitors were still to be seen as they emerged from the Carlton, the Negresco and the Hôtel de Paris to take a gentle stroll or a drive. In the summer wraps, if they were worn at all, were of towelling or canvas in startling colours, slung round the shoulders to be thrown aside on the beach to expose the long brown legs and bare backs of the sunbathers lying full length on the mattresses provided for their comfort. Many of the leading couture houses in Paris began to design special beachwear. Schiaparelli, a hard-working, hot-tempered Italian with a flair for producing original and startling garments, daringly brought out two-coloured beach dresses in 'shocking' pink and magenta that could be reversed and were tied loosely round the waist to reveal matching shorts underneath.

Vera Boréa designed elegant pyjama suits with flared trousers and neat double-breasted linen jackets to wear with a spotted silk scarf and a jaunty little sailor's cap or a large floppy hat.

Nothing like these clothes had ever been seen before in the English country or at the seaside. Women with boyish, slim figures went mad about them, and so unfortunately did those with rolls of fat in the wrong places, who endeavoured to diminish their flesh by dieting, eating nuts and bananas while everyone else was enjoying hot lobsters cooked in cream and *soufflé surprise*. Rich, middle-aged men, imitating the forgotten athletes of Sparta, suddenly appeared in bathing drawers, exposing their hairy chests and hairy legs to the sun without apparently any shame or any idea of how ugly they looked. For in spite of the collapse of the American stock market and the Depression in Britain, Cap d'Antibes and the other resorts were crowded all through the Thirties with English and American summer visitors seeking pleasure on the hot Mediterranean beaches.

The Hon. Mrs Reginald Fellowes, the Marquise de Casa Mauray, Lady Ashley, the Mosleys, Mrs Syrie Maugham and many other leading figures in society were spotted by Mariegold, the gossip-writer of the *Sketch*, who declared that 'pyjama suits were becoming gayer and gayer every week and "Plage Society" ever more chic and elegant'. Every hotel on the French and Italian coast was refurbished with new cocktail bars, dance floors and outdoor restaurants sprouting gay umbrellas and pots of flowers. Sartori's at Cap d'Antibes and Caramello's at St Jean-Cap-Ferrat were the last word in gastronomic delight. And the villas that had previously been closed all the summer were now filled with visitors from all over the world.

At Eze, Madame Jacques Balsan, the ex-Duchess of Marlborough, occupied a villa surrounded by cypress trees with a view that embraced the whole coast from Cannes to Rapallo. At St Jean-Cap-Ferrat, Somerset Maugham, now very rich on the proceeds of his books and plays and also somewhat bitter because the high-class literary critics tended to dismiss him as a 'popular' writer, rebuilt the Villa Mauresque in the style of a Moorish *hacienda*. Apparently he had everything anyone could possibly want: a swimming-pool among the red and white oleanders in his garden, a collection of French Impressionist paintings he had picked up for a song, Marie Laurencins in his

80 *Monte Carlo, magnetic centre for expatriate Britons, as it was during the thirties. This photograph shows the fashionable set taking tea at the Café de Paris before visiting the Casino, seen on the left. (Radio Times Hulton Picture Library)*

dining-room, cocktails ever on the mix before luncheon and dinner, a number of distinguished friends, and Gerald Haxton as a stimulating though capricious companion. Yet Maugham was by no means satisfied with the worldly success he had achieved and as a host he often failed to make his guests feel at home. He could be shy, tetchy and unpredictable, so that some of his visitors walked in fear of his cutting remarks and were shocked by the scenes he took pleasure in provoking. 'He liked people to behave badly,' according to Arthur Marshall, 'and when they did, he was amused.'

Michael Arlen, living in his light and airy villa on the hillside above Cannes, was less exacting and a good deal happier. His drawing-room had white walls that reflected the dazzling colour of the sea and the sky, blue curtains and a blue carpet, and his house guests were allowed to please themselves, to go off and play golf or to bathe and lie in the sun. He owned a huge speed-boat called *Swallow 2* with a windshield like a racing car and a pennant on the front, chiefly because he loved scudding through the bright water in a hair-raising swirl of rainbow-coloured foam and also because speedboats had become a status symbol of the rich in the Mediterranean. Every harbour all along the coast was crammed with them or with private yachts, gleaming with new paint and expensive, highly polished fittings to show off the affluence of their owners.

But it was not only the summer season on the Riviera that had become fashionable. Venice and the Lido were equally attractive, though the strip of sand on the Adriatic where Byron and Shelley used to ride together in the evenings had nothing very attractive about it until the rich international society of the Thirties suddenly decided it was THE place to go. Even then it could not boast of any beauty. It was dominated by the huge and ugly Hotel Excelsior, where the American-born Princess Jane di San Faustino, an imposing figure with white hair and a flowing white dress, resided like a queen. Every morning she held court, sitting outside her *capanna* on the beach while new arrivals were presented to her and their credentials carefully examined. Every afternoon she summoned those whom she considered worthy of her attention to play backgammon with her and if they proved socially acceptable, invited them to her evening parties and the charity galas she organized during the season, or recommended them to Countess Morosini who ruled the fashionable world in Venice with a similar authority. Not to be accepted by the Princess was a calamity for the *recherché* socialite and the snobbish climber. At first she frowned on Elsa Maxwell, disapproving of her vulgarity, but when she broke her hip and could only rule the Lido from her *chaise-longue*, she turned the upstart and ebullient Elsa into an ally, recognizing her quite extraordinary flair for attracting the gayest and wealthiest pleasure-seekers in the world to the Lido.

They spent their mornings bathing in the sea and lying in the sun, eating green figs and gossipping; their afternoons playing backgammon or bridge and lying in the sun again, soaking its rays into their soporific bodies and burning their skin a golden brown. That this suited some women and not others was quite beside the point. Sunbathing was the new cult. It belonged to the new freedom won from the restrictions of the past, to the concept of undressing instead of overdressing. Elizabeth Arden and Helena Rubinstein, bitter rivals in the beauty business, brought out special make-up to tone with the glamour of the new look, new lotions and scented oils to anoint the sun-worship-

pers in their ritualistic obsession with their bodies. A dark tan
was enviable—almost a necessity—and the traditional beauty
belonging to an English rose complexion rejected deliberately
for a more swarthy continental appearance.

The *Sketch* and the *Tatler* showed pictures of the Baroness
d'Erlanger, Prince and Princess Jean de Faucigny Lucinge,
Count Bestigui, Lady Mendl 'in a delightfully picturesque
summer attire', Serge Lifar and Mlle Nikitina, the Russian
ballerina, 'basking on the Lido sands', Mlle Nikitina wearing
'one of the new "backless" bathing-suits to allow the violet rays
of the sun as much area for their health-giving work as possible'.
Cecil Beaton, looking rather coy in a fez, was posed with Elsa
Maxwell; the Cole Porters were seen with Princess Marina
Ruspoli and Count Celani and Olga Lynn with Sacheverell
Sitwell's beautiful wife and the Hon. Mrs Fitzgerald. But when
the sun went down in a blaze of purple and gold and the colour
drained out of the sky, everyone withdrew from the Lido to
dress for the evening in Venice, where the gaiety began at
Harry's Bar and did not end until long after midnight. There
were balls and fancy dress parties in the fading Renaissance
palaces, concerts on the Piazza san Marco, mad moonlit escapades
on the Grand Canal and violent emotional scenes played out

81 *Sun- and fun-seekers at Deauville. It may have been less picturesque than the South
of France but it was near enough to attract week-end visitors from London. (Illustrated
Newspapers Group)*

against the backdrop of the most romantic city in the world. Venice hummed with the carnival spirit of the rich and the not-so-rich hangers-on living the high life before Mussolini and Hitler had begun to darken the night with their bellicose ravings. Apparently thoughtless, idle and selfish, the cosmopolitan élite of society had, none the less, a quality of elegance and a *joie de vivre* that the twentieth century would not see again, and in the dream world of Venice all things were possible, nothing could destroy the sensuous pleasure of the luminous evenings under the stars.

There were tennis courts at the Lido that were very seldom used except by the star players arriving for the tournament in the high season, and speedboat races which attracted an international following. But sport was taken more seriously at Deauville and Le Touquet, where polo, racing, golf and tennis were all energetically pursued by the summer visitors, the modern young women who enjoyed playing tennis imitating Suzanne Lenglen, the prima donna tennis star of the Twenties, whose short, crêpe-de-chine skirts and neat dark hair tied by a bandeau had created a sensation.

The *Sketch* reported that there was 'more to do in Deauville than in any other luxury town in the world' and that the Normandie, the Royal and the Golf Hotel were all full for the *Grande Semaine*. There were two golf courses where the Prince of Wales enjoyed playing and the informality of his golfing attire often roused considerable comment; the tennis club on a par with Wimbledon, and the polo ground which resembled a garden party on the days when Lord Louis Mountbatten and his team were playing against the Marquis de Portago and the Baron de Neufville. The race course was '*très Newmarket*', attracting all the leading racehorse owners and backers from England, Lord Derby, Lord Carnarvon, Sir Humphrey de Trafford and the Aga Khan studying form with M. Hennessy and Princess de Faucigny Lucinge. Fashion decreed the wearing of straw hats, cream-coloured suits and brown and white 'co-respondent' shoes for the men and smart summer dresses for the ladies; and besides the racing, the tennis and golf tournaments, there were the shops in Deauville and the Casino, and if the weather was fine, the crowded beach with everyone wearing the very latest and most exotic beach pyjamas that vied in extravagance with those to be seen on the Lido.

Dinner at the Ambassadeurs invariably led to an all-night visit to the Casino with its plush decor and shaded lights and the subdued murmur of bids followed by silence and a fearful concentration. At the big baccarat table with a minimum stake of 1,000 louis or £175, the regulars took their gambling in earnest while the bemused onlookers watched them raking in their winning counters or waiting with an expressionless face for their luck to turn. Mr Solly Joel, the financier and racehorse owner, was seen adding to his millions by a run of luck, with Lord Furness, Lord Carnarvon and the Sultan of Johore at his elbow and the rather sinister Zographos, leader of the world famous Greek gambling syndicate, on the other side of the table next to Mme. Dubonnet and the rich Mme. Martinez de Hoz.

Women were even more reckless than men as compulsive gamblers and none more so than that exigous pair of lollipops, the Dolly Sisters, now precariously balanced on the fringe of smart society through the wealth of Gordon Selfridge. He had first seen them doing a cabaret turn at the Kit-Cat Club in London and was so captivated by Jenny, there was nothing he would not do for her. He bought an interest in the Casino at Le Touquet so that she could enjoy unlimited credit there, and she once played all round the clock from a Friday until the following Tuesday, winning £70,000 on a run of luck, only to lose it again before she tottered back to her hotel in a state of exhaustion. Fragile-looking with her doll-like hair and liquid Hungarian eyes, Jenny got herself up like a jeweller's shop window, wearing a solitaire ring the size of a walnut on her finger and diamond bracelets reaching to her skinny elbows. But the gambling and the fun and the gifts from Gordon Selfridge could not last for ever and when he was unable to pay her debts of £90,000 from the profits of his department store, Jenny committed suicide and the Casino lost a very good customer.

Deauville and Le Touquet as a playground for the smart set had the advantage of being within easy reach of London for the week-end. The very rich now had their own private aeroplanes and Imperial Airways ran scheduled services from Croydon Airport to various parts of the Continent. The planes only carried eighteen passengers and a steward, and were very noisy and bumpy, so that the paper bags provided for the air-sick were very necessary and it was wise to plug the ears with cotton wool and also to dress sensibly for the high altitudes. Leather coats and flying-helmet hats as worn by Lady Louis Mountbatten and Princess Emmeline de Broglie immediately became fashionable, and a casual reference to hopping over the Channel to Paris or farther afield made a good impression at any cocktail party or social gathering. Cecil Beaton, nervously apprehensive of his first flight to Holland, felt it was 'a modern and commendable thing to do' to save time and enjoyed himself immensely, wondering afterwards why he had anxiously written all those 'important letters' to be opened in the event of an accident.

The speed of air travel seemed miraculous. Nothing quite like it had ever been known before, and after the pioneering long distance flights of Lindbergh and Amy Johnson which roused the public to an orgy of hero-worship, it was felt that the conquest of the air would draw the ends of the world together in peace and harmony. Though flying across the Atlantic was not yet a practical alternative to travelling by sea in one of the top-class liners and the terrible R 101 disaster in 1930 had put an end to all further development of airships, air travel shortened the distance between Britain and Central Europe and made Austria a favourite place to visit in the mid-Thirties by flying to Paris or Brussels and then on to Vienna.

The Prince of Wales went to Kitzbühel, his patronage transforming the quiet little mountain village into a winter sports resort that became more chic than St Moritz. Visitors went to the Grand Hotel or to the Schloss Mittersill, a very exclusive country club 3,000 feet up in the mountains, run by Count Hans Czernin and Baron Hubert Pantz, who were known to all their English friends as Hans and Pants and could arrange anything from a chamois hunt or a sleigh ride up the Grossglockner Pass to a *thé dansant* or a wedding breakfast. For skiing, Schiaparelli, as with her beach dresses, revolutionized the drab gaberdine trousers and jackets women had been accustomed to wear into gay and daring suits of bright colours with little fur caps and outsize gauntlet gloves; and there was a sudden craze for dressing in peasant costume—leder-hosen and Tyrolean hats with feathers in them, dirndls and embroidered aprons—so that quite distinguished men and women on returning home were to be seen at weekend house parties in the English countryside inappropriately garbed in Austrian fancy dress, only Lady

82 *Eden Roc, Cap d'Antibes. It was here that the fashion for a Summer Season began, and quickly spread to the entire French Riviera. (Illustrated Newspapers Group)*

Diana Cooper and Lady Birley wearing their Tyrolean capes and pointed hats with a panache that defied ridicule.

In the summer, Salzburg, the shimmering eighteenth-century Baroque town where Mozart was born, attracted everyone interested in music and a good many smart people who were not. Max Reinhardt lived in the splendid Rococo Palace of the Prince Archbishop and with his indefatigable major-domo, Rudolf Kommer, entertained a variety of guests all through the festival season. The Sitwells went there with William Walton, Harold Acton and Lord Berners, the Duff Coopers, Tilly Losch, Bruno Walter, Moissi, the great actor and Molnar, the playwright. Mozart's operas were performed by all the leading singers of the day at the Festspielhaus, and in 1935 the Salzburg Festival transcended all other musical events of the year when Toscanini consented to conduct four performances of *Falstaff* and *Fidelio*. '*Ardo o agghiaccio, non conosco tempore*'—'I burn or I freeze, I cannot be lukewarm'—the Maestro had written two years before in refusing to return to Bayreuth while Hitler's persecution of the Jews persisted, and it was not only the magic of his genius as a sublime interpreter of Verdi and Beethoven that excited his audience, but his courage and his integrity. The Austrian Chancellor Dolfuss had been assassinated by the Nazis in 1934 and Hitler had only refrained from overrunning the country because Mussolini had exploded with fury. But for how long could Austria survive? Travellers returning from Salzburg via Munich saw the sinister-looking SS guards standing at street corners and the new autobahn cutting like a knife through the countryside towards the frontier. It was quite a relief sometimes to get back to Paris or to London.

Paris did not appear to change very much or to have lost its elegance as the leading fashion centre in the world. The couture houses flourished in spite of the difficult economic climate of the Thirties and the new silhouette of the second decade after the War was more seductive and more attractive than ever before. Very short skirts, flat chests and bobbed hair were 'out'. Waists were put back where they belonged and rounded bosoms encouraged to offset the slim, long length of the new evening dresses created by Jean Patou and Mme. Vionnet. Women with beautiful legs protested—why should they cover them up? And the fashion journalists huddled together on little gilt chairs in the scented salon at the preview of Patou's new collection, refused to believe that anyone would wear a long skirt ever again. But they were wrong. In six months no well-dressed woman in society wished to be seen without one.

Mme. Vionnet, established in the Avenue Montaigne, invented the bias cut, which allowed the material of her dresses to be moulded round the bosom and to fall in soft, clinging folds round the legs. Lanvin, Poiret and the Irish-born Edward Molyneux created their own version of the same cut, using supple lamé or brocade in lovely colours or printed chiffons of a gossamer thinness that frilled out below the knees. Evening coats and wraps fell to the floor again, Molyneux creating a ravishing black velvet wrap edged with white fox for Gertrude Lawrence to wear over a slender white satin dress with long black gloves and diamond ribbon bracelets to accentuate her feminine allure.

Day clothes also had longer skirts, dominated by the expensive simplicity of Coco Chanel's suits or the more extravagant creations of Schiaparelli and the cocktail dresses in dark satin designed by Mainbocher and worn with a Reboux hat of cocks-feathers and a silver fox stole. Fox fur dyed in a whole range of colours was the last word in fashion. Coat collars submerged the face of the wearer and coat sleeves were trimmed up to the elbows with bands of fur; even muffs were revived with the head and the tail and the four paws of the fox dangling rather helplessly from its tormented body. Accessories of all sorts—real or artificial jewellery, flowers, scarves, bags, hats and gloves—became more romantic and more feminine, as the women who had been young and wild in the Twenties adopted the new fashions and found them more becoming. The Paris couturiers showed them how to look more beautiful and still youthful in their maturity, and the shops in the Rue de la Paix and the Faubourg St Honoré were as irresistible as ever. Dinner at Maxim's or luncheon at the Ritz, the races at Longchamp and the smart restaurants in the Bois de Boulogne saw the best-dressed women in the world of cosmo-

83 *Tiger-shooting was one of the more exotic leisure pursuits of the British in India. Trophies would serve as reminders of these colourful years.*

politan society at ease in the new style of the Thirties.

But Paris was not only the city of elegance, it was still the art capital of the world where the books that were banned in England—*Lady Chatterley's Lover, Ulysses* and Radclyffe Hall's notorious lesbian novel, *The Well of Loneliness*—could be bought and smuggled through the Customs at Dover; where a new generation of *avant garde* artists, writers and musicians of all nationalities worshipped at the shrine of Picasso, Jean Cocteau, Stravinski and Gertrude Stein. Almost everyone with any enthusiasm for what was most vital in the arts seemed to end up on the doorstep of Gertrude Stein's apartment which she shared with her inseparable companion, Alice B. Toklas. She was 'as much a part of Paris as the Eiffel Tower' according to Harold Acton, and rather more disconcerting. Her rooms were hung with the paintings of Picasso to whom she had been devoted for years, his vivid personality stimulating her own instinct for new forms in art and his own farouche experiments acting like a catalyst on her technique as a writer. She strung words together like raw pigments pasted on with a palette knife, divorcing them from their context and using them as symbols of sound rather than of sense; and whereas to some people this apparently insane repetition—'A rose is a rose is a rose . . .'—sounded like sheer gibberish, to the intelligentsia seeking originality and novelty in the arts, it was tremendously exciting and thought-provoking.

The Sitwells paid homage to Gertrude Stein as a doughty fighter in their own never-ending battle against the Philistines, entertaining her in London and escorting her and Miss Toklas to Oxford, where Harold Acton had arranged for her to give a lecture. 'She made a memorable entry on the platform,' he wrote, 'looking like a squat Aztec figure in obsidian, growing more monumental as soon as she sat down.' And what followed was even more surprising, since her homely American manner in contrast to her bizarre appearance disarmed and deflated the undergraduates who had come to laugh at her, and she answered them back with the greatest good humour when they heckled her. Acton himself found her very sympathetic and grew fond of her when he went to live in Paris. She was, he thought, 'a solid rock among the brambles of French literary society, too individual to be merged into any clique'.

84　*Afternoon tea in the air over London. The late Twenties saw the start of regular passenger flights between the British and French capitals and a whole new range of experiences was opened up. (Illustrated London News)*

Brought up in the pre-war world of aristocratic Florentine society, Acton was an aesthete by nature and by environment. At the age of six his favourite painter was Botticelli; at Eton he wrote poetry and read Andrew Marvell, John Donne, Aldous Huxley and the Sitwells. At Oxford he added Evelyn Waugh to his old-Etonian friends, Brian Howard, Peter Quennell, David Cecil and Robert Byron; was a member of John Sutro's Railway Club and of the Hypocrites, whose range of interests extended from a revival of Victoriana to the latest Harlem blues. Originality of thought and expression excited his enthusiasm without destroying his judgement. He enjoyed the all-night discussions on poetry, music and the arts and some of the wilder escapades of his friends. But when the University was invaded by the brash Bright Young Things from Mayfair and every party became an orgy of jazz and sex, 'when cocktails were substituted for Amontillado and conversation was stifled by the gramophone', he withdrew into his shell to some extent and soon after leaving

Oxford, escaped to Paris, living alone in a quiet apartment on the Left Bank.

'The Seine under the stars, the narrow streets jutting off at curious angles into the darkness, the glowing "ox-eyes" of mansard roofs, the multiple bridges with their mysterious arches, the parks locked up, only ponds and plants alive there, assuming marvellous shapes under the moon . . .' All this appealed to Acton's highly developed aesthetic sensibility and he never grew tired of exploring Paris at night. But he was wary of some of its alien inhabitants. He thought the antics of Ernest Hemingway and his boozing companions in Montparnasse were bogus, preferring the society of the artists Tchelitcheff, Christian Bérard and Tony Gandarillos, or the dazzling conversation of Jean Cocteau, still the *enfant terrible* of Parisian society and its most versatile poet, playwright, film-maker, designer, draughts-man and publicist.

None of the younger artists and writers of the post-war generation living, according to Acton, 'on the jagged brink of disillusion and pulled back periodically by Marx or Freud or some other esoteric sage', could match the speed and elegance of the scintillating images that flowed from Cocteau's brain, none had the magic of his febrile personality when he held court surrounded by beautiful young men and discoursed on the virtues of opium or the enchanting prospect of death. The young were suffering from a surfeit of experimental anarchy in the arts; they distrusted everything and depended on artificial stimulants to bolster up their self-esteem. Only James Joyce, who was no longer young and almost blind, remained aloof from their hysterical aberrations, like a pagan priest weaving his own ritual of words to evoke the underground stream of consciousness buried in the soul of mankind. Harold Nicolson called on him one day and found his little furnished flat in the Rue Galilée 'as stuffy and prim as a hotel bedroom' and Joyce himself rather unreal, 'like a very nervous and refined animal . . . with a brittle and vulnerable strangeness'.

Upper-class English visitors of a less intellectual calibre went to Paris for the night clubs, dancing to the negro bands and drinking a lot of expensive and rather inferior champagne before returning to their hotels with a hangover. They patronized the Boeuf sur Toit which Cocteau had made famous, the Rotonde and the Dôme and the cabarets round the Place Pigalle, and some of them sought out the seedier cafés on the Left Bank where the homosexuals and the lesbians defiantly drowned their sorrows in absinthe or brandy. Other visitors preferred Mistinguette, still appearing at the Folies Bergères in a frizz of feathers, furs and chiffon, her fabulous legs said to be insured for thousands of pounds, or Josephine Baker, the talented dark singer and dancer who had created a sensation at the Casino de Paris. Old men in the audience sat up higher in their seats to watch the erotic, semi-nude chorus girls kicking their legs in the air, their mouths watering like Pavlov's dogs at the sight of food; young men escorting the elderly American ladies hooked on the sights of 'gay Paree', did well for themselves in the wads of dollars they smirkingly accepted. What the tourists saw was not all that different from what the butler saw, but as everyone spoke and sang in French, it seemed naughtier and more shocking with continental overtones of the gay life that were missing in London and New York.

That London had Soho and New York Harlem was of no consequence. It was amusing and rather wicked to dig out the underworld of Paris, to go drinking and fornicating farther afield in Marseilles or Algiers where the Arab boys were lithe and beautiful, to cross the Tiber when in Rome to discover the obverse side of the coin belonging to the haughty Roman aristocracy, whose decadent exclusiveness was more marked than anywhere else in Europe. Sight-seeing covered a multitude of sins and could be interpreted in many different ways. Money could buy almost anything and even if the Americans had more dollars than the English had pounds, the English still expected to be treated with respect. At the British Embassies in the capitals of the world standards of behaviour, at least on the surface, were controlled by the conventions of the past. Presentation at Court provided the entrée into diplomatic society for ladies whether old or young, and if some of the young amused themselves with the up and coming pink-faced attachés, it was with discretion. The world of Henry James was not altogether dead. Young married women had more freedom than debutantes, but fun on the side was kept within bounds, for no young man however bold really wanted to risk his career by getting involved in a scandal.

Old-fashioned standards ruled even more strictly in the

outposts of the Empire and above all in India, where the Viceroy as H.M. King George V's representative maintained the traditional ceremonial dignity of the Court with the utmost regal splendour. Here there were still devoted and compliant servants and the power and prestige of the British Raj cast an aura of stately Edwardian opulence over its participants, in spite of Mahatma Gandhi's embarrassing meditations at Ahmedabad and his astute political scheming. To all outward appearances very little had changed. The Viceroy and his entourage went tiger-shooting with the Indian princes, sitting high up in the howdahs mounted on the elephants, and if the wounded tiger attacked, it was the mahouts leading the elephants or the carriers walking behind who got eaten, not the sahibs with their guns. Young cavalry officers went mad on pig-sticking and polo—keeping ponies was a lot cheaper in India than at home. Horse races were organized in the Hill Stations and hunting the jackal with hounds brought out from Melton on the long sea voyage from England. Clubs in the cities and the outstations were exclusive to the British, full of army officers and Indian Civil Service personnel and a sprinkling of traders, who were not quite the thing but if introduced by a member might just be tolerated and allowed to pay for their gin. Only a 'pukka' could run up debts at the bar, at bridge or the races, bluffing his way out by being a sporting chap and a gentleman. If he happened to be the younger son of one of the old aristocratic families or the brigadier's wife knew who his mother was, so much the better; and if he had charm and a good figure in his dress uniform, he could wheedle himself out of the scrapes he got into after a sound ticking-off from his superior officer.

For it was not that the British in India had no sense of duty. The honour of the regiment ranked high in the minds of the youngest and most foolish subaltern. Discipline and a sense of justice informed all ranks of the Civil Service. Loyalty, decency and courage far from home and the playing-fields of Eton set a good example. But the Indians were 'them' and the British were 'us' and each had observed the distinction since the days when Disraeli dazzled Queen Victoria with the title of Empress. The modern Viceroys—Lords Reading, Irwin, Willingdon and Linlithgow—were men of distinction and intelligence, yet the hierarchy they ruled was an intricate maze of out-of-date

85 *Air travel meant getting away from it all, and winter sports meant new fashion
ideas. This photograph shows British visitors enjoying a curling match at St Moritz.
(Popperfoto)*

protocol, precedence and social discrimination. Each official had
his own niche, and his wife—if he had one—knew her place, or
was very soon put firmly into it by the other mem-sahibs who
knew where she ought to belong. Leaving cards in the 'listed'
houses was a necessity for the new arrival, who otherwise would
not have been invited to any of the dinner parties that were the
backbone of society; and at these formal entertainments, the
governor of the district and his lady took their guests into the
dining-room paired according to their rank from the High Court
judges and the the generals to the youngest subaltern and the
newest debutante to have arrived off the boat from England.

Officially an almost Victorian attitude to women still
persisted and a voyage to India by P. & O. had much the same
significance as when the sisters and cousins of the Empire-
builders set off in the nineteenth century to visit their relations,
like a herd of pale milk and white does in search of a mate. Only

their luggage was different. Instead of the ruffled blouses and long serge skirts, the topees and the white parasols lined with green linen, the little vanity bags and the large feather-trimmed hats, the mosquito-nets and the butterfly-nets and the little sketch books and books on botany, the modern young women arrived with a handful of short-skirted cotton dresses, a lot of scarves and beads and pale flesh-coloured stockings, some flimsy underwear, a make-up box and perhaps a camera and a cigarette-case. The strange smells and the sights and sounds of India left them equally wide-eyed and agog with excitement when they got off the boat, though quite unprepared to find themselves in a society which could have been transplanted from Cheltenham or Salisbury, a society, moreover, stiff with Victorian prejudice, intolerance and snobbery, very self-centred and much addicted to gossip.

Yet there was fun to be had in India. There were picnics and parties and sight-seeing trips: the Taj Mahal by moonlight and the temples of Mysore with their jagged outlines and writhing oriental figures, the Great Falls of Gersoppa and its romantic fortress perched high on the rocks, and the jungles forever mysterious and secretive. There were amateur theatricals and early morning rides at the Queen of the Hill Stations, Ootacamund, affectionately known as Ooty, and both in its climate and its landscape reminiscent of a patch of England set high up in the Nilgiri Hills, its small Victorian villas and bungalows built in the 1860s surrounded by hollyhocks, roses and mignonette flourishing side by side with the exotic eucalyptus trees. Ooty, in fact, looked rather like Malvern in its Victorian heyday, just as the summer residence of the Viceroy at Simla with its fretted balconies and turreted towers resembled a Hydro in Harrogate, though it was within a bowshot of the jungle, where Lord Linlithgow loved to go hunting with his butterfly-net, and at night the screaming monkeys and parakeets settled into silence while the tigers and the jackals prowled noiselessly through the thick undergrowth.

Lord Linlithgow had all the virtues of his aristocratic ancestors and few of their failings. He was wise, courageous, absolutely honest and very patient in all his negotiations with Gandhi and the other Indian leaders. He disliked ostentation and preferred his butterfly-net to shooting tigers. But vice-regal society was of necessity formal and dignified. In Simla some relaxation was possible; in New Delhi it was not. Sir Edwin Lutyens started working on his grandiose plans for the Imperial city in 1913, consuming tons of marble in the process before the great domed and colonnaded residence of the Viceroy was ready in 1930 to receive Lord Linlithgow's predecessor, Lord Willingdon. A vast processional way isolated the residence from its surroundings and only came to life on state occasions when animated by rows of superbly accoutred British and Indian soldiers guarding the arrival of the Indian princes for the annual investitures. These surpassed anything to be seen at Buckingham Palace. In the Grand Durbar Hall, lined with mirrors and black marble, the Viceroy's bodyguard of huge men in turbans and scarlet coats, carrying lances with streaming pennants, formed the background, and everyone else was dressed in uniform: civilians in white knee-breeches, silk stockings and buckled shoes and the regiments in a gorgeous variety of gold laced tunics, plumed headgear, tight trousers and high boots clinking with spurs. The Viceroy, entering in procession, wore the superb sky-blue robes of the Star of India over a Privy Councillor's

86   *The dining-room of the Viceregal Lodge at Simla. Standards of elegance here remained unaffected by the rapid changes of style in Britain. (Central Press Photo Ltd.)*

uniform, and the Vicerine a tiara and all the jewels she possessed cascading down the bosom of her evening gown, the train of her purple velvet mantle held by the small sons of the Indian princes in bejewelled turbans and white satin suits trimmed with belts and buttons and layers of pearls. The Maharajas themselves wore long brocaded tunics and brightly coloured turbans loaded with diamonds, rubies and emeralds and their attendants fluttered round them like the exotic birds of the jungle, while the military bands played God Save the King and selections from the Gilbert and Sullivan operas.

It was the British version of the old Mogul Court, resplendent and satisfying. The Indians loved it and so did their Anglo-Saxon masters. But outside in the sultry air the Vicerine's English flowers wilted in the heat and Gandhi, as naked as God made him except for his loin-cloth, vowed himself to poverty and civil disobedience. Time was running out. The British in India had passed the peak of their achievement and the last stronghold of aristocratic power and privilege abroad would soon crumble away in the high tide of Indian nationalism, leaving an empty niche in the processional gateway where the statue of King George V had once looked down on the imperial pomp of New Delhi.

9 A CRISIS FOR THE NOBILITY

At home, in Britain, the Depression lifted slowly. Unemployment which had reached an all-time peak of just under 3,000,000 in January 1933 fell by half a million before the year was over. Industrial production recovered to the level of 1930 and continued to improve steadily, though not in quite the way the National Government anticipated. The basic industries of the North and the Midlands declined in favour of the new light industries in the South, where modern factories making electrical equipment, motor-cars and consumer goods of all kinds proliferated. These in turn stimulated a boom in the building of houses, schools, shops and cinemas—a ribbon development casually eating up the countryside in a suburban sprawl. New houses meant new furniture on the 'Never, Never' system (delivered by Mr Drage in a 'plain van' so that the respectability of his customers could not be called into question), new wireless sets and electric fires, new carpets, curtains and ornaments, mass-produced in 'modern' design and ranging from Art Deco figurines to parchment lampshades bearing pictures of Anne Hathaway's cottage.

It was all quite terrible in the eyes of anyone with taste and enough to give Lady Colefax or Mrs Syrie Maugham a heart attack. Yet the emancipation of the new workers in the suburbs was an important factor in the gradual movement towards greater prosperity; and although the Government, still preaching the virtues of economy, took the credit for these encouraging signs of recovery, it was really the people themselves acting in the opposite direction by spending their money instead of saving it who were responsible for the improvement in their circumstances.

They all aspired to owning a motor-car and many of them achieved it thanks to the Austin 7 and the Morris Cowley; they all tried to do on the cheap some of the things the rich did with their time off, playing tennis, dancing at the new road houses, swimming and picnicking at the seaside and skating on the new indoor ice-rinks. And all the girls and young women, workers themselves in the food factories, the cinemas and Lyons Corner House teashops, did their best to look like their favourite filmstars or the society beauties pictured in the newspapers.

But if the inhabitants of the new suburbs were on the up grade, the workers in the heavy industries were not. Neither the eloquence of MacDonald nor the platitudes of Baldwin could cure the evils of the antiquated coal-mines, shipyards and iron-works, and the gap between the lower and the upper classes, between the poor and the rich widened into a dark gulf; not so much in the country where the landowners were still the hub of the community, but in the towns and cities where derelict houses and slums left over from Victorian days were sometimes owned by aristocratic landlords and administered by hard-faced agents, or where the old type of family business had become out of date. The paternal image, except for men like the Earl of Derby, the Duke of Devonshire and a few of the more enlightened industrialists, was no longer effective; yet there was nothing to put in its place, only the intellectual theories of the Left-wing agitators or the dole with its even more humiliating and hateful adjunct, the Means Test, breeding bitterness in the midst of despair.

Various attempts to relieve the distress of the unemployed made by upper-class voluntary helpers with a conscience did something to brighten what was euphemistically called their 'enforced leisure'. But to the Prince of Wales, touring the depressed areas of Newcastle-on-Tyne, Liverpool and South Wales, it was shameful and demoralizing to see able-bodied men sitting about in rather dreary clubs hopefully organized to make their idleness more palatable. He was deeply shocked by what he saw and even more appalled by the attitude of MacDonald and Baldwin, who regarded any practical suggestions he made as an interference in political matters outside the province of the Heir to the Throne.

Political society was not very inspiring to anyone like the

87   *In Britain, the landscape of the Thirties was becoming ever more industrial with tall smoking chimneys and larger factories in every manufacturing town. (Radio Times Hulton Picture Library)*

Prince with a go-ahead kind of temperament. That Ramsay MacDonald, Baldwin and Neville Chamberlain were the only gentlemen in England except for a few professional undertakers to continue wearing a wing collar, showed something of their mentality. They belonged to the old-fashioned days of *laisser-faire* politics and, without the vigour but with all the complacency of their generation, were wedded to the pre-war image of Britain's supremacy among the nations of the world. MacDonald, growing older and greyer, pressed doggedly on from one conference to another, his speeches becoming more and more emotional, all their meaning lost in swirling clouds of rhetoric. Stanley Baldwin, considered by one of his ex-colleagues to be 'self-centred, selfish and idle, without a constructive idea in his head and devilish sly', carefully maintained his public reputation for honesty, virtue and lack of personal ambition, greatly assisted by Mrs Baldwin, whose hats were the object of Lady Cunard's hilarity and whose skirts, without the style of Queen Mary, reached down to her ankles.

It was, however, unwise to laugh at either of the Baldwins while he continued to lead the Conservative Party. Apparently dozing on the front bench, with a curious habit of sniffing his order paper and cracking his finger joints, his docile appearance belied an acute awareness of the mood of the House of Commons on every possible occasion, especially in a crisis when things seemed to be going against him. His deliberate technique of fumbling about with his notes was a masterly device for creating expectation and covering up his mistakes with a mixture of innocence, frankness and humility; while in the smoking-room or at tea on the terrace, he conveyed the idea that he only held on to high office out of a patriotic sense of duty and would have been happier in the country looking after his pigs or sitting by the fire in the slippered ease of a country gentleman. No one really noticed that he was creating a new pattern for the Conservative Party by guiding it away from the exclusive power and privilege of the aristocracy into the orbit of the middle classes who had previously voted for the Liberals, though in this he was assisted by his henchman, Neville Chamberlain, who was more practical and eager to get things done and had a zest for reform which resulted in some domestic improvements in housing and local government.

Younger politicians simply had no chance to get their nose in and there were very few of them anyway, except Anthony Eden, Duff Cooper and Hore Belisha, to reach Cabinet rank in the Thirties. The loss of a whole generation of brilliant young men in the years from 1914 to 1918 had left a gap which now could not be filled; for the Great War, as it was now called, had killed off many of those who might have taken responsibility for the conduct of the nation's affairs with a more forward-looking sense of urgency than that of the ageing wing-collared brigade, forever seeking to solve the problems of the modern world with the methods of the past.

No one felt this void more keenly than the Prince of Wales. As a public figure much was expected of him, yet his position was highly equivocal, for he was powerless in reality to influence the policy of the Government. Anything, moreover, that he did or said which could be construed as 'mixing in politics' immediately roused the wrath of King George and caused a rumpus, as when the Prince in a speech to the British Legion Festival in 1935 suggested, without consulting the Foreign Office first, that some members of the group should visit Germany as a gesture of good will. With his long experience of state affairs, the King was probably right in believing such a statement could be interpreted as too pro-German, but the Prince did not think so or take kindly to being reprimanded as if he were still an irresponsible schoolboy. Since the King's serious illness in 1928, he had taken on more and more of his father's burdens, standing at his mother's side through all the social functions of the Court, receiving Ambassadors from overseas and playing his part with charm and dignity. Yet his feeling of frustration was intensified. He was still not allowed access to state papers or given the opportunity of learning the ins and outs of parliamentary government; he was still regarded in the sober atmosphere of the elderly Court as a rather naughty and impulsive young man, and still treated by his father as Queen Victoria had treated her son, King George following the fatal pattern of disapproval and lack of understanding that his grandmother had shown towards the future King Edward VII—an attitude all the more tragic, since his own relations with his father in the last years of King Edward VII's

88 *The Baldwins were against too intellectualized an approach to politics. Here Mrs Baldwin presents a challenge cup at the Northaw point to point, 1924. (Radio Times Hulton Picture Library)*

reign had been particularly harmonious and agreeable.

1935, however, was the twenty-fifth anniversary of King George V's accession to the throne and to mark the recovery from the worst of the Depression, it was decided by the Government that this should be celebrated in the manner of Queen Victoria's Golden Jubilee with a state drive through London and a service of Thanksgiving at St Paul's, coinciding with similar services in the provinces and a night of bonfires, fireworks and dancing on the village green. Political controversy it was hoped would die away—and for the time being it did, for the public of all classes turned the occasion into a holiday of national rejoicing and took not the slightest notice of Sir Stafford Cripps when he sourly criticised the celebrations as 'a lot of political bally-hoo'.

May 6 happily was brilliant and sunny—'royal weather'. Chips Channon and his wife, Lady Honor, walked from their house in Belgrave Square through the Green Park to the Ponsonbys' apartment in St James's Palace, where they and a group of privileged friends had been invited to watch the procession. The Mall was crowded, people who had been there all night, fainting and jostling each other for position behind the Guards and the benevolent police lining the route, cheering the appearance of a road sweeper lifting a spadeful of horse dung from the empty roadway, laughing good humouredly at everything and nothing. Then the first coach appeared, carrying the black and gold robed Speaker of the House of Commons—Lady Honor Channon's cousin—followed by the Prime Ministers of the Dominions and Ramsay MacDonald with his daughter, Ishbel. 'He looked grim and she dowdy. No cheers.' Then the Lord Chancellor, 'wig and all'; then the minor royalties—'a few cheers'. Then masses of troops, magnificent and virile, resplendent in grand uniforms, the sun glistening on their helmets. 'Then thunderous applause for the royal carriages. The Yorks in a large landau with the two tiny pink children . . . the Kents, that dazzling pair [Prince George had been created Duke of Kent on his marriage to Princess Marina of Greece in 1934] and the Prince of Wales, smiling his dentist smile and waving to his friends', paired with his elderly aunt, the Queen of Norway, who looked 'comic'. Then more troops and suddenly the coach with Their Majesties. 'All eyes were on the Queen in her white and silvery splendour. Never had she looked so serene, so regally

89 *The first meeting of the controversial National Government, 1931. Included in the picture are the Premier, Ramsay MacDonald, J. H. Thomas, Stanley Baldwin, and Neville Chamberlain. (Radio Times Hulton Picture Library)*

majestic, even so attractive. She completely eclipsed the King . . .' and suddenly had become 'the best dressed woman in the world'.

The enthusiasm of Chips Channon was shared by the crowd. Queen Mary—wisely—had never changed her style. Every inch of her was royal. The toques and the tiaras she wore, her bejewelled gowns from the House of Reville and Rossiter, her gloves and her long-toed satin shoes with buckles on them suited her stately Edwardian figure and by disregarding the vagaries of fashion, she had created an indelible picture of how a queen should look and behave. But the Jubilee was a triumph for the King also. Though frail and visibly ageing, his integrity and steadfastness through all the angry phases of transition and disbelief in the past twenty-five years, now commanded more respect and admiration than ever before. He was surprised by the warmth of the reception he received, not realizing perhaps that through the invention of the wireless, his homely

90 *A splendid royal occasion. The Lord Mayor presents a pearl sword to King George V at Temple Bar during the Silver Jubilee celebrations, 1935. (Popperfoto)*

Christmas broadcasts to the nation had brought him in touch with his people as no other monarch before his time, and not aware, so modest was his own opinion of himself, that the incorruptible honesty and good faith he had shown throughout his reign set a standard of decency all the more unique in a world torn with disruption and discontent. Never had any monarch been greeted from the lowest to the highest rank of his people with such an uprush of loyalty and affection. In the East End when he drove through the streets with Queen Mary in his high-backed Daimler, the cheers and the excitement, especially of the children, the home-made decorations and the flags and the bunting, moved him deeply. In the West End, gay with flowers and flags and the brilliant floodlighting of the public buildings which gave London a new magic by night, Buckingham Palace became the focus of high society attending the official balls and banquets and thousands of Londoners milling round its gates with the visitors from overseas.

Chips said the evening of the Jubilee was like Ascot on Gold Cup Day. Walking down St James's Street 'one met everyone'—and by 'everyone', of course he meant all the high

91 *Meanwhile, in the streets of Paddington, it was accordians and songs. (Radio Times Hulton Picture Library)*

ranking people in society he entertained so assiduously at his house in Belgravia; for Chips, as all his English friends called Henry Channon, had 'arrived' and was a connoisseur in the art of living in the high style of the English aristocracy he had so successfully conquered. The only child of a very rich Chicago businessman, he despised America and all it stood for, developing a taste for European culture while working in Paris for the Red Cross as a young man at the end of the War. Then he went to Oxford and fell in love with London, sharing a house there with Prince Paul of Yugoslavia and Viscount Gage, making friends easily in the glittering social world of the younger set and becoming a naturalized Englishman. Marrying the eldest daughter of Lord Iveagh, Lady Honor Guinness, he entered parliament as the Conservative member for his father-in-law's former constituency, Southend, bought an old manor house at Kelvedon in Essex and moved into Belgrave Square in 1935.

Harold Nicolson dined there one evening and wrote to his wife, Vita Sackville-West: 'Oh my God how rich and powerful 'Lord' Channon has become! There is his house in Belgrave Square next door to Prince George, Duke of Kent, and Duchess

223

of ditto and little Prince Edward. The house is all Regency upstairs with very carefully draped curtains and Madame Récamier
sofas and wall-paintings. Then the dining-room is entered
through an orange lobby and discloses itself suddenly as a copy
of the blue room of the Amalienburg near Munich—baroque
and rococo and what-ho and oh-no-no and all that. Very fine
indeed.' But Chips was not only very rich and grand—the
Amalienburg dining-room cost over £6,000 and Napoleon's
gold-plated dinner service more than that—not only a social
climber and a snob; he had a genuine belief in the country of his
adoption and a very agreeable personality. 'Never was there a
surer or more enlivening friend,' Lady Diana Cooper wrote of
him. 'He installed the mighty in his gilded chairs and exalted the
humble. He made the old and tired, the young and strong, shine
beneath his thousand lighted candles. Without stint he gave of his
riches and his compassion.'

People told him their secrets and he observed their antics
with his boot-button brown eyes, meticulously recording in his
Diaries the small change of history in the day-to-day happenings
of the upper-class world in the 1930s. He knew the Marlboroughs,
the Duchess of Sutherland, the Londonderrys, Lord Derby's
family, Lord Beaverbrook and Winston Churchill, and was very
intimate with the Duke and Duchess of Kent. He worshipped
Lady Diana: she was 'supreme among mortals. Adorable, divine,
inspired creature, the character of the age; glamorous, gay and
good.' And he was fascinated by Emerald Cunard, finding her
'as kind as she was witty' and her house in Grosvenor Square with
its 'rococo atmosphere, the conversation in the candle-light, the
elegance, the bibelots and the books', unique as a rallying-point
for most of London society, only those who were 'too stupid or
too stuffy' to be invited being 'disdainful' of her charms. He
disliked Lady Astor, his American counterpart in the House
of Commons; though 'breezy and funny in a queer combination
of warm-heartedness, originality and rudeness, she was *antipatica*,
an unconscious snob and a hypocrite'. Not a great woman or even
a clever woman, like Lady Oxford, who looked like 'a mad raven
and could be rude, dictatorial and magnificent . . . her crisp,
penetrating phrases riveting'—especially in the fierce battles she
had with Lady Cunard, which roused the wickedness in both
of them and were a constant source of entertainment to everyone

else.

According to the Mad Raven, the Yellow Canary *thought* she was a clever woman, but was not. 'Women,' said Margot Oxford, 'were barren and could do nothing without the stimulus of a man's love.' Yet all through the summer of 1935, Emerald Cunard was at the height of her glory and her mischief-making as the *confidente* of the Prince of Wales in the most recent of his love affairs. 'There is tremendous excitement about Mrs Simpson,' Chips wrote eight days after the Jubilee procession. 'I find the duel over the Prince of Wales between Mrs Simpson, supported by Diana Cooper and strangely enough, Emerald, and the ———— camp, most diverting. The Prince is obviously madly infatuated and she, a jolly unprepossessing American, witty, a mimic, an excellent cook, has completely subjugated him. Never has he been so in love. She is madly anxious to storm society while she is still his favourite, so that when he leaves her (as he leaves everyone in time) she will be secure.'

Though Chips was wrong in his final analysis, he had some reason to doubt the Prince's staying power, for his favourites among the young married women of the smart set had come and

92   *The summer exhibition at the Royal Academy was always on the list of society events. The Countess of Oxford and Asquith (centre) is pictured here with her son, Anthony Asquith and Princess Bibesco at Burlington House in 1926. (Radio Times Hulton Picture Library)*

gone through the years, much to the dismay of Queen Mary and the people who believed it was his duty to find a suitable wife and settle down. After Mrs Dudley Ward, he was attracted by Thelma Furness, one of the Morgan twins, of whom Cecil Beaton wrote in his *Book of Beauty*: 'The Morgan sisters, Lady Furness and Mrs Vanderbilt, are as alike as two magnolias, and with their marble complexions, raven tresses and flowing dresses, with their slight lisps and foreign accents, they diffuse an Ouida atmosphere of hothouse elegance and lacy femininity . . . They should have been painted by Sargent, with arrogant heads and affected hands, in white satin with a bowl of white peonies near by.'

Not that there was anything in the least Edwardian about the Morgan twins, except their preference for wearing long instead of short-skirted evening dresses in the Twenties. They belonged to the hectic, glamorous post-war world of high fashion on both sides of the Atlantic and were often to be seen in Paris, at Deauville, Monte Carlo or Biarritz. As the daughters of an American Consul and his half-Spanish wife, passionately proud of her aristocratic descent, their background had always been cosmopolitan, and the end of the War found them, at the age of sixteen, living on their own without a chaperone in an apartment in New York. Thelma eloped with a glib young man twice her age, James Vail Converse, known as 'Junior', married him in Maryland and after a blissful honeymoon at the Everglades Club at Palm Beach, discovered that his rakish behaviour was not so attractive as she had thought. Gloria married one of the Vanderbilts and was whirled into the Fifth Avenue Set, still dominated by her eighty year-old mother-in-law, Mrs Alice Vanderbilt, who always wore black and a dog-collar of diamonds and pearls round her neck worth a fortune.

Gloria was years younger than Reggie Vanderbilt, but the marriage was a success. A daughter, 'little' Gloria, was born and the whole family travelled to Europe in high style, followed by valets, footmen, nurses and a load of cabin trunks. Thelma joined them at the Ritz in Paris, after a trip to California to get a divorce from Junior Converse and an abortive attempt to become a film-star; and besides having a wonderful time on the Vanderbilt money, buying a trousseau of new clothes from Chanel, Lanvin and Vionnet, racing at Longchamp, dining at Maxim's and

93   *Not Heath Row but Waterloo was the terminal for the elegant trans-Atlantic travellers of the twenties and thirties. Lady Furness, the former Thelma Morgan, is shown here meeting her sister, Mrs Gloria Vanderbilt. Lady Furness was a friend of the Prince of Wales and it was through her that he met Mrs Simpson. (Radio Times Hulton Picture Library)*

finishing the evening at the Montmartre night clubs, she was pursued by Lord Furness, a bold buccaneering Yorkshireman with red hair and blue eyes, who suddenly discovered he had a great deal of business to attend to in Paris.

Marmaduke—or Duke Furness, as he was known to his friends—was fifty-five and a widower, with a son at school and a daughter from his first marriage only a year or two younger than Thelma, who was not yet twenty-one. He was extremely rich on the proceeds of the shipping companies his father had founded, and a viscount. This made him very exciting to Thelma, even if to the older ranks of the English aristocracy the Furness title was too new to count for much. '"Milord" was always bowed by the *maitre d'hôtel* to the best table,' she wrote in her autobiography, *Double Exposure*. 'Other women would look up with what I thought to be a little envy as we entered a restaurant.' And the fact that Furness often drew the attention of everyone by his loud and 'picturesque' language learnt in the stables in Yorkshire, most of his comments beginning with 'What the bloody hell—' only added to his attraction, to the sense of power and purpose that in Thelma's eyes set him apart from other men.

She married him in 1926, a year after Gloria's husband Reggie Vanderbilt had died suddenly in America. Duke Furness had a house in Arlington Street, a hunting lodge called Borrough Court in Leicestershire and another in the North of Scotland for the deer-stalking. London society accepted his new and attractive American bride and she enjoyed every moment of her first Season. She was presented at Court and went everywhere. 'Duke, I was convinced, was the ideal husband—intelligent, worldly and fun to be with,' she wrote. 'We were blissfully happy those first few months. I had never had so much attention showered on me. Duke delighted in giving me gifts—large and small . . . I was utterly content in his love and firmly believed it would always be that way.'

But it was not. Hunting and horses bored Thelma. After the London Season was over there was nothing to amuse her in Leicestershire; and what was worse, Duke Furness had a roving eye, which began to rove rapidly in other directions after their son was born. He went off to Monte Carlo on his own and was seen at parties in London with another woman while his wife moulted in Borrough Court, until as it happened the Prince of Wales came to Leicester Fair to hand out rosettes to the prize-winning cows. After the ceremony he quite casually walked over to talk to Lady Furness, who was more than grateful for his attention and delighted when he made a date for her to dine with him at York House. 'The Prince seemed to me to be winsomely handsome,' she wrote. 'He was the quintessence of charm. And after the swaggering earthiness of Duke, his natural shyness and reserve had a distinct appeal.'

Duke Furness could not very well object and Thelma found it more convenient than she had thought to accept the fact that in English society it seemed quite the usual thing for husbands and wives to go their own way without rushing into the divorce courts as in America. Neither of them paid much attention to the inevitable gossip. Duke Furness was a man of the world—he took his wife's friendship with the Prince in his stride. And it was perhaps fortuitous that he had arranged a safari in Africa at the very moment when the Prince had decided to visit Nairobi as a guest of the Governor General. Furness tactfully went off big game shooting with his gun in one direction, while the Prince did his shooting with a ciné camera in another part of the jungle and invited Thelma to join him. His camp was the acme of comfort and convenience with 'portable bath tubs, dining-tables, wine-coolers and the finest mosquito-proofed nets', and at night when the stars came out in the wide sky and the glow of the camp fires began to die away, they were together. 'This was our Eden,' Thelma wrote ecstatically, 'and we were alone in it.'

Back in England the Prince got busy making his own garden of Eden at Fort Belvedere, a pseudo-Gothic, turreted house on the edge of Windsor Great Park, which had once been inhabited by one of George IV's mistresses and still belonged to the Crown. With the eager enthusiasm he always showed for anything he had not done before, he took to gardening in a big way, hacking

94　*The face that shook the British monarchy. Wallis Simpson, in traditional debutante's dress, when she was presented at Court. (Popperfoto)*

down the trees and the undergrowth himself, supervizing the building of a swimming-pool, digging the soil and laying out the tennis court. Apart from the pleasure he took in having a new hobby, the exercise he thought was good for him, for he shared the mania for keeping fit that swept the nation at this time, everyone doing gymnastics in the morning or rushing off to play squash and golf as part of the ritual of remaining slim and athletic looking.

Yet the Fort, as the Prince called it, meant more to him than that. It represented a home of his own in the country, a refuge from the nervous strain of always being in the public eye, a haven of peace where he could enjoy the kind of domestic life that so far had eluded him and now, at the age of thirty-five, seemed more desirable. Thelma Furness came down every weekend, sometimes on her own and sometimes with a few close friends. They went for long walks with their dogs and dived in and out of the swimming-pool, the Prince played the bagpipes and Thelma's father, on a visit there, read aloud from the works of Charles Dickens, while she worked at her embroidery. It was all very homely and rather old-fashioned, not at all the kind of modern orgy of dissipation that the society gossips could get their teeth into; and Queen Mary must have been quite startled when she received an embroidered paper-weight as a birthday present from her eldest son, worked by his own hands under the guidance of the elegant and sophisticated young American staying at the Fort.

Gossip, of course, did begin to circulate. The older aristo-cracy resented what they called the Americanization of the Prince —he even picked up a bit of an American accent, which sounded rather common; and he looked a bit of a bounder in his grey flannel trousers and checked socks, with a scarf round his neck and his hair ruffled. In public he seemed more at ease with the lower classes—they responded to the magic of his smile and his democratic friendliness; at balls and parties and state functions, he often looked rather bored and lonely, nervously twitching his tie and wondering how soon he could make his escape.

Thelma took a house of her own in London and it was here that she first entertained Mr and Mrs Ernest Simpson, who were friends of her elder sister, Consuelo. Wallis Simpson was 'fun'— they got on well together; and when she was presented at Court

95 *King Edward VIII and his brother, the Duke of York, walking in the funeral procession of the late King George V. Not long after this poignant picture was taken, the new King had to make the momentous choice between the throne and marriage to a divorcée. (Popperfoto)*

by the American Ambassador's wife, Thelma lent her the feathers and the train she had worn at her own presentation. She looked immaculate in her borrowed plumage, cool and collected in her white satin sheath and long white gloves. The Prince, having made her acquaintance at Thelma's house, singled her out when her turn came to curtsey to his father and mother in the ballroom at Buckingham Palace. He was 'struck by the grace of her carriage and the natural dignity of her movements'.

The Simpsons had a very modest flat in Bryanston Square, though according to the Prince, 'Everything in it was in exquisite taste and the food unrivalled in London. Having been raised in Baltimore, where a fine dinner is considered one of the highest human accomplishments, Wallis had an expert knowledge of cooking. But beyond all that, she had a magnetic attraction for gay, lively and informed company . . . The talk was witty and crackling with the new ideas that were bubbling up furiously in the world of Hitler, Mussolini, Stalin and the New Deal . . .' and Wallis herself never failed 'to advance her own views with vigour and spirit', a trait in her character the Prince found enchanting, accustomed as he was to the deference most people paid to him on account of his royal status.

Thelma Furness had no interest in politics or current affairs
—they bored her as much as hunting. She did, however, regard
Wallis Simpson as one of her best friends in London and when
she went off to California in 1934 to visit her sister, Gloria, she
jokingly asked Wallis to take care of 'the little man', as they
called the Prince, while she was away. On her return six weeks
later, having travelled on the same boat as Aly Khan who filled
her cabin with red roses and danced with her every night, she
was mystified by the Prince's coolness towards her. He seemed
preoccupied—perhaps jealous of Aly Khan, though according
to Thelma quite without cause. Indeed, for anyone who had
packed so much experience of the devious world of smart society
into so short a time, Thelma was still, apparently, extraordinarily
naïve. She consulted Wallis Simpson, who assured her that
nothing could possibly be wrong; then they all went down to the
Fort for the week-end, and during dinner on Saturday night,
Thelma noticed that the Prince and Wallis seemed to be bent on
deliberately excluding her from their little private jokes. 'Once
he picked up a piece of salad in his fingers and Wallis playfully
slapped his hand. I, so over-protective of heaven knows what,
caught her eye and shook my head at her,' wrote Thelma. 'She
knew as well as everybody else that the Prince could be very
friendly, but no matter how friendly, he never permitted familiar-
ity.' Wallis, however, looked straight at Thelma and 'that one
cold, defiant glance' told her everything.

Thelma packed and left the Fort the next morning and a
week later was on her way to Spain with Aly Khan, driving his
high-powered motor at 100 miles an hour. The Simpsons
continued to spend their week-ends at the Fort and in September
1934 the Prince took a short holiday in the South of France with
them. *Time Magazine* reported: 'Such fun was Edward of Wales
having at Cannes with the beauteous Mrs Wallace (sic) Wakefield
(sic) Simpson, that he sent back to Marseilles an airplane he had
ordered to take him to Paris.' This was probably the first mention
of Mrs Simpson in the American press. *Time Magazine* did
not know how to spell her name; the English press did not know
she existed.

In Mayfair, however, the gossip and the speculation increased. All through the Jubilee celebrations the Prince divided

his time between the Court balls and banquets that were invariably dull and the pleasures of Mrs Simpson's astringent and stimulating company. For Ascot he had his own house party at the Fort with Emerald Cunard acting as hostess to the Simpsons and the Duff Coopers among his guests. At the flat in Bryanston Court he was very much the *jeune homme de la maison*, mixing the cocktails and pouring them out while Ernest Simpson hovered discreetly in the background. At the opera in Lady Cunard's box, he was seen paying rather more attention to Mrs Simpson than to Lily Pons on the stage, and three days later, somewhat dwarfed by his bearskin, riding behind his father for the ceremony of Trooping the Colour. The Court turned a deaf ear to the gossip, Queen Mary, ever reserved and dignified, seeking to protect her ailing husband from the distress it would cause him and perhaps hoping that her eldest son's latest folly was only another of his 'fads' which would fade away in time.

But there was no time—or not enough. The King caught a cold after Christmas and died at Sandringham on January 20, 1936, with all his family at his bedside—and the Prince was embarrassed when his mother unexpectedly took his hand in hers and kissed it in a gesture of homage to the new monarch.

Comment in the press on his accession to the throne was highly flattering. The *Times* extolled the virtues of the new King and so did Dr Lang, the Archbishop of Canterbury, and Mr Baldwin, the Prime Minister. The *Illustrated London News* wrote: 'In ascending the throne at the age of 41, King Edward VIII brings to his high task a unique experience of men and the world, along with a singularly winning personality. Wherever he has gone he has won all hearts by his unassuming friendliness, humour and sportsmanship. He is the first bachelor King of this country since George III in 1760 succeeded to the throne before his marriage. Edward VIII has also made history since his accession by being the first British Soverign to travel in an aeroplane, for on Jan. 21., the first day of his reign, he flew from Sandringham to London, accompanied by his brother and Heir Presumptive, the Duke of York.'

A modern King, proclaimed with all the splendour of a mediaeval pageant by Garter King of Arms and the Heralds, to the sound of trumpets; a King who had made history on the first day of his reign, travelling by air . . . While the nation hailed

96   *King Edward VIII and Mrs Simpson in the informal fashion of the day. The*
photograph was taken during a cruise in the Adriatic in 1936. (Popperfoto)

the new King with rapture, the Court remained sceptical. The
aristocray, the bishops, the elderly members of the House of
Lords and the House of Commons were on the side of the trumpets, the traditional ritual, the outward and historic semblance of
royalty. They had served the late King with devotion and rectitude; they were averse to change, to any yielding of the privileges
and the influence they had enjoyed from one generation to the
next. The monarchy was 'the fountain of honour', unsullied in its
most recent years by scandal, above the immorality of the age,
an institution to be upheld and protected. Was the new King
aware of what was at stake? It seemed doubtful from the company
he kept.

Even Harold Nicolson, dining at Bryanston Court in April
with Lady Cunard, Lady Colefax and Lady Oxford, found the
whole setting of the Simpson *ménage* 'slightly second-rate' and
wrote: 'I do not wonder that the Sutherlands and the Stanleys
are sniffy about it all.' The King looked very well and gay and the
drawing-room was filled with arum lilies and orchids; but it was
evident that Lady Cunard was 'incensed by the presence of Lady
Colefax and Lady Colefax furious that Lady Cunard should also
have been asked', while Lady Oxford appeared to be 'astonished

97 *The panoply of state. King Edward VIII prepares for the opening of Parliament,
1936. (Popperfoto)*

to find either of them at what was to have been a quite intimate party'.

Between the devilry of his friends and the critical grey sea of the Court, the King was, indeed, in a dilemma, which hardened his obstinacy and deepened his determination to solve the problem of his personal life in his own way. He believed he could have his cake and eat it, though he had no intention of becoming a hypocrite. It had been easy enough for his grandfather, King Edward VII, married to Queen Alexandra, to ride in the state landau beside his Queen Consort in the morning and to leave his private motor outside the door of Mrs Keppel's house in Grosvenor Street the same afternoon. But 1936 was not 1906. The ethics of society had been refashioned by more than a quarter of a century of change, by the revolt of the younger generation in search of freedom from the suffocating conventions of the past, the craze for youthfulness, gaiety and independence, the new ideas on sex and psychology, the open honesty and gregariousness in matters that had always been concealed beneath a polite layer of discretion. And King Edward VIII belonged to his generation. His success as Prince of Wales, his charm, his lack of formality, his friendliness were all geared to it, to the hectic pace of the years since the War, to the royal aeroplane instead of the royal Daimler, to golf and tennis and dancing in the West End night clubs, instead of to shooting, philately and grand balls in the spacious houses of the nobility.

In the crisis which soon came upon him, he misjudged the puritan instinct in the vast majority of the British people and failed to realize how shallow the effect of the new morality was, except on the smart set surrounding him as in a masquerade. Outside the Amalienburg dining-room of Chips Channon and the salon of Lady Cunard, who visualized Wallis Simpson as Queen of England and herself at last as Mistress of the Robes, he had few friends to advise him and when their advice proved unpalatable, he brushed it aside. Mrs Simpson's name appeared in the Court Circular when she dined at York House. Mrs Simpson—without her husband—went abroad the *S.S. Nahlin* with the Mountbattens, the Duff Coopers, the Brownlows and Lady Cunard as a guest of the King. In August she was invited to Balmoral, the King driving to meet her instead of keeping an appointment to open the Infirmary in Aberdeen, and in October her divorce case was heard in the law court at Ipswich. The fat was in the fire and simmering dangerously.

By November Mr Baldwin, coming and going in his small black motor-car between Fort Belvedere and No. 10 Downing Street, was cracking his finger joints more than ever under the strain. Neither he nor his friend Geoffrey Dawson, editor of the *Times*, ever thought of sharing Lady Cunard's vision of Mrs Simpson as Queen of England or even as the morganatic wife of their Sovereign, while the Archbishop of Canterbury, though icily silent on the subject, succeeded in conveying the message of his holy office through his minions in the church—there would be no Coronation if the King persisted in associating himself with a woman who had divorced two husbands. The American press thought otherwise. Under the banner headline QUEEN OF ROMANCE, one journalist wrote: 'Wallis Simpson IS a queen—the queen of romance, of glamour and the unfulfilled longings of a love-starved world. She is the queenly heroine of a love story, that, touching these two—Edward VIII, monarch of the British Empire, and Wallis Simpson of America—touches millions.' There were pictures of Wallis Simpson as a girl, of her first marriage to Winfield Spencer; pictures of the King and Wallis on board the *S.S. Nahlin*, in the sea and out of the sea; pictures of Balmoral, Buckingham Palace and Ipswich—and although the distributers of *Time* excised the more compromising photographs before circulating the magazine in England, there were many English people who obtained the unexpurgated editions and were not amused.

For the crisis of the King, even before it became known to the general public, was a crisis for the aristocracy, who saw the monarchy losing prestige abroad and tottering beneath the weight of the scandal at home. If the monarchy should fail then the function of the nobility as its supporters would wither and die and their very survival would be at risk, or at best an anachronism. That the danger did not come from without, from the Communists or the Fascists or even from the proletariat in Britain, but from the Trojan horse within, from the King himself and his raffish friends, made the situation all the more alarming and deplorable. But it was also rumoured that Mrs Simpson was in league with the German Ambassador, Herr von Ribbentrop, that the King was very pro-German and aimed at making himself a dictator in Britain, that the Crown jewels were being reset for Mrs Simpson and the King was insane about her—all of which made the whole affair still more inflammable. The best and the worst instincts of the upper classes rose to the surface: all their loyalty to the Crown and devotion to their country, all their snobbery and belief in their own superiority to this nonentity from Baltimore without so much as a drop of blue blood in her veins. Whole families were split down the middle into Cavaliers and Roundheads, into pro-Simpson and anti-Simpson factions, into those who disliked Baldwin and the Archbishop and believed a modern King should be allowed to please himself and those who saw the Court in danger of becoming tarnished and Buckingham Palace drifting into the status of an American night club.

The King was trapped and when the cloud no bigger than a man's hand developed into a deluge of lewd publicity, he sent Mrs Simpson off to Cannes with Perry Brownlow, his Lord in Waiting, and retired to the Fort. Lord Beaverbrook, summoned home when he was half way across the Atlantic and hoping to unseat Baldwin at last, counselled patience and geared his newspapers to the support of the King. Winston Churchill

98 *The immediate pre-war years were a period of gloom and heightening drama for the Royal Family, shown here by the tension on the faces of King Edward and his brother, the Duke of York. (Popperfoto)*

thrice intervened in the House of Commons in defence of the King and the third time was shouted down. Geoffrey Dawson, the sinister Jekyll to Mr Baldwin's honest Hyde, set the *Times* in motion to review the life of Mrs Simpson and to expose the King's offence. Even Chips Channon, scurrying hither and thither in search of news, began to wonder whether the King's obstinacy did not make him unfit to rule. Only at Marlborough House, now the residence of Queen Mary, did calm prevail, the distressed elderly Queen showing no outward sign of anxiety when she drove out to view the ruins of the Crystal Palace, which had gone up in flames on the night of November 30.

Then, suddenly, the crisis was over. On December 11 the King abdicated in favour of his brother, and Queen Mary, breaking her long silence on the subject, was heard to say that she thought 'the Yorks would do it very well'. Once more the trumpets sounded and this time for a King who was a family man with a charming wife and two engaging little daughters, a King, moreover, with a sense of duty and simple tastes like his father, whose service to the public, though less spectacular than his brother's, had already won him respect and affection. The traditional Christmas party at Sandringham and the new King's broadcast, achieved with great courage in overcoming his stammer, showed that things were back to normal. The monarchy had been shaken, it had not fallen; and Mr Baldwin had proved to his own satisfaction that it was only the icing on top of the British plum cake that was frivolous—the rest of the nation was as solid and respectable as the filling inside.

10 THE LAST YEARS OF PEACE

Queen Mary with her long experience of the needs of the monarchy was right—the Yorks did it very well indeed, better than anyone had expected. The country admired King George VI for taking on a difficult job and watched him grow in stature, helped by his lovely, smiling Queen, whose radiant charm and poise endeared her to everyone.

There had not been a Coronation for twenty-six years and never before had the event been given such world-wide publicity. News film cameras and B.B.C. commentators were allowed into Westminster Abbey for the first time, so that the ceremony of the King dedicating himself to the service of his people amidst the splendour and brilliance of a superbly staged royal pageant could be shared by the whole population and was not simply an occasion witnessed by the privileged few with seats in the Abbey and their packets of sandwiches conveniently stowed in their coronets.

It was, none the less, a day of glory for the high aristocracy of England; for it was not Lady Cunard and Lady Colefax or Chips Channon who were the King's supporters, but the peers and peeresses of the realm, whose hereditary services to the reigning monarch dated from the fifteenth century and whose names rolled off the tongue with a Shakespearean cadence. Bernard, Duke of Norfolk, as Earl Marshal of England, the Marquess of Salisbury as Lord High Steward, the Duke of Somerset bearing the orb on a purple velvet cushion, the Duke of Sutherland carrying the sceptre, the Lord Great Chamberlain girding on the sword of state and the spurs and four Knights of the Garter—the Duke of Abercorn, the Marquess of Londonderry, the Earls Stanhope and Lytton—holding the embroidered silk canopy above the King for the anointing. Four beautiful duchesses—Norfolk, Rutland, Roxburghe and Buccleuch—held the canopy over the Queen, and six lovely aristocratic young girls in white, watched over by the Duchess of Northumberland as Mistress of the Robes, held her long purple train lined with ermine and embroidered with gold thread.

No one put a foot wrong as the complicated ritual proceeded on the floor of the Sanctuary. The various performers moved with grace and dignity like a colourful mediaeval Book of Hours suddenly brought to life, the kaleidescopic patterns changing and re-forming under the brilliant lights gleaming on the jewelled crown, the encrusted copes of the bishops, the crimson velvet and ermine, the white ruffles and white knee breeches of the pageboys, the banners of the heralds embossed with furious gold lions and prancing unicorns and the silver trumpets that sounded the hair-raising *vivats* through the ancient silence of the Abbey. Elderly peers, dripping with stars and orders and enveloped in huge velvet mantles, managed to kneel to their Sovereign and retire backwards without accident, and in the tiers of seats in the North Transept reserved for the peeresses, there was a sudden swirl of white-gloved arms like a skein of swans in flight, when they lifted their coronets to their elegant, aristocratic heads in one concerted movement.

No stage director, not even Max Reinhardt, could have produced a more magnificent scene; and it was astonishing that this effulgent display of the historic power and privilege of the nobility, the rivières of diamonds, emeralds and rubies seen at the Coronation, the dog-collars of pearls, the velvet and the ermine, the satin slippers and long kid gloves, the knee breeches and silk stockings did not appear in the least out of harmony with the year 1937. Foreign visitors were amazed by the beauty of it all; and outside the Abbey in the streets hung with flags, the crowds waited for the long and sumptuous procession to weave its way through the afternoon back to Buckingham Palace, the King and his Consort riding in the dazzling golden coach and waving gently to the cheering multitudes, with the very grand,

99 *Was he a reluctant king? Distressed over his brother's abdication, the Duke of York nevertheless saw it his duty to take the throne. His coronation as King George VI in May 1937 had the full pomp and ceremony of tradition. Here the Peers of the Realm pay homage to a new monarch. (Associated Press Ltd.)*

very austere yet lovable dowager Queen Mary in a second glass coach, accompanied by her two excited little grand-daughters, Princess Elizabeth and Princess Margaret.

London was *en fête* for the whole of the summer, the splendour and the opulence of high society apparently undiminished by the hectic years between King George V's Coronation in 1911 and that of the new King twenty-six years later. Indeed, very little change, except in fashion, was to be seen at the grand ball the Duchess of Sutherland gave at Hampden House on May 15. The ornate tiaras and jewels of the ladies, the decorations and sashes of the gentlemen, the exotic uniforms of the foreign princes and the *Corps Diplomatique* belonged to the pre-war era of wealth and stability. Even fashion in the marvellous Winterhalter confection of tulle and lace the English couturier, Norman Hartnell, designed for the new Queen had a romantic air of the past recreated in modern terms; and although Chips Channon thought the Queen's tiara was less impressive than his wife's, he described the Sutherlands' ball as 'a dazzling night'. The ball-room was hung with tapestries and much to his satisfaction 'all the Royalties of the earth' were gathered on the red-carpeted dais. Chips had not forgotten Wallis Simpson and the ex-King, but not to have been accepted by the new regime would have been a social disaster for the Channons, so he was quite overwhelmed with delight when King George and Queen Elizabeth smilingly talked to him and Queen Mary greeted him kindly. The whole evening was 'an exalted success' and as 'the Royalties processed into supper they formed a formidable crocodile of crowned heads'. It was not, however, until after supper when the King and Queen and Queen Mary had gone, that Emerald Cunard appeared, looking very small and fragile and by no means so buoyant as usual in a filmy white dress of floating ostrich feathers.

The royalties, the Americans and the continental visitors stayed on after the Coronation at Claridges, the Ritz and the Savoy, or at the new Dorchester Hotel which had risen out of the ground in Park Lane in 1931 like a glorified cinema organ with Art-Deco trimmings, its vulgar exterior and plushy interior designed to attract the wealthy tourists travelling across the Atlantic in the giant luxury liner *Queen Mary*. There were still things to be seen in London that could be found nowhere else in the world—the historic Abbey, the Tower, Carlton House

100　*No casinos, no leisure clothes, but dinner jackets and evening gowns on the transatlantic run. This picture shows the magnificent dining-room of the Queen Mary with (facing) an illuminated map of the north Atlantic on which the giant ship's course was charted hour by hour. (Radio Times Hulton Picture Library)*

Terrace and the royal parks, Fortnum & Mason's and the shops in St James's Street; and the brilliant flood-lighting of the Coronation Season enhanced the beauty of the city at night, while helping to conceal the damage being done to it in the daytime by the greedy speculators in property. For the tide of destruction begun in the Twenties was continuing at a pace. Many of the upper-class residential areas, like the east side of Berkeley Square where twenty famous houses were destroyed in 1937, were changing in character at a deplorable rate, their aristocratic owners selling out to the developers for demolition or conversion into commercial premises. Chesterfield House, Lansdowne House and the Adelphi, designed by Robert Adam and inhabited by many celebrated people, all vanished in a heap of rubble; and the modern architects or engineers building in a bastardized trans-Atlantic style combined with the ill-digested functionalism

243

of Le Corbusier, had nothing of any aesthetic value to contribute to the pattern of London's streets and squares. One observer of this appalling trend suggested that people no longer worthy of palaces destroyed them, and declared that if this vandalism continued, London would soon become a characterless city of concrete and glass wholly devoted to commercialism.

Except for Lord Derwent and a handful of his friends who founded the Georgian Group to protect and preserve the domestic architecture of the eighteenth century, the upper classes did not seem to care very much. They minded more about the desecration of the countryside and the decline of their ancestral homes under the pressure of rising taxation and death duties, finding a champion in Lord Lothian, who sponsored a new act of Parliament whereby the Government agreed to accept certain houses and their contents to be administered by the National Trust in lieu of a cash payment after the death of the owner. But aristocratic patronage of the arts which had given England some of the most beautiful houses and gardens in the world, was virtually at an end. It was difficult enough to keep together what had been created or collected in the past, let alone to commission new work. Talented sculptors like Eric Gill, Epstein and the young Henry Moore, and artists like Rex Whistler, Oliver Messel and John Piper had to pick up what they could from the more enlightened institutions and commercial groups, Eric Gill decorating the new Broadcasting House in Portland Place and Rex Whistler painting a mural for the tea room at the Tate Gallery.

Uncertainty of taste, veering from the traditional to the ultra-modern, ruled in the interior decoration of the houses and flats belonging to the rich. Tubular steel and glass furniture, black and white kid-skin chairs, Lalique wall lights and ornaments, black glass pilasters and Venetian red walls with concealed flood-lighting, abstract designs in rugs and curtains, flower arrangements of dead grass, cabbage leaves and poppy heads by Constance Spry and bathrooms with apricot-tinted glass engraved with fish and air bubbles, were some of the experiments tried and often abandoned after a little while for something more new-looking, for what was fashionable one day was out the next. Lady Melchett's bedroom had lacquered gold pilasters against shiny blue walls, Lady Drogheda's dining-room

101 *John Gielgud as Hamlet gave one of the most memorable performances of the Thirties. (Radio Times Hulton Picture Library)*

was lined with black glass and Noel Coward's studio done up in zebra stripes of off-white and dark brown. Finally the Surrealism of Dali came in, though no one in London went quite so far as Schiaparelli in Paris, who had a divan in her salon made in the form of a giant pair of scarlet lips.

Some of the younger artists and designers fortunately found rewarding work in the theatre and through the medium of their stage sets and costumes had a considerable influence on fashionable taste. Rex Whistler evoked the atmosphere of the eighteenth century for a dramatized version of Jane Austen's *Pride and Prejudice* in 1935, and in 1937 was responsible for the decor of *Victoria Regina*, Laurence Housman's play which started at the Gate Theatre Club with Pamela Stanley as Queen Victoria and had a stimulating effect on the revival of Victorian taste in decoration. Oliver Messel, an old-Etonian and a stage designer of genius, began his long and fruitful association with the theatre by doing the sets and costumes for a number of Cochran revues in the late Twenties and early Thirties, then for A. P. Herbert's musical comedy *Helen* in a ravishing white and gold pseudo-classical setting, and for *The Country Wife* starring Edith Evans, Michael Redgrave and the American actress, Ruth Gordon, his extravagant baroque style and marvellous sense of colour a delight on the eye.

Audiences now had a far wider range of entertainment in the theatre to choose from than in the Twenties when the West End was dominated by drawing-room comedy and melodrama, and they responded eagerly. The fashionable playgoer was more intelligent and more perceptive. Shakespeare in the West End was no longer a doubtful proposition; Chekhov, Oscar Wilde and Restoration comedy seen through the eyes of a new generation of producers and actors outrivalled and eclipsed the theatre of Gerald du Maurier, Freddy Lonsdale and Tallulah Bankhead. For Lilian Baylis at the Old Vic and Salder's Wells had done her work valiantly and her prayers had been answered; God had sent her the best young actors and producers and when they arrived in the Waterloo Road she kept them working hard until they had proved themselves worthy of their art and were ready to emerge triumphantly into the starry firmament of the West End.

John Gielgud, richly endowed with a romantic stage presence and the melodious voice of the Terrys, having cut his teeth on *Hamlet, Richard II* and *King Lear* at the Old Vic, dazzled the West End all through the Thirties, not only with his own subtle and brilliant characterization of parts as different from each other as Romeo, Trigorin, Hamlet and John Worthing, but in the company he gathered round him, Peggy Ashcroft, Edith Evans, Gwen Ffrangçon-Davies, Laurence Olivier, Jack Hawkins, Frank Vosper and Michael Redgrave. Their team-work was a revelation. Each performer, including Gielgud himself, played with a delicate perception of the whole pattern of the play in question, unlike the star actor managers of the past who tended so often to sacrifice the play to their own performance and to leave the rest of the production to chance. For Gielgud had absorbed the new conceptions of Granville Barker and of Stanislavski's Moscow Arts Theatre, and these creative ideas were reinterpreted by Komisarjevsky and by Michel Saint-Denis, the founder and producer of the *Compagnie des Quinze*, who first came to London in 1931 with *Noé* and *Le Viol de Lucrèce*, returning later to direct Gielgud, Peggy Ashcroft and Gwen Ffrangçon-Davies in a superb production of the *Three Sisters*. Connoisseurs of acting believed quite rightly that they had never seen anything better in the theatre and even James Agate, whose column in the *Sunday Times* could sway the opinions of intelligent society in favour or against a new production, gave unstinted praise.

This exciting renaissance in the theatre of the 1930s was achieved without any subsidy from public funds, entirely through the enthusiasm of a few highly creative individuals; and it was matched by a still more remarkable development in the ballet, which after the death of Diaghilev had dwindled into a second-rate entertainment, such artists as Serge Lifar and Nikitina dancing in Cochran's revues or as part of the variety

102   *Robert Helpmann and Margot Fonteyn in* Giselle, *in 1936. Young stars of the Sadler's Wells Ballet, which under the direction of Ninette de Valois was soon to achieve an international reputation.*

theatre programmes in the West End and the provinces. That English dancers—even with Russianized names—could ever reach the standard of Diaghilev's original company seemed highly improbable. Yet once again a miracle was achieved through the enthusiasm of two extremely talented individuals: Marie Rambert, a Polish–Russian dancer married to the English writer Ashley Dukes, and Edris Stannus from County Wicklow, who took the name of Ninette de Valois when she joined the Diaghilev Ballet in 1923. Marie Rambert founded the Ballet Club in a church hall in Notting Hill Gate and, warmly supported by the Sitwells and the *cognoscenti* in the world of art, inspired Antony Tudor and Frederick Ashton to compose their first ballets, while Ninette de Valois joined forces with Lilian Baylis in 1931 and with a troupe of six dancers at Islington started the Vic Wells Ballet, soon to become known as the Sadler's Wells Ballet and later as the world-famous Royal Ballet.

Single-minded in her purpose, a brilliant organizer and indomitable, de Valois had a genius for fostering the artistic talents of the young people she drew into her orbit and by establishing a ballet school in the first year of her association with Lilian Baylis, ensured the future of their joint enterprise. Alicia Markova—a Londoner, whose real name was Alice Marks and who had danced with the Diaghilev company as a child—came to Sadler's Wells in 1932, with an Irish boy, Anton Dolin, and their ability to dance the classical rôles of the Russian ballet encouraged de Valois to revive *Giselle* and *Lac des Cygnes* under the direction of Nicolas Sergueyev, the former *régisseur* of the Maryinski Theatre in St Petersburg.

Yet even this enormously exacting and ambitious programme did not exhaust Ninette de Valois's powers of concentration and her zeal for the task she had undertaken. With her marvellous gift for attracting the best available talent to what was still a perilous adventure, she made Constant Lambert, the witty, precocious, 'roaring boy' of music in the Twenties, musical director of the ballet company, the exotic brilliance of his personality inspiring the dancers and luring the élite of intellectual society to Islington. She also gave Frederick Ashton the opportunity to develop his unique talent as a choreographer and saw the potentiality of the dark-eyed, chubby little girl called Margaret Hookham long before it was visible to anyone else—the future *prima ballerina assoluta* of the world, Margot Fonteyn, dancing her first leading rôles in Ashton's *Le Baiser de la Fée* and *Apparitions* at the age of sixteen and then a *Giselle* that revealed the lyrical beauty and the magic of this young artiste for the first time. Before long the association of Ashton as choreographer with Fonteyn as the leading exponent of his subtle and brilliant work had given the Sadler's Wells ballet a distinctive style that no other ballet company possessed, as well as a growing reputation which finally conquered the world.

That the English could also challenge the world in providing a standard of opera equivalent to the Salzburg Festival was yet another improbability that was swept aside in the Thirties by an equally indomitable individual, who was the very last patron of the arts bold enough and rich enough to do his own thing against all the odds of the twentieth century. John Christie was forty years old and still a science master at Eton when he inherited Glyndebourne, a delectable Tudor manor house set in the folds of the Sussex downs near Lewes. As a landowner he took his responsibilities seriously and, being a man of great determination with strong views on the obligations of the gentry towards the people in the district, he set about establishing the Ringmere Building Works, which developed from a small estate facility into one of the biggest building concerns in the south-east. Music was his hobby. He regularly visited the summer festivals at Bayreuth, Salzburg and Munich with his old friend Dr Lloyd, the Precentor of Eton, who was a very fine organist; and it was characteristic of his open-handed generosity that when his old friend refused to stay at Glyndebourne because there was no organ, Christie decided to build one and a special room to house it. Dr Lloyd died before he ever played on the organ, but when the Organ Room was finished, visitors to Christie's house parties, both amateur and professional, gave concerts there for the pleasure of their host and his guests. On one occasion a young soprano from the Carl Rosa Opera Company came down to sing—Audrey Mildmay, daughter of the Rev. Aubrey St John Mildmay, the 10th baronet—and was so charming and fascinating, Christie fell in love with her and married her in 1931.

The idea of building an Opera House attached to the old Tudor manor house was born in their first summer together at Glyndebourne, though it was not until three years later after many difficulties had been surmounted that the opening performance of *Le Nozze di Figaro* was given under the direction of Fritz Busch and the producer, Carl Ebert. The first night audience was a very distinguished one; it included the Duchess of Norfolk, Princess Hohenloe, Lady Diana Cooper, Maurice Baring, the Hon. James Smith, Lord Gage and many other connoisseurs of music, some of whom had travelled down on the special train from London. But on the second night, for *Cosi Fan Tutte*, only seven people got out of the special train and the audience was so sparse it looked as if Christie and Audrey Mildmay were heading for failure. The impact of the performance, however, was exhilarating. Sung in Italian with a cast of English and foreign singers, impeccably rehearsed and produced with great elegance on the small stage, it was a revelation of how Mozart's operas could be done and never had been done in England until now.

The word went round that Glyndebourne was something very special indeed, not just a rich man's folly or a society outing, but a festival worth going to and worth dressing up for at 3 o'clock in the afternoon. For Christie insisted from the very beginning that the audience should wear evening dress, and in spite of the anomaly of gentlemen in white ties and tails and ladies in long gowns moving down the platform at Victoria Station in the middle of the afternoon, his intuition that this would create a sense of occasion was right. With those who accused him of kotowing to the snobbish elements of high society, he argued pertinently that if the performers took the trouble to do their parts exceedingly well, so must the audience. Moreover, he received the patrons who had paid for their tickets as if they were his private guests, allowing them to wander through his glorious garden in the long dinner interval in the pastoral beauty of the summer evening, with the sheep cropping the short downland grass beyond the hedge and the sun setting behind the hills. Very good food and excellent wine in the restaurant added to the pleasure of the opera enthusiasts and by 1937, when the season was extended to include five of Mozart's operas, the optimism of John Christie's first prospectus claiming that he hoped to make Glyndebourne 'an artistic and musical centre to which visitors would come from all over the world' was triumphantly justified.

But 1937 was the last year of the decade when English

103   *The British war cabinet that faced the sombre tapestry of a war-benighted Europe.*
The group includes Kingsley-Wood, Winston Churchill, Hore Belisha, Lord Halifax and
Neville Chamberlain (the Premier). (Popperfoto)

society could still ignore what was going on in Europe. In March
1938 Hitler grabbed Austria and was apparently greeted with
jubilation by the populace. Mussolini looked on. Britain and
France dithered. France had no government at all at the crucial
moment. Britain had Neville Chamberlain, who had succeeded
Stanley Baldwin as Prime Minister at last, having waited a life-
time for him to die or retire. Once described by Lloyd George as
'a good lord mayor of Birmingham in a lean year', Chamberlain,
if anything, was even more insular than Baldwin, more bigoted
and more impatient of criticism. He believed he knew more about
foreign affairs than his younger and more virile Foreign Secretary, Anthony Eden, and this led almost immediately to a con-

flict between them over negotiations with Mussolini. Eden resigned and Chamberlain appointed Lord Halifax, an ex-Viceroy of India, to the Foreign Office, finding him a good deal more amenable to his guidance and to the idea of making friends with the Dictators. Halifax had already visited Berlin in 1937 as a guest of Hermann Goering, ostensibly to join a hunting party in the private capacity of an English gentleman interested in sport; but this ill-timed gesture of *bonhomie* had not met with much enthusiasm in some political circles. Indeed, to Claud Cockburn, a Left-wing journalist, the whole affair looked like a sinister conspiracy cooked up by what he called 'the Cliveden Set' of influential people entertained by Lady Astor in her enormous mansion near Maidenhead.

Still riding high on the dazzling reputation she had originally made for herself in society as a young and vivid American married to a very rich husband, Nancy Astor was notoriously self-opinionated. To her friends she was fascinating and irresistible; to her enemies—and they were many—a vain, boisterous, indiscreet exhibitionist, who thought she knew everything and said as much in a strident voice. In Parliament her influence was negligible, but with Lord Astor as co-proprietor of the *Times* and its self-righteous editor, Geoffrey Dawson, believing devoutly in reconciliation with Germany at any price, her week-end house parties at Cliveden were a hot-bed of intrigue and politically orientated towards the policy soon to be known publicly as the policy of appeasement.

Chamberlain, of course, had inherited an impossible situation—a Britain rearming at a snail's pace and an electorate so pacific at heart it would do almost anything to avoid the calamity of a new war. But the rape of Austria, so soon to be followed by the Führer's demands on Czechoslovakia, was the signal for society to take sides and to wonder whether the skiing at Kitzbühel would ever be the same again, in spite of the assurances of the travel agents that Nazi occupation of the winter sports resort would make no difference at all. Chips Channon, who had been fêted by Goering, Goebbels and Ribbentrop at the Berlin Olympic Games in 1936, shocked Harold Nicolson profoundly when he declared: 'We should let gallant little Germany glut her fill of the reds in the East and keep decadent France quiet while she does so. Otherwise we shall have not only reds in

the West, but bombs on London, Kelvedon and Southend.'
Nicolson argued that the Nazis stood for violence, oppression,
untruthfulness and bitterness and the English 'for a certain type
of civilised mind, for tolerance, truth, liberty and good humour'.
But the dilemma persisted—in Parliament and out of Parliament,
in society and out of society.

Many people in high places shared Chips Channon's views
and expressed these views to Herr von Ribbentrop, the aristo-
cratic-looking, very correct and very charming German Ambassador, who sent his son to an English public school, though he
was not in fact an aristocrat at all but an ex-champagne salesman
with a sparkling veneer of distinction. Many other people—
Harold Nicolson himself, Anthony Eden, Lord Cranborne, heir
to the Marquess of Salisbury, Duff Cooper and Winston Churchill
—dissented strongly from the insidious idea Herr Ribbentrop
was only too willing to believe, that the upper classes in Britain
would not oppose Hitler's designs on Europe provided he left
the Empire alone. Yet, with aerial warfare an unknown quantity
and its horrors in a way greatly exaggerated, even Winston

104 *One of the first women parliamentarians, Lady Astor was a militant supporter of*
many causes. Here she is seen campaigning in Plymouth in her usual vigorous style.
(Central Press Photos Ltd.)

Churchill recognized the dilemma when he admitted after the Austrian *débâcle*: 'We stand to lose everything by failing to take strong action. Yet if we take strong action, London will be a shambles in half an hour.'

Churchill was still a voice crying in the wilderness. Since the beginning of the decade he had been warning the Government and the country of Britain's weakness. In 1930, in the Romanes lecture, he said: 'We see our race doubtful of its mission and no longer confident about its principles, infirm of purpose, drifting to and fro with the tides and currents of a deeply disturbed ocean.' In 1933 when Hitler seized power in Germany, he alone realized that the absurd-looking little Charlie Chaplin figure in boots might become dangerous. And again in 1936 when the Nazi leader reoccupied the Rhineland and Mussolini sent his troops into Abyssinia, he confronted Baldwin with the frightful deficiencies of Britain's air defences and got no answer. No one believed him—or wanted to believe him.

He was too pugnacious, too bold, too much in love with danger: a warmonger, a turncoat, an opportunist, who smoked cigars in bed and drank brandy. How could his judgement be trusted when you looked at his past history, shifting from one political party to another with no sense of loyalty to either? Look at his disastrous promotion of the Gallipoli campaign, his poor performance as Chancellor of the Exchequer, his irreconcilable attitude to India, his championship of King Edward VIII. In his sixties now, though still a shrewd and quick-witted opponent, a man of vintage character and of strong-minded independence, the gay and brilliant promise of his youth seemed to have led nowhere, to a seat below the gangway in the House of Commons, to shouts of 'scaremonger' and 'sit down' from the blind and ageing schoolboys who occupied the Front Bench. Yet he bore his colleagues no ill-will and he did not give up. As the policy of appeasement gathered pace down the hill towards disaster, he continued to warn and to admonish. To Harold Nicolson he spoke of 'this great country nosing from door to door like a cow that has lost its calf, mooing dolefully now in Berlin and now in Rome—when all the time the tiger and the alligator wait for its undoing'. And there was not much time left.

It was still possible to escape—or so people thought. There was the London Season with its annual events: the Derby, the

105 *Was this the ill-starred occasion which turned the fate of Poland and Czechoslovakia? Hitler greets Neville Chamberlain in Godesburg for the famous night conference of September 23, 1938. (Associated Press Ltd.)*

Courts, Ascot, Goodwood and Cowes. There was Douggie Byng at Monseigneur, and in the theatre, Lynn Fontanne and Alfred Lunt in *Amphitryon '38*, Noel Coward and Gertie Lawrence in *Red Peppers*, and at Drury Lane, the handsome, romantic King of Ruritania, Ivor Novello, in one dazzling uniform after another in *Glamorous Night, Careless Rapture* and *The Dancing Years*. The restaurants were full. The season of grand opera at Covent Garden was successful and Lady Cunard's luncheon parties continued with Herr von Ribbentrop and Count Grandi among her favourite guests. Then society went off to the sun, to the Lido and Cap d'Antibes, while others observed the sacred Twelfth of August on the grouse moors in Yorkshire and in Scotland.

There was plenty of escapist talk, too, some of the wishful

thinking inspired by German agents posing as anti-Nazis. The
Hitler regime was on the point of collapse, they said, the German
army had no boots, their tanks were made of cardboard. Hitler
was bluffing, some people thought, and Mussolini could still be
wooed with buttered parsnips. And there was Stalin and the
great unknown Russian continent, dedicated to the Communist
principle of the brotherhood of mankind. Books in yellow jackets
poured out of Victor Gollancz's Left Wing Book Club explaining
what could and should be done. American journalists travelled all
through Europe, describing their experiences, speculating,
advising, drawing conclusions . . . And finally there was the Prime
Minister of Britain with his wing collar, his trilby hat and his
umbrella, flying to Germany at the age of sixty-nine—a Daniel in
the lions' den of Berchtesgaden who came home thinking he was
unscathed.

It was all of no avail—or at most only a breathing-space;
short enough, yet long enough after the Munich agreement had
proved to be another illusion for public opinion to change, as the
fanatical voice of the Führer came screaming over the air, harsh
and vindictive and at last unmistakable. The pro-German
faction in society looked a little ashamed, the appeasers were in
confusion and in the last precarious moment of peace, the faces
of the Left-wing enthusiasts were red with embarrassment when

106 *The end of the Long Party—September 1939. (Central Press Photos Ltd.)*

it became known that Stalin had signed a pact with Hitler.

Reality could no longer be ignored. The euphoria, the fun and the dissipation of the Twenties had already dissolved into the air like Prospero's insubstantial pageant and the more sober amusements of the Thirties were now abruptly curtailed. England was in danger. The aristocracy and the gentry prepared to gird on their swords again, only their swords were not much use to them. They needed machine guns, bombs, torpedoes and the tanks and aircraft they had not got. They needed all sorts of mental and physical weapons they did not yet understand and would have to learn about if they were to survive the new holocaust of 1939; for this was a war they shared with the whole nation and that tested their powers of adaptability beyond all other wars they or their ancestors had known. Happily by accepting change as part of the fun of being alive and by throwing away the exclusiveness, the stuffiness and prudery of the past, the frivolous young of the Twenties, now older and wiser, had forged a new society, more flexible and less vulnerable to defeat. They did not know exactly where they were going or what was coming to them, but their instinct for survival was as strong as ever. There was not much flag-wagging and very little jingoism—only the wailing of the first air-raid siren on Sunday morning, September 3, and then the silence of the imponderable future.

Bibliography

ACTON, Harold. **Memoirs of an Aesthete.** *Methuen, 1948.*

ARLEN, Michael. **The Green Hat.** *Heinemann, 1924.*

ARLEN, Michael J. **Exiles.** *André Deutsch, 1971.*

BAILY, Leslie. **B.B.C. Scrapbook.** *Frederick Muller*, Vol. 2. *1918–1939.*

BEATON, Cecil. **The Glass of Fashion.** *Weidenfeld & Nicolson, 1954.*

BEATON, Cecil. **The Wandering Years: Diaries, 1922-1939.** *Weidenfeld & Nicolson, 1961.*

BEDFORD, John, Duke of. **The Flying Duchess.** *Macdonald, 1968.*

BEHRMAN, S.N. **Duveen.** *Hamish Hamilton, 1972.*

BLYTHE, Ronald. **The Age of Illusion: England in the Twenties.** *Hamish Hamilton, 1963.*

BYNG, Douglas. **As You Were.** *Duckworth, 1970.*

CARTLAND, Barbara. **We Danced All Night.** *Hutchinson, 1971.*

CHANNON, Sir Henry (Chips). **Diaries, 1934-1940.** Ed. Robert Rhodes James. *Weidenfeld & Nicolson, 1967.*

CHURCHILL, Randolph. **Lord Derby, King of Lancashire.** *Heinemann, 1959.*

COOPER, Lady Diana. **The Rainbow Comes and Goes.** *Rupert Hart-Davis, 1958.*

COWARD, Noel. **Present Indicative.** *Heinemann, 1937.*

DAY LEWIS, Cecil. **The Buried Day.** *Chatto & Windus, 1960.*

DEAN, Basil. **Seven Ages.** *Hutchinson, 1970.*

DONALDSON, Frances. **Freddy Lonsdale.** *Heinemann, 1957.*

DU MAURIER, Daphne. **Gerald: a Portrait.** *Gollancz, 1934.*

EELLS, George. **The Life that Late He Had: Cole Porter.** *W.H.Allen, 1967.*

FIELDING, Daphne. **Emerald and Nancy.** *Eyre & Spottiswoode, 1968.*

FIELDING, Daphne. **Mercury Presides: Autobiography.** *Eyre & Spottiswoode, 1954.*

FITZGERALD, Scott. **The Great Gatsby.** *Penguin, 1925.*

GARLAND, Madge. **The Indecisive Decade.** *Macdonald, 1968.*

GRAVES, Robert, and HODGE, Alan. **The Long Week-End.** *Faber & Faber, 1950.*

HARRISON, Michael. **Lord of London: The Duke of Westminster.** *W.H.Allen, 1966.*

HOLROYD, Michael. **Lytton Strachey.** Vol. 2. *Heinemann, 1968.*

HUXLEY, Aldous, **Crome Yellow.** *Penguin, 1921.*

HUXLEY, Aldous. **Antic Hay.** *Penguin, 1923.*

Illustrated London News.

ISRAEL, Lee. **Miss Tallulah Bankhead.** *W.H.Allen, 1972.*

LAVER, James. **Between the Wars.** *Vista Books, 1961.*

LAWRENCE, Gertrude. **A Star Danced.** *W.H.Allen, 1945.*

LEWIS, Wyndham. **Collected Writings on Art.** Ed. Walter Michel and C.J.Fox. *Thames & Hudson, 1969.*

MANNIN, Ethel. **Young in the Twenties.** *Hutchinson, 1971.*

MITFORD, Jessica. **Hons and Rebels.** *Gollancz, 1960.*

MITFORD, Nancy. **The Pursuit of Love.** *Hamish Hamilton, 1945.*

MUGGERIDGE, Malcolm. **The Thirties.** *Collins, 1967.*

NICOLSON, Harold. **King George V.** *Constable, 1952.*

NICOLSON, Harold. **Diaries and Letters, 1930-1939.** *Collins, 1966.*

NICHOLS, Beverley. **Twenty-five.** *Jonathan Cape, 1926.*

NICHOLS, Beverley. **The Sweet and Twenties.** *Weidenfeld & Nicolson, 1958.*

POPE-HENNESSY, James. **Queen Mary.** *Allen & Unwin, 1959.*

POUND, Reginald. **Arnold Bennett.** *Heinemann, 1952.*

SITWELL, Osbert. **Laughter in the Next Room.** *Macmillan, 1949.*

The Sketch

SYKES, Christopher. **Nancy: the Life of Lady Astor.** *Collins, 1972.*

The Tatler

TATTERSALL, E.H. **Europe at Play.** *Heinemann, 1938.*

TAYLOR, A.J.P. **English History, 1914-1945.** *Pelican, 1970.*

THOMSON, George Malcolm. **Lord Castlerosse.** *Weidenfeld & Nicolson, 1973.*

The Times
TREWIN, J.C., with MANDER and MITCHENSON. **The Gay Twenties.** *Macdonald, 1958.*
TREWIN, J.C., with MANDER and MITCHENSON. **The Turbulent Thirties.** *Macdonald, 1960.*
TURNBULL, Andrew. **Scott Fitzgerald.** *Bodley Head, 1962.*
VANDERBILT, Cornelius, Junior. **Farewell to Fifth Avenue.** *Gollancz, 1935.*
VANDERBILT, Gloria, and FURNESS, Thelma, Lady. **Double Exposure.** *Frederick Muller, 1959.*
WAUGH, Evelyn. **Decline and Fall.** *Chapman & Hall, 1927.*
WAUGH, Evelyn. **Vile Bodies.** *Chapman & Hall, 1930.*
WAUGH, Evelyn. **A Handful of Dust.** *Chapman & Hall, 1934.*
WESTMINSTER, Loelia, Duchess of. **Grace and Favour.** *Weidenfeld & Nicolson, 1961.*
WINDSOR, H.R.H. Duke of. **A King's Story.** *Cassell, 1951.*
WOOLF, Virginia. **Mrs Dalloway.** *Hogarth Press, 1925.*
WOOLF, Virginia. **To the Lighthouse.** *Hogarth Press, 1927.*

Index

Indexer's note: Royal personages are indexed by Christian names, e.g. Edward, Prince of Wales. Similarly, other people may be found under either the maiden name or the married name, and commoners will be found under either the family name or the title; readers are invited to look in both places, though all references to persons with changed names will be found in only one place.

* = photograph

Abdication issue 230–8
Abdy, Lady 73*
Accession of King Edward VIII 233
Accra 35*
Acton, Harold 90, 203, 206, 207, 208
Adam, Robert 54
Aga Khan 200
Agate, James 247
Ainley, Henry 113
Aircraft, Duchess of Bedford's 64, 68*
Airships 202
Air Travel 202, 207*
Albert, King of the Belgians 22
Albert, Prince, Duke of York 2*, 11, 14, 15*, 32–3, 94, 177, 220, 231*, 233, 238*, 239–40, 241*, 242
Aldington, Richard 184
Alexander, Sir George 108
Alexandra, Queen 5
Alfonso XIII, King of Spain 69*
Alington, Napier 124
Allahabad 27
Altman, Mr 74
Aly Khan 232
Ambrose and his band 36
Antic Hay 150
Apple Cart, The 142
Aquitania, S.S. 73

Aragon, Louis 92
Arden, Elizabeth 198
Aren't We All? 110
Argyle House, Chelsea 95–6
Ark Club 84
Arlen, Michael 48, 126, 159–60, 161*, 162, 197
Armistice (1918) 1, 6
Arundel Castle 22
Ascot 16, 17, 19*, 67*, 255
Ashcombe, Wilts 76, 77*, 78
Ashcroft, Peggy 246–7
Ashley, Edwina 39, 52, 93*, 100, 202
Ashley-Cooper, Lady Mary 47*
Ashton, Frederick 76, 248–9
Asquith, Anthony 225*
Asquith, Herbert 11
Asquith, Margot 92, 93, 224–5*, 234
Astaire, Fred 44, 128
Astley, Philip 121–2
Astor family 58
Astor, Nancy, Lady 224, 252, 253*
As You Were 131
At the Cottage Door 74
Auden, W. H. 141*, 179, 190
Aylesford, Lady 57

Baker, Josephine 209

Bakst, Leon 87, 152
Baldwin, Stanley 22–3, 51–2, 62, 168, 172, 176, 184, 216–18, 236, 238
Balfour, Patrick 48, *see also* Kinross
Ballet, revival of 248–9
Balsan, Consuelo 57, 58
Balsan, Colonel Jacques 57
Bankhead, Tallulah 116–17, 123*, 124, 126, 161
Bannerman, Margaret 106
Bara, Theda 128
Baring, Maurice 42
Baring, Poppy 40
Barnard, Captain 64
Bath, Marquess of 67–8
Baylis, Lilian 114, 248
Beaton, Cecil 48, 65*, 76, 77*, 78, 84, 86, 87, 96, 97, 103, 126, 129, 156, 199, 202, 226
Beaton, Nancy and Baba 76
Beaumont, Hugh 112
Beaverbrook, Lord 138, 172–3, 175*, 224, 237
Beddington, Mrs Claude 139*
Bedford, Duchess of 62–4, 68*
Bedford, Duke of 79, *see also* Woburn
Beecham, Sir Thomas 77, 84, 87–9
Beerbohm, Max 79, 95
Beggar's Opera, The 114
Belgravia 70
Belisha, Hore 218, 251*
Bell, Clive 144, 154
Bell, Vanessa 144
Belloc, Hilaire 42
Belvedere, Fort 229–30, 236
Belvoir Castle 59, 65
'Bend Or', *see* Westminster, Duke of
Bennett, Arnold 95, 133–7*, 138–9
Bennett, Constance and Joan 129
Bentinck, Lord George 55
Berenson, Bernard 95
Berlin, Irving 44, 122
Berners, Lord 96, 157*, 203
Bernhardt, Sarah 77
Best, Edna 116
Bill of Divorcement, A 112
Birkenhead, Lord 46, 136
Birley, Lady 203
Birley, Oswald 156
Bitter Sweet 119
Black Man and White Ladyship 94

Blandford, Lord 101*
Blaney, Nora 44
Blenheim Palace 54, 57
Blood and Sand 127
Blue Boy 72–4
Boar hunting 71
Bolton Abbey 60
Book of Beauty 84, 226
Boote, Rosie 106
Bow, Clara 128
Bowes-Lyon, Lady Elizabeth, *see* Elizabeth, Queen (Mother)
Braithwaite, Lilian 114–15*
Brecknock, Lord 100
'Bright Young People' 46–52, 68, 99–100
Britannia (racing yacht) 25
British Empire Exposition 31*
British Gazette (newspaper) 51–2
British Museum 75, 92
British Union of Fascists 170
Brownlow, Lady 39
Buchanan, Jack 45
Buckingham Palace 6–8, 14
Burlington, Lord 54
Byng, Douglas 130, 131*, 132, 255

Café de Paris 44, 130
Café Royal 91
Café society 85
Calthrop, Gladys 116
Campbell, Mrs Patrick 43, 106–7, 113*, 119, 141
Canalettos 24, 64
Careless Rapture 255
Carmichael-Anstruther, Lady 47*
Carolus-Duran 95
Cartland, Barbara 105, 132, 173
Cassel, Sir Ernest 39
Castlerosse, Lord 48, 173–4, 177*
Cavalcade 119, 177, 178
Cavendish, Andrew 191
Cecil, David 148, 207
Cecil, Lord Hugh 84
Chaliapin, Feodor 42, 84, 87
Chamberlain, Lady Austen 95
Chamberlain, Neville 172, 217–18, 251*, 255*
Chanel, Gabrielle (Coco) 69–70, 73*, 204
Channon, Sir Henry 'Chips' and Lady Honor 220–5, 238, 242, 252–3
Chaplin, Charles 98, 128

Charleston 44, 100
Charlot, André 120
Charlot's Revue 113, 122
Chatsworth 59–60
Christie, John 249–50
Christopher, Prince and Princess (of Greece) 102
Churchill, Lady Randolph 56
Churchill, (Sir) Winston 11, 51–2, 136, 156, 168, 224, 237–8, 251*, 253–4
Clayhanger 136
Clemenceau, Mons. 11
Cliveden 252
Clynes, J. H. 13
Cochran, Charles B. 116–17*
Cocteau, Jean 206, 208
Cody, Lew 121*
Colefax, Lady 94–6, 98, 102, 122, 138, 234
Conference on Ireland 13*
Conrad, Joseph 136
Constant Nymph, The 113, 118
Cooper, Lady Diana (Diana Manners) 29*, 40, 41*, 42, 43, 52, 65, 101, 202–3, 224
Cooper, Gary 129
Cooper, Gladys 105–6, 110, 111*, 125*
Cornwallis-West, Captain 107
Coronation (1937) 239–41*, 242–3
Corrigan, Laura 98–102
Costume Jewellery 70
'Coterie' set 40
Country Wife, The 246
Courtauld, Samuel 88
Covent Garden 88, 255
Coward, Noel 66, 96, 102, 104, 114, 115*, 116, 117*, 118, 119*, 120, 132, 139, 151, 161, 178, 245, 255
Cowes Week 23–4, 255
Craven, Earl of 46
Crawford, Joan 129
Cripps, Sir Stafford 220
Crome Yellow 148–9
Crowder, Henry 92–3
Cry Havoc! 185
Cunard, Sir Bache 85, 87, 89
Cunard, Lady (Maud) 'Emerald' 84–6, 87*, 89, 90, 92, 93, 94, 217, 224–5, 233–4, 236, 242, 255
Cunard, Nancy 86*, 90–2, 94, 149
Cunningham-Reid, Captain and Mrs 39

Curzon, Lady Cynthia 22
Curzon, Lord 22–3, 38
Curzon, Frank 110
Cust, Sir Charles 9
Cutty Sark 71

Dali, Salvador 152
Dalton, Canon 6
Dalton, Murray 45
Dancers, The 123
Dances, new kinds of 44
Dancing Years, The 255
Dare, Zena 106
Dawson, Geoffrey 236, 238, 252
Day Lewis, Cecil 179
Dean, Basil 106, 112–13
Death of a Hero 184
Deauville 199*, 200–1
de Casa Mauray, Marquis 39
de Clifford, Lord 46
Decline and Fall 158
de Flairieu, Countess 101*
de Laszlo, Philip 156
Delavigne, Doris 174
Delius, Frederick 113
Delysia 44, 130
Depression, The Great (1931) 163–7*, 168–75, 180*, 215
Derby, Earl of 14, 55, 60–2, 67*, 200, 216, 224
Derby (Epsom) 16, 61–2, 254
Derwent, Lord 244
Desmond, Florence 130
de Valois, Ninette 248
Devonshire, Duke of 14, 17*, 55, 60, 191, 216
Diaghilev, Sergei 87
Dietrich, Marlene 126, 129
Disraeli, Benjamin 55
Divorce 49, 88, 159, 236
Doble, Francis 118
Dolfuss, Chancellor 204
Dolly Sisters 194, 201
Double Exposure 227
Douglas, Norman 92
Draper, Ruth 84
Dryden, John 45
Duff Gordon, Lady (Madame Lucile) 18
Du Maurier, Gerald 105, 108, 109*, 110
Duveen, Sir Joseph 72–5
Dwight, H. G. 74

Eastlake, Lady 55
Eaton Hall 71
Eden, Anthony 218, 251–3
Eden Roc 203*
Edward VII, King 4–5, 56, 98, 219, 235
Edward VIII, King, see Edward, Prince of Wales
Edward, Prince of Wales 2*, 11–12, 15*, 17*, 19*, 27–8, 31*, 32, 33*, 34, 35*, 36*, 37–9, 44, 62, 94, 121, 170*, 177, 200, 202, 216, 218, 220, 225, 228–31*, 232–4*, 235*, 236, 237, 238*
Eiffel Tower Restaurant 91–2, 126, 157
Elgar, Sir Edward 139*
Eliot, T. S. 139
Elizabeth II, Queen 33, 242
Elizabeth, Queen (Mother) 33, 241–2
Embassy Club 36–9, 43, 68, 161
Eminent Victorians 142
Empire Crusade 172
Epstein, Jacob 153*, 154, 244
Eton and Harrow Match 23
Evans, Edith 114, 246

Fabians 50, 140
Façade 150
Fairbanks, Douglas 127–8
Fallen Angels 116, 124
Farquhar, Lord 8
Farrar, Gwen 44
Fellowes, Hon. Mrs Reginald 196
Fifth Avenue Set, New York 58
Fitzgerald, Hon. Mrs 199
Fitzgerald, Scott and Zelda 166, 195
Flies in the Sun 125
'Flying' Duchess 64–5, 68*
Folies Bergères 209
Fonteyn, Margot 248–9
Forster, E. M. 144
Forsyte Saga, The 134
Forty-three Club (Gerrard St) 35, 45–6
Fraser, Lovat 114
Frick, Mr 74
Fry, Roger 144, 154
Furness, Lord Marmaduke 227–8
Furness, Lady Thelma 226, 227*–32

Gable, Clark 129
Gainsborough 72–4
Galsworthy, John 133–4
Gambling 201

Gandhi, Mahatma 27, 210, 214
Garbo, Greta 127*, 129, 161
Garsington, Oxfordshire 147–9
Gellibrand, Paula 39, 196 (Marquise de Casa Mauray)
General Strike 47*, 50*, 51*–2
George V, King 2*, 4, 6, 7*, 8, 9*, 10–19*, 22, 24, 25*, 28, 60, 61, 71, 80, 176–8, 218–23*, 233
George VI, King, see Albert, Prince, Duke of York
George, Prince, Duke of Kent 2*, 12, 31*, 40, 94, 121, 220, 223, 224
Gershwin, George 44, 122
Gertler, Mark 148
Gibbons, see Grinling Gibbons
Gielgud, John 96, 245*, 246
Gilbert, John 121, 161
Gill, Eric 244
Gish, Lillian 127
Glaenzer, Jules 122
Glamorous Night 255
Glyn, Elinor 18, 49
Glyndebourne 249–50
Gold Standard 177
Goodbye to All That 184
Good Soldier Schweik, The 184
Goodwood 23–4, 255
Gosse, Sir Edmund 144
Grace and Favour 71
Grafton Hunt, Brackley 63*
Grand National 61
Grant, Duncan 144, 148
Graves, Robert 184
Great Gatsby, The 166
Green Hat, The 124, 159–62
Green Mansions 154
Greville, Hon. Mrs Richard 94–5
Grinling Gibbons carvings 24, 60
Guinness, Bridgit 103
Guinness, Bryan 187–8
Guinness, Lady Honor 223
Gwalior, India 33*

Halifax, Lord 251*, 252
Hall, Radclyffe 206
Hammersley, Lily 56
Hammerstein, Oscar 122
Harewood, Earl of 13–14
Harlow, Jean 128
Hartnell, Norman 242

Hasek, Jaroslav 184
Hassan 112–13
Haxton, Gerald 96, 197
Hay Fever 117–18
Headfort, Marchioness of 18, 106
Helen 246
Hemingway, Ernest 208
Henderson, Arthur 168, 178
Henley regatta 23
Henry, Prince, Duke of Gloucester 2*, 11–12
Herbert, (Sir) Alan P. 246
Heygate, John 159
Hitler, Adolf 181–2, 189, 190*, 204, 251–5*, 256
Hitler Youth Movement 181*
Hons and Rebels 189
Hoover, President Herbert 163–4
Howard, Brian 48, 207
Howland, Lord 63
Hudson, W. H. 154
Hungaria Restaurant 45
Hunger marches 178
Hunting 39, 53, 59, 63*, 85
Huntington, Collins 73
Huntington, H. E. and Arabella 73–4
Hurlingham 23
Hutchinson, Leslie 130
Huxley, Aldous 148, 149*, 150, 158, 207

India 23, 210–14
Isherwood, Christopher 141*
'It' 49, 128
Iveagh, Earl of 223

James, Henry 133, 209
Jeffries, Ellis 112
Joad, C. E. M. 184
Jockey Club 62
Joel, Solly 201
John, Augustus 143*, 145, 147–8, 155–7
Johnson, Amy 202
Joyce, James 208
Joynson-Hicks, William 35–6
Jumper suits, introduction of 70, 73*
Jungman Sisters 46–7, 104
Justice 134

Kelly, Gerald 156
Kent, William 54
Keppel, Mrs George 98, 235

Kern, Jerome 44, 122
Keynes, John M. 144, 179
King's Story, A, (Windsor) 27
Kinnoull, Lord 46
Kinross, Lord (formerly Patrick Balfour) 89
Kipling, Rudyard 172
Kit-Cat Club 35, 133, 201
Knoblock, Edward 136
Knowsley Hall 60–2
Kreisler, Fritz 84
Kress, Mr 74

Lady Chatterley's Lover 206
Lamb, Henry 148
Lang, Archbishop Cosmo G. 233, 236
Lansbury, George 168, 170
Last of Mrs Cheyney, The 108, 110
Lavery, Lady Hazel 81, 82*, 155*, 156
Lavery, Sir John 82, 155*, 156
Lawrence, D. H. 146–7, 160
Lawrence, Gertrude 106, 116, 119*, 120–2, 255
Lehmann, Lotte 88
Leider, Frida 88
Lenglen, Suzanne 200
Leslie, Shane 156
Le Touquet 200–1
Let Us Be Gay* 123
Leverhulme, Lord 72
Lewis, Wyndham 154–5
Light of Common Day, The 47
Lillie, Beatrice 45, 121*, 122
Linlithgow, Lord 210, 212–13
Lloyd George, David 10–13*, 168
Lloyd George, (Lady) Megan 18
'Lollipops', Beecham's 88
London Calling 116, 151
Londonderry, Marquess and Marchioness of 80–5*, 156, 224
Londonderry House 80–4
London Venture, The 160
Longleat House 54, 67–8
Lonsdale, Lord 14
Lonsdale, Freddy 110, 112, 133
Lord Northesk Cup 68*
Lord Raingo 138
Lothian, Lord 244
Luigi 36
Lutyens, Sir Edwin 213
Lygon, Hugh 158

Lygon, Lady Lettice 100
Lynn, Olga 124, 132, 199

MacDonald, Ramsay 12, 75, 84, 142, 163–5*, 168, 170, 176, 178, 184, 216–17, 220
Macmillan, Lady Dorothy 17
Macmillan, Harold 17
MacNeice, Louis 179, 190
Maid of the Mountains, The 106, 110
Man from the North, A 134
Manhattan Club 46
Markova, Alicia (Alice Marks) 248
Marlborough, Duke of 57–8
Marlborough, Duchess of 56–7, 104, 224
Marxism 179
Mary, Princess Royal 2*, 12–14
Mary, Queen 2*, 4–7, 14, 18, 19*, 22, 24, 25*, 30, 60, 61, 80, 177, 220, 221–3*, 226, 230, 238, 242
Matriarch, The 107
Matthews, A. E. 112
Maugham, Somerset 95, 133, 135*, 136, 137, 138, 196, 197
Maugham, Syrie 96–8, 126, 196
Maxton, James 178
Maxwell, Elsa 102–4
Mayfair 20–1, 40, 52, 70, 76, 97, *see also* 'Bright Young People'
Means Test 216
Melchior, Lauritz 88
Memoirs of an Infantry Officer 184
Mendl, Lady 98–9, 199
Mentmore Towers 56
Mercury Presides 68
Messel, Oliver 76, 244–5
Metcalfe, 'Fruity' 38–9
Metropolitan Opera House, New York 28, 88
Meyrick, Kate 35, 45, 46
Midnight Follies 130
Mildmay, Audrey 249
Milestones 136
Millar, Gertie 106
Mind in Chains, The 179
Miracle, The 29*, 42
Mistinguette 195, 209
Mitford family 186–91
Mitford, Unity 188–90*
Modern Comedy, A 134
Molyneux, Edward 204

Monte Carlo 197*
Moore, George 86–7, 90, 93–4, 160
Moore, Henry 244
Morgan Twins, Gloria and Thelma 226–32
Morrell, Lady Ottoline 145*, 147–9
Mosley, (Sir) Oswald 22, 170, 172–3*, 183, 188
Motor cars, cheap 215–16
Mrs Dalloway 146
Mrs Siddons as the Tragic Muse 73
Mountbatten, Countess, *see* Ashley, Edwina
Mountbatten, Earl Louis ('Dickie') 30, 39, 200
Murphy, Gerald and Sara 191

Nahlin, S.S. 236–7
Nares, Owen 105
National Gallery 75
National Government 176, *see also* MacDonald, Ramsay
Nevill Holt, Northants 85–6
New Party, The 170
Nichols, Beverley 43, 96, 98, 185
Nicholson, Harold 96, 208, 223, 234, 252–3
Night Clubs 34–6
No, No, Nanette 44, 113
Norfolk, Duke of 24, 239
Norman, Montagu 176
Northcliffe, Lord 11
Norton, Hon. Mrs Richard 39, 52, 128
'Not Forgotten Association' 36*
Novello, Ivor 91*, 96, 118, 139, 255

Old Vic 114
Old Wives' Tale, The 136
On Approval 110
On With the Dance 116
Ootacamund 212
Operette 66
Orators, The 179
Orpen, Sir William 155
Orwell, George 190
Oxford and Asquith, Countess, *see* Asquith, Margot

Pacifism 186
Palazzo Mocenigo, Venice 101
Parker, Dorothy 122

Parliament, opening of 16, 235*
Peace Pledge Union 186
Pearson, Joan 111*
Picasso, Pablo 152, 154, 206
Pickford, Mary 127
Playfair, Nigel 114
Plunket, Lady 100
Polesden Lacey 94–5
Polo 27, 200, 210
Ponsonby, Elizabeth 130
Ponsonby, Sir Frederick 9
Ponsonby, Loelia 47–8, 50, 71, 75*
Porter, Cole 44, 103–4, 199
Poulsen, Mr 44
Present Indicative 116
Private Lives 119*, 120
Pursuit of Love, The 187

Quaglino's 45
Queen Charlotte's Ball (1931) 21*
Queen Mary, RMS 242, 243*
Queen was in the Parlour, The 118
Quennell, Peter 148, 207

Rachmaninoff, Sergei 84
Rainbow Comes and Goes, The 42
Ranelagh 22
Read, Herbert 154
Redesdale, Lord and Lady 186–7, 190
Red Peppers 255
Reinhardt, Max 42, 203
Rembrandt 61
Renown, HMS 30
Ribblesdale, Lady 104
Ribuffi, Luigi 46
Riceyman Steps 138
Richmond, Duke of 24–5*
Rockefeller, John D. 74
Rogers, Ginger 128
Romilly, Esmond 186, 190–1
Romilly, Giles 186
Romilly, Lord 59*
R.101 Disaster 202
Rosebery, Earl of 56
Rosebery, Lady 157*
Rothenstein, John 148
Rothermere, Lord 170, 172
Rothschild family 55–6
Rowley, Violet 71
Royal Opera House, Covent Garden 88, 255

Royal Yacht Squadron, Cowes 25, *see also* Cowes Week
Rubenstein, Arturo 84
Rubenstein, Helena 198
R.U.R. 113
Rush, Richard 54–5
Rutland, Duke of 40, 55, 59, 65
Rutland, Duchess of 42

Sackville, Lady 90
Sackville, Lord John 53
Sackville-West, Diana 59*
Sackville-West, Edward 148
Sackville-West, Vita 223
Sadler's Wells 76, 114, 248–9
St Joan 114
St Moritz 211*
St Paul's Cathedral 6, 220
Samuel, Sir Herbert 176
Sandhurst, Lord 8
Sandringham 5
Savoy Hotel 97*, 130
Scarborough, Lady 42
Selfridge, Gordon 194, 201
Shanghai Express 126
Shaw, George Bernard 50, 95, 114, 136, 139*, 140–2
Sheppard, Canon Dick 186
Silver Box, The 134
Silver Jubilee (1935) 220–2*, 223*
Silver Slipper Club 46
Simla, India 213*
Simon, Sir John 183–4
Simpson, Wallis 225, 227, 229*, 230–4*, 236–8
Sirocco 118
Sitwell, Edith 76, 150, 151*, 152, 203
Sitwell, Osbert 75, 95–6, 150, 151*, 152, 203
Sitwell, Sacheverell 1, 150–2, 199, 203
Skin Game, The 134
Smith, Lady Eleanor 46–7
Some 121
Sovrani's 45
Spender, Stephen 179, 190
Spring Cleaning 110
Squire, Ronald 112
Stamfordham, Lord 9, 12, 13
Stanley, Pamela 245
Steeplechasing 32
Stein, Gertrude 206

Stephen, Sir Leslie 144
Stop Flirting 44
Strachey, Lytton 142–4, 147–8
Stravinski, Igor 87, 152, 206
Strife 134
Supervia, Conchita 88
Surrealism 245
Sutherland, Duchess of 101*, 224, 242
Swanson, Gloria 128

'Talkies', arrival of 128
Tate Gallery 75
Taylor, Laurette 122
Teck, Duchess of 30
Tempest, Marie 117
This Year of Grace 118
Thomas, J. H. 170
Thomas, Linda Lee (Mrs Cole Porter) 103
Thorndike, Sybil 114
Three Sisters 247
Thynne, Henry 68
Tiger-shooting 205*, 210
Tit-Bits (magazine) 134
Titheradge, Madge 116, 118
Toklas, Alice B. 206
Toscanini, Arturo 183
To the Lighthouse 146
Trade Union Congress 51–2
Treasure Hunts 47
Tree, Sir Herbert 108
Trooping the Colour 15*, 233
Tucker, Sophie 45

Ulysses 206
United States, Prince of Wales's visit to 27

Valentino, Rudolph 127, 195
Vanderbilt, Cornelius 58
Vanderbilt, Gloria 226, 227*, 228, 232
Vanderbilt, William 57–8
Vane-Tempest-Stewart, Charles 82, see also Lord Londonderry
Vane-Tempest-Stewart, Lady Helen and Lady Margaret 85*
Venice 101, 198–200
Versailles, Treaty of 8
Viceroys of India 210–14
Victoria, Queen 4–5
Victoria and Albert (HMY) 24

Victoria Regina 245
Vile Bodies 158
Vivian, Daphne 67–8, 100
von Ribbentrop, Herr 237, 252–3, 255
Vortex, The 96, 114, 115*, 116, 118, 161

Walter, Bruno 203
Walton, (Sir) William 150, 203
Wandering Years, The 76
War cabinet 251*
Ward, Hon. Mrs Dudley 36, 44, 226
Waugh, Evelyn 48, 157*, 158–9, 207
Way of the World, The 113
Way the World is Going, The 140
Webb, Mr and Mrs Sydney 50, 168–9*
Weddings: Lady Elizabeth Bowes-Lyon 32; Lady Cynthia Curzon 22; Diana Mitford 187–8; Princess Mary 14; Diana Sackville-West 59*
Well of Loneliness, The 206
Wells, H. G. 133, 136–40
West, Rebecca 140
Westminster, Duchess of, see Ponsonby, Loelia
Westminster, Duke of 70–5*, 139
Westminster Abbey 14, 33, 239
Westmorland, Earl of 39
Weymouth, Lord 67, 100
What Are We To Do with Our Lives? 140
Whistler, Rex 76–7, 96, 244–5
White, Jimmie 45
Wilde, Oscar 133
Wilson, President Woodrow 6–9*, 11
Windsor Castle 16
Windsor, Duke and Duchess of, see Edward, Prince of Wales, and Simpson, Wallis
Woburn 61–5
Women in Love 148
Woolcott, Alexander 122
Woolf, Virginia 144–5, 148
Wyatt, Benjamin 80
Wyndham, George 70
Wysard, Tony 174, 177

York Cottage, Sandringham 5–6
York House, Piccadilly 31
Young Woodley 113

Ziegfeld Follies 28
Zinkeisen Sisters 156